# Histoire des idées et critique littéraire

Vol. 331

ULLRICH LANGER

# PERFECT FRIENDSHIP

*Studies in Literature*
*and*
*Moral Philosophy*

*from Boccaccio to Corneille*

LIBRAIRIE DROZ S.A.
11, rue Massot
GENÈVE
1994

100431952S

ISBN: 2-600-00038-0

Copyright 1994 by Librairie Droz S.A., Geneva (Switzerland)

*For Susan*

I am grateful to the National Endowment for the Humanities for a year-long fellowship that enabled me to write major portions of this book; I am no less grateful to the Graduate School Research Committee of the University of Wisconsin which has provided various forms of financial assistance. I have been fortunate to be able to work closely with my colleagues Jan Miernowski, whose knowledge and indefatigable enthusiasm have been of immense help, Douglas Kelly, whose erudition and good counsel I have always been able to rely upon, and François Cornilliat, whose perspicaciousness and intellectual sympathy have been a constant inspiration. My conversations with Steven Winspur have given me a perspective on the ethical side of literature, and have opened important and fruitful avenues. Susan J. Erickson has provided me with substantive criticism and encouragement at every stage of this study. Joshua Scodel gave the manuscript a careful reading; his comments were enormously helpful. I wish to acknowledge as well the comments and help of Jean Céard, Tom Conley, Martine Debaisieux, Gérard Defaux, Philippe Desan, John Dillon, Richard Goodkin, Timothy Hampton, Patrick Henry, C. Stephen Jaeger, Christopher Kleinhenz, Laurent Pernot, François Rigolot, Robert J. Rodini, Jane Tylus, and Abby Zanger. I have profited from various conversations with many other friends and colleagues, in many different settings. Errors and infelicities remain, of course, my own. I am especially thankful to Melanie and Sigmund Suomi, whose warm presence has been constantly reassuring.

A note on the translations: non-English quotations in the main body of the text have been translated in the footnotes. Whenever it is not indicated otherwise, the translations are my own. In most cases I have opted for a close, literal translation.

Portions of this book have appeared in shorter form elsewhere: Chapter III in *Common Knowledge*, 3 (Spring 1994): 40-53; Chapter V in French translation in eds. François Cornilliat, Mary Shaw, *Rhétoriques fin de siècle* (Paris: Christian Bourgois, 1992), pp. 68-80.

Finally, I wish to thank Ruth Fivaz-Silbermann of Editions Droz for her help in guiding the book to publication.

# INTRODUCTION

This book is about the interplay between literary worlds and moral philosophy in the early modern period. It talks about the choices fictional characters make in their worlds, choices that define their relationships to other characters, in terms that bridge the literary and the ethical. It assumes that when crucial choices are made, enacted, discussed and defended within the confines of an imaginary world, these choices constitute interventions in the ongoing reflection by early modern culture on the status and nature of relationships of human beings with each other. In other words, the literary world always also has a specifically ethical function. This ethical value of the literary character's choice does not always coincide with the overall esthetic design of the literary work, nor does it always, strictly speaking, reflect the intention of the author. For, seen from its context, the literary work does not just intervene on the scene of moral philosophy by providing an elaborate representation of human relationships. Rather, certain moments in the literary work become crucial precisely because they are so charged with ethical resonance. In other words, the literary work does not just augment, criticize or subvert an ethical tradition by strategies inherent to its art. The salience of certain moves within the literary world is *already* determined independently of the intentional thrust and design of that world. In that sense the ethical-intellectual context of the literary work can impel the reader to a primarily topical approach to the text. To modern minds formed in the spirit of literary autonomy, this approach seems to fragment the text, seems to ignore the esthetic freedom of the work. In my view, however, the selectivity of a topical reading, that is, the favor accorded to moments determined by their contextual resonance, is perhaps not such a bad thing: the momentum of an historical ethical reading of literature should go precisely against a closed-off sense of the work. I am tempted to say that *any* reading that focuses on the interplay between the ethical gestures of literature and ethical reflection in culture as a whole must to some extent select exemplary moments, when an option is critical to the nature of a relationship, and is critical because it allows discussion, reflection, imitation (or not, as we sometimes see). This selectivity of an "ethical" reading does not mean that these moments are not linked in intricate ways with an extended narrative: in some cases the very effectiveness of an ethical gesture depends on a pattern of behavior and relationships that is represented in a complex way over time.[1]

One of the aims of this book is to show why certain gestures in literary worlds are crucial, constitute interventions in ethical thought, for the early modern period. In order to do this, I have introduced both philosophical material - classical, medieval, and early modern - and literary analogues or sources, while elucidating the choice or choices that certain literary characters make. To some readers, intent upon literary interpretation only, this procedure may seem inordinately digressive. The value, however, of such postponing of the literary reading is that it sets up the literary world as a reaction to, a product of, a transgression of an intellectual-moral context. This context is accessible, and it is provocative, too: it poses central questions, it evaluates certain relationships in ways not entirely foreign to our thinking. It is also this provocation that my inclusive procedure is attempting to tease out, with the extraordinary help of the literature around which my book is organized.

Pantagruel's offers his friendship to Panurge, in Rabelais's *Pantagruel*, and Panurge's subsequently refuses to help his friend in epic combat; this refusal does not lessen the friendship. In a novella from

---

[1] This is the case with Corneille's *Rodogune*: see my discussion in Chapter VII. See, for an often subtle general reflection on the relationship between moral philosophy and literature, Martha C. Nussbaum, *Love's Knowledge: Essays on Philosophy and Literature* (New York, Oxford: Oxford University Press, 1990), especially pp. 3-53. Nussbaum's study juxtaposes classical ethical notions, derived mostly from Aristotle, and mainly modern novels, in a style that itself attempts to demonstrate the value of knowledge conveyed by literature, a value denied by the very form of much of current philosophical argumentation. My own study focusses on important modifications of the interplay between literature and ethics during the early modern period.

Marguerite de Navarre's *Heptaméron*, the female protagonist Floride attempts to uphold an "honest" friendship with Amadour, who is incapable of responding in kind. In Montaigne's essay on friendship, he removes his feeling for his friend from any exemplary discourse of motivation. In Madame de Lafayette's *La Princesse de Clèves*, the princess is unwilling to say why she remains faithful to her dead husband. In Corneille's play *Cinna*, the emperor Augustus offers friendship to his bitter enemy; in *Rodogune*, the tyrant Cléopâtre self-destructs, crushed by the friendship of her two sons for each other. These are all moments, I believe, that are ethically charged, first by the way in which they speak to us today, but above all by the way in which they intervene in a tradition of reflection on the duties, possibilities, and political and theological ramifications of friendship. It is around these moments that the following chapters are organized.

This book is also intended for a reader seeking information about friendship as a subject of theoretical reflection and as a theme in literature of the early modern period. Although the index will be the most detailed guide, there are general theoretical lines according to which the chapters are organized. The commonplaces of friendship constitute a constant backdrop, especially the Aristotelian typology of friendship (useful, pleasurable, and perfect), the similarity and equality of friends, and the requirement of mutual absolute honesty. The persistence of these commonplaces does not prevent historical modification in the definition of the perfect love that friendship is said to be: the nature of a love "for someone's own sake" and the explanation of such a love move through historical, theological, and political paths that are traced in several chapters.

Friendship narratives are also pervasive in early modern France and Italy: apart from the afore-mentioned works, I have found material in writers and genres as diverse as Boccaccio and his imitators, the sentimental romance (Helisenne de Crenne, Nicolas Denisot, and later on Madeleine de Scudéry), the chivalric romance or epic (*Amadis de Gaule*, Ariosto, and shorter prose narrative), lyric poetry (Etienne Jodelle), and para-literary texts such as Traiano Boccalini's pieces and a wealth of dialogues and semi-philosophical texts (by Leon Battista Alberti, most extensively, but also Estienne Pasquier, Giovambattista Giraldi Cintio, Pierre de la Primaudaye, Pierre Charron, etc.). Editions, commentaries, translations, prefaces, and florilegia constitute another important source, not only for friendship but for the discussion of any

moral philosophical issue in the early modern period. I will begin by
introducing some of the common elements of all these sources.


## 1. Commonplaces of Friendship

> L'amicitia è un amore tra tutti gli altri eccellente, & le cose
> eccellenti sono poche, & però fra pocchi si ritrova la vera
> amicitia, non pure ne nostri tempi, ma ne gli antichi anchora,
> perche si vede, che in tutta la antichità si fa mentione appena di
> due, ò tre paia di veri amici. (Giovambattista Giraldi Cintio)[2]

True friendship is exceedingly rare.   True friendship almost
always belongs to a more or less distant *past*, since the present time is
thought to exclude perfect relationships, which friendship surely is.
Renaissance compendia of examples used to illustrate moral philosophy
privilege classical, especially Roman, Antiquity.   In the case of
friendship this privilege is overwhelming: in Theodor Zwinger's
*Theatrum humanae vitae* most examples in the sections devoted to
friendship are Greek or Latin, with the biblical friendship between
Jonathan and David thrown in.[3]   In Battista Fregoso's compendium
there are ten classical or biblical examples, and only one friendship
figures in the category of the *recentiora*.[4]  Partly, this predominance of
certain classical friendships in treatises of moral philosophy can be
explained by their tendency to follow the model of Valerius Maximus's

---

[2] "Friendship is a love excelling all others, and excellent things are few in
number, and therefore among few is true friendship found, not only in our
times, but in ancient ones as well, for one sees that in all of antiquity mention
is made but of two or three pairs of true friends." *Dialogues philosophiques et
tres-utiles, Italiens-François, touchant la vie Civile*, trans. Gabriel Chappuis,
(Paris, Abel l'Angelier, 1584), f. 373v.

[3] *Theatrum humanae vitae* (Basel: E. Episcopius, 1586), Vol. 18, Liber 2,
pp. 3315-3316, and Vol. 22, Liber 1, pp. 3896-3897.

[4] *Baptistae Fulgosi opus incomparabile, in IX libros digestum, de dictis &
factis memorabilibus*, trans. Camillus Gilinus (Basel: Westhemerus, 1541),
Liber 4, cap. 7.

*Facta et dicta memorabilia* (4.7), whose examples are standard for the Renaissance, but there is also a real sense of friendship's extreme infrequency.

No one illustrates this feeling of friendship's near-anachronism better than the essayist Michel de Montaigne. In his paean to his dead friend Etienne de La Boétie, Montaigne gives what he considers to be salutory advice about having friends. Do not trust friendships, unless they are the sort of perfect friendship La Boétie and he had enjoyed. In ordinary friendships, Montaigne holds Aristotle's well-worn proverb to be true: "O mes amis, il n'y a nul amy" (*Essais*, 1.28).[5] The way in which the essayist introduces Aristotle's maxim seems to imply an imaginary, melancholy scenario: Aristotle wistfully exclaims to his friends that there is no friend, as if he were suggesting that they, too, cannot be real friends. Far from being an insult, however, his maxim provides them with useful, prudent advice. The scene also seems to contradict the message offered: Aristotle is surrounded by his friends, and the lack of true friends he appears to bemoan entails not physical solitude, but, strangely enough, a sort of proliferation of present relationships, of "false" friendships. It is as if, contrasted to multiple, empty relationships, the existence of the true friend entailed a deep mental solitude, as one always feels alone in his absence, and especially in the company of others. Indeed, it does for the otherwise sociable Montaigne, whose inaccessible, unique love for the dead La Boétie is a figure for his own intense self-involvement. In the context of Montaigne's essays, Aristotle's exclamation is also a product of *experience*; it is at the end of one's life, when one has felt the pain of betrayal often enough, that one can come to this regrettable conclusion.

In fact Aristotle's exclamation, as understood by Montaigne, also figures in Renaissance moral philosophy. True friendship in virtue is an immutable and stable love, according to Mario Equicola: because the philosopher found extremely few friends possessing the required virtuous

---

[5] "Oh my friends, there is no [true] friend." Ed. Pierre Villey, V.-L. Saulnier (Paris: Presses univ. de France, 1965), p. 190.

affection, he was forced to proclaim loudly "O amico, amico niuno."[6]
Equicola interprets this to mean that the laws of friendship are just too
difficult to observe.

Montaigne's little phrase, presumably culled from Aristotle, "O
mes amis, il n'y a nul ami," in its expression of melancholy solitude in
the midst of others, recalls the first poem of a brief sonnet sequence
(printed in 1574) addressed by Etienne Jodelle to his friend (and patron)
Philippe de Boulainvilliers, who had become the Comte de
Fauquemberge:

> Quand seul sans toy je suis, car rien que ton absence
> Ne me fait trouver seul, tant que je serois
> Avecq' tous les humains seul je me jugerois,
> Car plus que tous humains m'est ta seule presence.[7]

These lines illustrate remarkably the rarefied yet intimate, nearly
redundant style through which perfect friendship is often evoked. The

---

[6] "Per ritrovarli [gli amici] rarissimi in questa affettione fu sforzato
Aristotele con alta voce dire, o amico, amico niuno: percio che è troppo difficil
cosa servare le leggi dell'amicitia vera, secondo da scrittori et philosophanti si
danno" (*Libro di natura d'amore*, rev. ed, Vinegia, Gioanniantonio & Fratelli
de Sabio, 1526, f. 106r).

[7] "When alone without you I am, for nothing except your absence makes me
find myself alone, so much so that if I were with all human beings I would still
judge myself to be alone, for more than all human beings is for me your
presence alone," "A M. le Comte de Fauquemberge et de Courtenay," 1.1-4,
in Jodelle, *Oeuvres complètes*, ed. Enea Balmas (Paris: Gallimard, 1965), vol.
1, p. 138. See, on the evolution of the friendship relationship in these eight
sonnets, the excellent analysis by François Cornilliat, "Morales du sonnet: le
vers et la vertu dans les sonnets de Jodelle à M. de Fauquemberge," *RHR
(Réforme, Humanisme, Renaissance)*, 24 (June 1987): 47-63. Commenting on
the first sonnet, Cornilliat says: "la poésie 'brûle' le discours amoureux, elle le
communique déjà communiqué" (p. 51). The second part of the sentence
applies, it seems to me, to much of represented friendship. The subtext to the
interplay of presence and absence in the sonnet is perhaps Petrarch:
"Innumerabiles causae segregant amicos, amicitiam veram nullae qua praesente
amicus absens esse non poterit" (*Epistolarum familiarum libri XIV*, Lyons,
Samuel Crispin, 1601, 2.6, p. 61).

interplay and closeness of the personal pronouns are a simple but an effective means of signalling the presence of the other: he is not signified but referred to, evoked, by the voice of the I. The contrast between the solitude of the poet and presence of the other is mediated by "tous les humains"; a radical distinction is set up between all other relationships and the friendship, but also between all others and myself, *except* the friend. This exception is expressed by Jodelle in the phrase "ta seule presence," recalling the three previous uses of "seul" to designate not the uniqueness of the friend, but the solitude of the poet. The solitude of the poet is, then, enabled by his unique friendship, very similarly to the way in which the dead La Boétie allows his friend Montaigne's self-reflection, although in fact in the case of Philippe de Boulainvilliers the friend is not dead, but only imagined to be absent. On the other hand, this solitude is felt precisely in contrast to the many (false) relationships other human beings may offer: "O mes amis. . . ." Nostalgic true friendship implies a simultaneous emptying-out and multiplying of other friendships.

Finally, Jodelle's lines and Aristotle's exclamation are semantically impoverished. The effectiveness of their language is based on referential language (exclamation, first and second person pronouns) and on the repetition of key words: "ami," "seul," forms of "être."[8] In Montaigne's version of Aristotle, "O mes amis, il n'y a nul ami," through a simple, paradoxical negation the word "ami" in its singular form attains a "singularity" that is retroactively denied its plural, affirmative, thoughtless use. Jodelle takes this play of negation one step farther. In his juxtaposition of "absence"/"presence" and "tous"/"seul" we find a rendering of Aristotle's singularization of the friend. But Jodelle has driven negation to its limits: "rien que ton absence / Ne me fait trouver seul" (nothing but your absence makes me find myself alone, i.e., only your absence has the power to make me feel alone). In the French the highly negated sequence of words suggests that the friend's absence is more "nothing" than "nothing," a greater nothingness than

---

[8] For this play on personal pronouns, see also Marie de Gournay, in her preface to Montaigne's *Essais* (1595): "Lors qu'il me loüoit, je le possedois; moy avec luy, et moy sans luy, sommes absoluement deux" ("Préface à l'édition des *Essais* de Montaigne," ed. François Rigolot, *Montaigne Studies* 1 [1989], p. 51).

nothing. This paroxysm of negation corresponds, however, to the fourth line's paroxysm of affirmation: "Plus que tous les humains m'est ta seule présence." The feeling of solitude is, because of the friend's singularity and his simultaneous absence, the most intense proof of the perfect relationship, a mirror to the intensity of his presence. Jodelle's elaborate yet semantically simple formulation is a remarkable version of the hyperbolically inward, "subjective" feeling that what I call nostalgic friendship sometimes becomes in the Renaissance.

I emphasize "Renaissance." For Aristotle did not say what Montaigne has him say. Of course we do not know what he really said; the source of this particular maxim is commonly assumed to be the description of Aristotle's life and philosophy in Diogenes Laertius. His compilation was available from the late fifteenth century on in printed form in both Latin and Greek, and Montaigne often borrows from the 1570 edition that includes the Latin translation.[9] In Diogenes Laertius, Aristotle says "ᾧ φίλοι οὐδεὶς φίλος," literally, "to whom there are friends no one is a friend." In other words, true friendship can involve only one other person, not many. However, in Greek editions of Diogenes Laertius before the addition of Isaac Casaubon's critical apparatus in 1593, the phrase is "ὢ φίλος, οὐδεὶς φίλος" (Oh friends,

---

[9] In his edition of the *Essais* Pierre Villey lists *Diogenis Laertii clarissimi historici de vitis ac moribus priscorum philosophorum libri decem* (Lyons, 1556) as the translation Montaigne must have used. I have consulted *Diogenis Laertii de vita et moribus philosophorum libri X. recens opera Ioannis Boulieri ad fidem Graeci codicis diligenter recogniti* (Lyons: Antoine Vincent, 1556), p. 303, where in this case the text is identical to the Latin text in the edition preferred by Edilia Traverso, in her *Montaigne e Aristotele* (Florence: Le Monnier, 1974, p. 30 n. 18), by Henri Estienne (ΔΙΟΓΕΝΟΥΣ ΛΑΕΡΤΙΟΥ ΠΕΡΙ ΒΙΩΝ . . . *Diogenis Laertii de vitis, dogmatis & apophthegmatis . . .*, Paris, Henri Estienne, 1570). Traverso discusses several instances of Montaigne's quoting of Aristotle through Diogenes Laertius, but does not mention this instance. Dorothy G. Coleman examines the Greek edition of Diogenes Laertius that Montaigne owned (the 1533 Frobenius edition) and finds no evidence of annotation by Montaigne, although that is not, according to Coleman, a sign of its not having been used. See "Notes sur l'édition grecque de Diogène Laërce que possédait Montaigne," *Bulletin de la société des amis de Montaigne* 27-28 (1978): 93-95.

nobody is a [true] friend).[10]  In sixteenth-century Latin versions, including the ones Montaigne may have consulted, the translation is "O amici amicus nemo," reflecting the (faulty) Greek edition before Casaubon's emendations, and thus taking the relative pronoun as an exclamation (Oh!) and the nominative plural as a vocative plural (friends!).[11]  The corrected Greek version, underlining the impossibility of multiple friendships, is pretty much a commonplace: this is the gist of what Plutarch, in his treatise *On Having Many Friends*, also maintains.[12]  The reasons for the exclusive nature of true friendship are the long time spent together, the required similarity between friends, the fact that the friend is another self.  But what Aristotle, in Diogenes Laertius's Greek version, has exclaimed is not a melancholy reflection on the disillusionment that the passage of time brings with it, but instead a theoretical ethical point: given the nature of true friendship as defined in the *Nicomachean Ethics*, say, the reasonable conclusion is that it is impossible to have many friends.  Montaigne's nostalgic scenario, derived from contemporary Latin versions, transforms what is a statement founded on dialectical or logical thought into something

---

[10] Such as in the Henri Estienne edition of 1570, part 1, p. 172 (Greek) and part 2, p. 155 (Latin), and in the 1533 Frobenius edition (Greek) which was in Montaigne's library.  Although the Greek and Latin texts still contain the prior, probably corrupt version, in ΔΙΟΓΕΝΟΥΣ ΛΑΕΡΤΙΟΥ ΠΕΡΙ ΒΙΩΝ . . . *Diog. Laert. de vitis, dogm. & apophth. clarorum philosopharum Libri X* (Paris: Henri Estienne, 1593), in the *Notae* (p. 75) of that edition Casaubon proposes ᾧ φίλοι, preferring that reading also to ᾧ πολλοὶ φίλοι, which is based on *Eudemian Ethics*, 7 (1245b 21).

[11] I have found the same translation in the following editions: Jehan Petit, 1510; Henri Estienne, 1570; Jacques Chouët, 1595.

[12] See Giovambattista Giraldi Cintio, whose philosophical dialogues were translated into French during Montaigne's time: "molti sono amici di nome ... ma in fatto se ne ritrovano ne bisogni pochissimi: la onde è nato il proverbio, CHI MOLTI AMICI VUOL, NE PROVI [sic] POCHI" (*Dialogues philosophiques*, f. 374v).  According to Diogenes Laertius, however, the Stoics believed "that it is a good thing to have many friends" (*Lives* 7.124 [Zeno]).

produced by the weight of experience, and tinged by feeling: the feeling of age, of solitude in the midst of friends.

Montaigne's transformation of the theoretical statement into an expression of feeling stands for a good deal of what happens in his essay on friendship, which is one of the most moving pieces of writing in the Renaissance. But whatever the inflections and deformations we observe in French and Italian Renaissance writers, the idea of friendship is very much connected to the theoretical discourse of moral philosophy, to a set of commonplaces, and to a few - surprisingly few - examples.

Friendship (*philia*) is generally distinct from desire, concupiscence, or erotic love (*eros*) and from simple good will (*eunoia*) or, later on, Christian charity and the love of God (*agape*). It is, after Aristotle, generally divided into three types: friendship through usefulness, through pleasure, and perfect friendship, a relationship of good men with each other through their goodness. This perfect friendship is often expressed in terms of loving another "for his own sake."[13] One of the first important humanist commentators on Aristotle's *Nicomachean Ethics*, Jacques Lefèvre d'Etaples, formulates it succinctly: "Est enim amicitia per se, qua quis suiipsius, & boni gratia quod intra se est, amatur."[14] Friendship is possible only when the persons involved are similar to each other, when they have gained knowledge of each other through a long and agreeable time spent together, and when they are both virtuous. Jean des Caurres, in his *Oeuvres morales et diversifiées*, summarizes the necessary elements of friendship:

---

[13] I have opted generally for the masculine pronoun in situations in which both women and men may be designated, or when God is designated. The reason is simple: the theory of friendship in classical times, and in its medieval and Renaissance versions, almost always concerns men, and is conceived of as a particularly male relationship. See chapter IV on the "maleness" of friendship theory. The designation of God with a female personal pronoun would introduce an even greater anachronism into the discussion.

[14] "[Perfect friendship] is truly friendship for its own sake, through which someone is loved because of himself, and because of the good which is between the friends." *Moralis Iacobi Fabris Stapulensis in Ethicen introductio, Iudoci Clichtovi Neoportuensis familiari commentario elucidata* (Paris: Simon Colin, [1535]), fs. 31r-31v.

> Que ces trois choses sont bien requises & necessaires pour
> fonder & asseurer ceste amitié: la vertu, comme honneste: la
> conversation, comme agreable: & l'utilité, comme secourable:
> qui est à dire, recevoir l'Amy, apres l'avoir cogneu &
> esprouvé: s'esjouir de sa compagnie, & se servir de luy au
> besoin, tout ainsi que nous desirons qu'il en use avec nous.[15]

Friends demonstrate their friendship by performing good actions for each
other; often these actions are of exemplary nature and have political
consequences.  Cicero's treatises on friendship (*Laelius de amicitia*) and
on duties (*De officiis*), and Seneca's treatise on favors (*De beneficiis*) and
some of his letters to Lucilius, reflect elaborately on the nature of perfect
friendship in the civic realm and the sort of actions entailed by such a
relationship.  In his *Libro di natura d'amore*, Equicola provides a brief
list of the signs of a true friend:

> De vera amicitia li segni se dicono essere se ti fa partecipe
> d'ogni suo secreto, se te exhibisce ogni generation d'honore, se
> confidentemente tua familiarita usa, se volontieri te dona, se
> con diligentia ha cura di tua salute, se essendo teco in qualche
> differentia, non cessa pero procurare tuo honore & utile, se in
> tuoi bisogni ti visita, se in cose dubie te conseglia, se in affanni
> te soccorre, se in dolor te conforta, se parimenti te fa partecipe
> della autorita & potesta sua.  Quello reputamo vero amico che
> è stabile & fermo persevera, ne qual Protheo si trasforma, ne

---

[15] "The following three things are necessary in order to found and render
sure this friendship: (honest) virtue, agreeable conversation, helpful usefulness,
that is, receiving the friend after having known and tested him, enjoying his
company, and having him be useful to us, as we would want to be useful to
him." *Oeuvres morales et diversifiees en histoires, pleines de beaux exemples,
enrichies d'enseignemens vertueux, & embellies de plusieurs sentences &
discours* (rev. ed. Paris: Guillaume Chaudiere, 1584), Livre 1, chap. 51, f. 96r.
This passage is taken from Equicola's *Libro di natura d'amore*: "Tre cose
richiede la vera amicitia, virtu, perche poco tempo dura l'amicitia che non è fra
virtuosi: & sententia di Sophocle è li amici dever bene amare, & ben operar
insieme, non haver in odio & far male: La seconda consuetudine, como
dilettevole, & percio non senza ragione li antiqui cresero, propinqui alla amicitia
habitar le gratie & Cupido: La terza lo uso, como necessario, dice Plutarcho piu
di bisogno esser l'amico, che non è il fuoco & l'acqua. . ." (f. 103r).

como ombra muta luogo, & quasi specchio, non riceve ogni
imagine: Quello istimo vero amico, il qual in tempo opportuno
ne incita & rafrena con libera ammonitione. . . (fs. 104r -
104v).[16]

Another elaborate Renaissance summary of the duties of friends is found
in Zwinger's *Theatrum humanae vitae*, in the section devoted to
distributive justice: friends show their *fides*, their moral commitment to
each other by protecting or conserving the other's life, by detecting or
indicating plots against the other, by defending and not abandoning the
other in dangerous situations, by freeing the other from prison, by
improving the other's habits, by not revealing the other's secrets, by
providing for the other's children, and by regretting the friend's
death.[17]   Zwinger provides several examples of this behavior taken
mostly from Antiquity.

The friend is thought of as another self, or friends as one soul
living in two bodies.  Friendship is generally thought of as incompatible
with the pursuit of wealth and ambition, and incompatible with tyranny,
although whether it survives best in a good monarchy or a republic is
open to question.  Aside from Plato's *Lysis*, a somewhat inconclusive
dialogue, Aristotle's *Nicomachean Ethics* and *Eudemian Ethics*, Cicero's
and Seneca's treatises and letters, there are many ancillary classical

---

[16] "The signs of true friendship are said to be that he lets you share in every
secret, that he displays for you honorable actions, that he uses your familiarity
in a trustworthy way, that he gives freely to you, that he cares for your good
health, that, when he has some difference with you, he does not for that reason
cease to procure useful things and honor for you, that he visits you in need, that
he counsels you in difficult matters, that he helps you when you are in need,
that he comforts you in pain, that on an equal basis he lets you share in his
authority and power.  We call him a true friend who is stable and perseveres,
who does not transform himself like Proteus, nor change places like a shadow,
nor receive every image like a mirror: we consider him a true friend who in
opportune time exhorts and restrains by freely admonishing [us]."

[17] *Theatrum*, pp. 3315-3316.  In book 17, under the heading "Amicitia
mutua arctissima quorumlibet inter se" Zwinger provides 37 examples of pairs
of friends, and lists peoples who maintained a cult of friendship.

writings on friendship by writers and moral philosophers such as Lucian, Plutarch, and Epictetus.[18]

Classical literary treatments of friendship become commonplace examples of friendship couples cited in post-classical moral philosophy and literature: especially Orestes and Pylades, but also Achilles and Patroclus, Aeneas and Achates, and occasionally Damon and Phintias. Often cited in medieval Christian treatments of friendship is the Biblical example of Jonathan and David. The list is not very long, once one leaves behind the most detailed compendia of *exempla*, and the examples are usually nothing but ciphers. In part, the very limitedness of the examples is a proof of the perfection of the friendships involved; perhaps perfection is obscurely felt to be redundant, and the small number undoubtedly is deemed to be sufficient.

The Middle Ages were not unconcerned with friendship, partly because the Church Fathers are imbued with a Latin moral philosophical tradition: Augustine reflects on friendship in many of his writings, although it is clear that for the bishop of Hippo God is the author of friendship, and its final cause. In this sense charity is an extension of friendship.[19] Lactantius is a favorite source for maxims on the nature of true gifts and genuine love of the other. Treatises by Ethelred of Rievaulx and Pierre de Blois discuss the Ciceronian ideal and the relationship between friendship and charity. The views of both Cicero and Aristotle are known and widely commented upon. Medieval theology is more concerned than one may think with *amicitia*: Peter Abailard uses Ciceronian maxims from the *De amicitia* in his compilation of theological opinions, the *Sic et Non*, when treating gratuitous love.[20] Saint Thomas Aquinas analyzes the concept of friendship in relation to charity, in the *Summa theologiae* (II-2 qu 23), and considers the status of ethical relationships and the love of virtue in

---

[18] For a wide-ranging philosophical treatment of the classical concept, see Jean-Claude Fraisse, *Philia: La notion d'amitié dans la philosophie antique* (Paris: Vrin, 1984).

[19] See Marie Aquinas McNamara, *L'amitié chez Saint Augustin* (Paris: P. Lethielleux, 1961), especially pp. 169-192.

[20] Question 138 (ed. Blanche B. Boyer, Richard McKeon, Chicago, Univ. of Chicago Press, 1976, pp. 472-473).

the *Summa contra gentiles* (3.34). The dominance of Aristotle in scholastic theology ensures a continued presence of books 8 and 9 of the *Nicomachean Ethics* in theological thought; the *Eudemian Ethics* and their discussion of friendship in book 7 are not well-known until the end of the Middle Ages. However, in the literary tradition the Ciceronian commonplaces seem to have had more resonance, although on many points it is difficult to distinguish between the two traditions: the figure of Reason, in Jean de Meung's continuation of the *Romance of the Rose*, advocates a quasi-classical friendship, and refers to Cicero himself. At the end of the Middle Ages Petrarch's *Epistolae de rebus familiaribus* (especially 18.8) and his *De remediis utriusque fortunae* contribute to the diffusion of Senecan and Ciceronian commonplaces on friendship.

If the theoretical discussion of friendship in the Middle Ages inevitably involves charity and its inherent superiority, the issues raised in the classical ethical texts find perhaps their most interesting development in medieval and especially late medieval treatments of the creature's love of God. For it is here that the often laborious calculus of the gratuitousness of perfect love meets its greatest challenge: how, on the model of Aristotle's definition of the highest form of love, can one love God *for his own sake*? If any love carries an interest, pleasure or usefulness, with it, it is surely this kind of love. However, to love God because he is good, or because he has promised us salvation, is an imperfect love, since it submits God to a condition, to an end more important than himself. The possibilities of perfect love of God were raised most forcefully by Augustine in his *De doctrina christiana*, but they were elaborated by a long line of succeeding theologians, from Peter Lombard in his *Sentences* to the scholastics active in the early sixteenth century. I believe that this scholastic experimentation with the paradoxes of love for the truly Other constitutes an important contribution to the *imagined* possibilities and requirements of human friendship. For the problems debated by the scholastics involve a love that is at least conceptually disjoined from the pursuit of virtue, and in this sense goes beyond the classical paradigm of friendship between good men *qua* their goodness. The love of God logically involves a reduction of the object of love to what amounts to a pure otherness, and it becomes increasingly possible to envisage human relationships in similar terms.

The literary works that will be the focus of this book were written by persons who for the most part were more sympathetic to the remnants of the classical tradition than to medieval theologians and their fifteenth and sixteenth-century epigones.  When these writers, especially on the French side, use theological material, it tends to be taken directly from the New Testament, or perhaps from Augustine.  The scorn of Renaissance authors such as Erasmus, Rabelais, Marguerite de Navarre, and Montaigne for the sophistry of the scholastic tradition is a well-established and entirely justified commonplace of literary history. Moreover, when considering the concept of friendship alone, the very form which much humanist writing took favors a neo-classical bent.  For the proto-Republic of humanist letters was literally an epistolary world: the correspondences of Erasmus and More, of Ulrich von Hutten, of the Florentine humanists, but also of the evangelical Reformers in general, are witnesses to this practice.  In that sense Cicero's and Seneca's letters were perhaps the most important model, especially since in many cases the letters themselves were written to friends, proclaimed the writer's love for his friend, and acted as a sort of *beneficium* (benefit or favor), in the form of counsel, consolation, encouragement, etc.  In spite of the fact that friendships between father and son are not always thought of as perfect, Gargantua's famous letter to his son Pantagruel, in Rabelais's *Pantagruel*, is a good example.  The very form of the letter, usually addressed to one person, underlines the intimacy and exclusiveness that perfect friendship is taken to incarnate.  Petrarch's personal letters, the *Epistolae de rebus familiaribus*, give an emotional, subjective twist to the Roman models.  But there is also a practical side: friendship prudently chosen enables one to survive the trials of adversity as well as the deceptions of good fortune.  It can serve didactic purposes, by presenting the letter-writer with occasions to proclaim the virtue of the educated few.[21]  Petrarch's widely read symposium *De remediis utriusque fortunae* contains sections on friendship and its value in good and hard times.  Any consideration of humanism's success must include the

---

[21] See Charles E. Trinkaus, *Adversity's Noblemen: The Italian Humanists on Happiness* (New York: Columbia Univ. Press, 1940), especially pp. 60-61. Trinkaus, though, emphasizes the relatively impersonal nature of the "friendship" of some humanists, such as Coluccio Salutati.

function of correspondence and the multiple uses of ancient moral philosophy in the maintaining and advertising of personal friendships.[22]

In this book, however, I will not be concerned with humanist or other epistolary friendships, as I will focus on the imaginary worlds that literature represents. How do relationships represented in literature work out ethical and theological issues debated in intellectual culture? More specifically, how is love for the "other" communicated in a fictional setting? In the Renaissance such a problem, for reasons that will become clearer in the following chapters, inevitably involves considering the meaning and consequences of "gratuitousness." The discussion of this concept entails the use of cultural material that explores the imaginative and logical possibilities of human relationships in a moral philosophical setting.    The imagining of gratuitousness also entails, for the Renaissance, consideration of the limit-concept of culture, God.    More generally the appropriation of classical moral theory cannot be separated from theological discourse through which moral philosophy is often filtered, although some literary texts seem to want to do just that. It is for this reason that I give some weight to the Christian theological revision of the teleology of friendship, and its most intricate conceptual elaboration in scholasticism.

This book also represents an attempt at a certain historically based "ethical" criticism.    I attempt to give a fair picture of the varied development and nature of "friendship" mostly in the sixteenth century, but my primary interest lies in the exploration of certain perhaps exemplary issues.    In this sense the reader will not find an exhaustive presentation of moral philosophy and all of its repercussions in the literature of the Renaissance.    I will concentrate on certain works that represent situations or relationships that imply moral philosophical

---

[22] See, for a subtle and wide-ranging consideration of humanist correspondence as the practice of friendship, Nancy S. Struever, *Theory As Practice: Ethical Inquiry in the Renaissance* (Chicago: University of Chicago Press, 1992), especially pp. 14-28 and 47-55. Struever contrasts Petrarchan and Erasmian epistolary friendship: "Petrarchan friendship is first of all a research field, a domain of discovery; Erasmian friendship is a constraint, an institutional guarantee; there is a movement from disciplinary topic to discipline" (p. 55). Struever also emphasizes Marc Fumaroli's claim that the essay form as practiced by Montaigne has its roots in the epistolary intimacy of Petrarch's letters (pp. 33-34).

problems. Before delving into the literary selections, I indicate in the first part (chapters I and II) the directions that my later analyses will be taking. This initial part is perhaps an extended introduction to the more "practical" analyses in the following parts of the book, but it, too, considers mainly particular problems, rather than attempting to "cover" the field:

- the incompatibility of ethical (lack of) motivation and literary motivation in the representation of perfect relationships: why does one love someone?;

- the problem of defining personal identity as independent of personal attributes (especially in Antoine Hotman's paradox on friendship): whom does one love?.

The second part (chapters III, IV, and V) deals with particular literary worlds; the theoretical direction set by the first section determines my reading of these works as the representation of friendship relationships:

- the gratuitous, unjustifiably exclusive love of someone not worthy of that love (in Rabelais's books);

- the improbability of female-male "perfect" friendship (in the 10th novella of the *Heptaméron* by Marguerite de Navarre);

- the nostalgic attempt at an a-teleological love, that is, one that refuses an end other than the relationship itself (in Montaigne's essay on friendship and Madame de Lafayette's *La Princesse de Clèves*).

In the third part (chapters VI and VII), through the reading of a para-literary and two dramatic texts, I will consider the imagined function of friendship in a larger political context, Florence of the early fifteenth century, and the French absolutist state of the mid-seventeenth century. Again, certain problems will constitute the focus of the readings:

- the "usefulness" of moral philosophy and friendship in particular, in an environment of pragmatic, interested relationships (Leon Battista Alberti's *De amicitia*);

- the efficacy or inefficacy of friendship as an instrument of political betterment (in Pierre Corneille's plays *Cinna* and *Rodogune*).

In each case I illuminate the literary interpretation by considering aspects of the moral philosophical tradition, the theological tradition, or of contiguous contemporary disciplines, such as the theory of usury or anti-Machiavellian political theory. The represented relationships are played off against the possibilities that contemporary intellectual culture had to offer.

The ethical perspective brought to literary works is first an outgrowth of the topic itself, as friendship is conceived of as a touchstone of moral philosophy, the perfection of human relationships. But I conceive this perspective also as a refusal of a purely estheticist-formalist or a purely antiquarian reading.[23] This perspective, however, has its costs: if one takes seriously fictional relationships, this means considering them as if they were real. This in turn entails a certain neglect of a literary work's symbolic or esthetic coherence, a certain neglect of generic constraints, and in the end a certain neglect of biographical, referential factors. The way Rabelais constructs the relationship between Pantagruel and Panurge must, at least for a moment, be understood independently of the symbolic and generic precedents the epic couple may have had. But it also must, I think, be understood independently of real relationships Rabelais may have had with his contemporaries. In part, this (always provisional) independence characterizes literary worlds in general. Perhaps, more importantly, literature in this period is becoming more and more the ground for imaginative experimentation, for experimentation with the multiple codes and values of an expanding civilization. On a different level, "taking literature seriously," that is, assuming it to be a useful representation of human beings and their choices, is also one of the ways in which the modern reader can perform interpretative work that reproduces something of what Renaissance readers themselves sought in literary fictions. For the "usefulness" of literature was a topos of early modern poetics, and it generally implied a simple allegorical reading, or one that took the represented actions to be models for imitation. For a modern reader, this sense of literature's "usefulness" is obviously inadequate. But there is another way in which the very fictionality and hypotheticalness of literary worlds are eminently useful, as well as pleasurable. Part of this non-exemplary but useful nature of certain

---

[23] In this regard I am emulating aspects of the courageous study by Robert E. Proctor, *Education's Great Amnesia: Reconsidering the Humanities from Petrarch to Freud: With a Curriculum for Today's Students* (Bloomington: Indiana Univ. Press, 1988), although I disagree with some of the interpretations of Renaissance intellectual culture.

literature is its requirement that the reader perform two seemingly conflicting operations: the relationships represented should be assumed to be real, and yet they should be taken as an exploration, a trying-out, a testing, of options.  The very work of trying-out provisionally real options provides the pleasure and the usefulness, not the subsequent imitation of the model, that is, its exemplary force.  While it would be difficult to locate such a sense of the "usefulness" of literature in any of the explicit poetics of the period, it seems clear that this sort of trying-out of hypotheses, of situations, was very much part of the intellectual culture of the Renaissance, in the scholastic tradition of commentary, in the early humanist argumentation *in utramque partem*, and perhaps most permanently in the legal professional milieu with which so many writers of the period were familiar.

Yet for today's reader of literature written in the past there is something more at play here.  Renaissance literature's usefulness also involves the attempt to understand the work on the terms of the intellectual culture out of which it arose; I do not think that Renaissance texts should simply be playgrounds of our fantasies, and I think that it is to our advantage not to let them become that.  The very problem of the love of an other cannot be separated from the act by which we explore that problem in a period fundamentally different from our own. Our reading of other worlds involves, in curious ways, the combination of an affective and a cognitive relationship that in that very combination comes close to the questions of moral philosophy.  For us to ignore the conditions under which older writers produced what they produced would entail a similar blindness when it came to our relationship to others and, in the end, to ourselves.  This in no way means that we should love the Renaissance "for its own sake": the pitfalls of such a love are examined throughout this book.  But it does mean that as modern readers we cannot help but be implicated in the ethical relationships we are studying.  It also means, conversely, that we have a certain historical responsibility, or that a certain historical approach and an ethical concern imply each other.

## 2. Friendship and Time

Friendship conveys a sense of completeness and completion that in linguistic terms is perhaps most characteristic of the perfect tense.  It is present to us, but has always already actualized itself, "perfected" itself. The development of friendship is the unfolding of what is already there, a sort of repeated showing of its completedness: just as the similarity of the friends ties them to each other, so does temporal development fail to introduce anything different, for each successive event is a confirmation, a demonstration of what has been perfected. Friendship entails a looking-back, its goal is already contained in its existence, in its birth. When Pantagruel meets Panurge, the latter puts on a dizzying and frustrating display of his knowledge of foreign languages, after which the giant tells him:

> Je vous ay jà prins en amour si grande, que, si vous condescendez à mon vouloir, vous ne bougerez jamais de ma compaignie, et vous et moy ferons ung nouveau per d'amytié, telle que fut entre Enée et Achates.[24]

The relationship is already determined *ab ovo* by Pantagruel ("je vous ay jà prins"), although, in Rabelais's usual fashion, the object of his gigantic affection is left to choose to accept or not to accept the favor (Panurge, in fact, knowing when a good deal is offered, does not hesitate to accept). It is as if the goal were already achieved, and the future set not as a quest, but as a repetition of the initial scenario of friendship: you will never be without me, we will be a pair, just like other famous pairs. These connotations are, I believe, characteristic of many literary treatments, although the temporal shortening that perfect friendship seems to entail is not part of its classical philosophical treatment. In Boccaccio's novella centered on friendship, the story of Tito and Gisippo (*Decameron*, 10.3), many lines of the text are devoted not to the development and enrichment of the friendship, but to a sort of deductive reasoning by which one friend proves to the other that friendship entails this or that favor. Gisippo proves to Tito in a lengthy speech that their friendship entails the sacrifice of his own fiancee to Tito, and in another lengthy speech Tito proves to the family of the unfortunate woman that

---

[24] "I have already taken you into such love that, if you agree to my wish, you will never leave my company, and you and I will be a new friendship pair, such as Aeneas and Achates." François Rabelais, *Pantagruel*, ed. V. L. Saulnier (Geneva: Droz, 1965), chap. IX, p. 54. Unless indicated otherwise all translations are my own.

this sacrifice is not only a consequence of the friendship bond but that the switching of bridegrooms is to the family's advantage, as well. The final events of the story are then related relatively briefly, as if in any case they were only repetitions of the initial *beneficium* of friendship. In spite of the highly dramatic nature of the sacrifices to each other, a story of friendship often gives a static impression.

In the Western literary tradition there are few literary works as antithetical to the static world of perfect friendship as the great early sixteenth-century romance-epic of desire, Ariosto's *Orlando furioso* (1516, 1532). Ariosto's poem was already known in the Renaissance for its depiction of indefatigable desire as constant movement. Montaigne, in his friendship essay, contrasts love with the more stable relationship of friends:

> En l'amitié, c'est une chaleur generale et universelle, temperée au demeurant et égale, une chaleur constante et rassize, toute douceur et pollissure, qui n'a rien d'aspre et de poignant. Qui plus est, en l'amour, ce n'est qu'un desir forcené apres ce qui nous fuit: *Come segue la lepre il cacciatore* . . . (Montaigne quotes four lines of the *Orlando furioso* [10.7.5-8]; *Essais*, 1.28, p. 186).[25]

The associations evoked by the concept of friendship - universality, temperedness, constancy, smoothness - are reproduced in the binary, repetitive style of the sentence, contrasting with the "madness" of the hunter chasing the erratic movement of the hare. In the case of desire, nothing but movement is left: we do not follow anything specific, merely that which flees us, "ce qui nous fuit."

In the *Orlando furioso*, from which Montaigne so tellingly quotes, the narrator follows the varied adventures of several pagan and Christian heroes, their military and amorous pursuits, in a way that suggests endless desire for satisfaction and offers little hope of attaining it. The self-conscious narration plays with the reader's desire for closure,

---

[25] "In friendship, it is a general and universal warmth, moreover tempered and equal, a constant and calm warmth, entirely sweetness and smoothness, which does not contain anything harsh and stinging. In addition, in love, it is nothing but a mad desire of that which flees before us: *As the hunter follows the hare* . . . ."

deferring the resolution of episodes and suggesting new bifurcations of the plot. This feverish movement comes to a Virgilian ending, although the extent to which the text comes to a full closure is a matter of critical debate.[26]

Friendship is not absent from Ariosto's poem: in imitation of Statius's Hopleus and Dymas (*Thebaid*, 10.347-448) and Virgil's Euryalus and Nisus (*Aeneid*, 9.176-445), two pagans, the robust hunter Cloridano and the angelic youth Medoro, stand united in friendship.[27] In a desperate act of loyalty both to each other and to their slain lord Dardinello d'Almonte, they decide to infiltrate by night the camp of Charlemagne in order to recover his dead body. They slaughter many Christian warriors, find the corpse, but cannot return without being attacked by the Christians. Cloridano suggests they leave the corpse and flee (18.189.5-8), and, thinking that Medoro has in fact done so, he leaves in great haste. Medoro, however, loves his lord more than Cloridano does, and continues to carry the heavy burden. Surrounded by Christians, he is gravely wounded by an impetuous warrior. Cloridano realizes his error, returns to find Medoro lying on the ground, lashes out in desperation at the Christians, and dies, apparently united with his friend (19.15). This epic pair is emblematic of an active friendship: no time is spent telling us why they are friends, or how they came to be friends, and much of the narrative involves their deeds for each other. In contrast, however, to the heroic-virtuous treatment especially in Virgil, in the *Orlando furioso* the heroes' feelings for each other tend to be emphasized more, and Medoro's loyalty to Dardinello becomes a more personal, melancholic one.[28]     Most importantly,

---

[26] See most recently Joseph C. Sitterson, Jr., "Allusive and Elusive Meanings: Reading Ariosto's Vergilian Ending," *Renaissance Quarterly* 45 (1992): 1-19. Sitterson usefully rehearses the various critical points of view - both Renaissance and twentieth-century - concerning the closed or open nature of the *Furioso*'s ending.

[27] They are, says the narrator, an "esempio raro di vero amore" (*Orlando furioso*, ed. Lanfranco Caretti, Torino, Einaudi, 1971, 18.165.3-4).

[28] See, on this more subjective emphasis, Walter Moretti, *Cortesia e furore nel rinascimento italiano* (Bologna: Pàtron, 1970), especially pp. 26-27, and the interesting discussion of Hegel's distinction between loyalty among equal friends

Ariosto is not content with the depiction of their death for each other and
their lord, and refuses a real stop, a real resolution.  In both Virgil's and
Statius's poems the two friends die more or less together, and thus
immediately constitute a finished, accomplished *exemplum*.  In contrast,
Ariosto reintroduces movement into their ending by making Medoro
survive, and survive in order to be reinserted into the movement of
desire.  For he will be found by chance ("Gli sopravenne a caso,"
18.17.1) and nursed back to health by, of all people, Angelica, who is
the proud emblem of desire.  The (almost) incessantly fleeing Angelica
causes various characters - among them the "hero" Orlando - to fall
desperately in love with her, chasing her along the forest paths and
*stanze* of the poem.  She, however, is not impervious to the ubiquity of
desire, and falls in love with someone who cannot chase her, the
severely injured Medoro.  She propositions him, allows him to enjoy
what so many others worked in vain to merit, and they are married.
Angelica cannot, as it were, get enough of him:

> E piú d'un mese poi stêro a diletto
> i duo tranquilli amanti a ricrearsi.
> Piú lunge non vedea del giovinetto
> la donna, né di lui potea saziarsi;
> né per mai sempre pendergli dal collo,
> il suo disir sentia di lui satollo. (19.34.2-8)[29]

In spite of the "tranquil" nature of their lovers' idyll, Angelica and
Medoro do not escape from the insatisfaction that desire implies.  The
evocation of their pleasures is one-sided: it is written from Angelica's
point of view.  There is never any satiety, any real rest; when Ariosto
goes on to describe her search for pastoral hideaways, the allusion is to

---

and loyalty to a lord, in connection with the Cloridano-Medoro episode, in
Eduardo Saccone, *Il "soggetto" del furioso e altri saggi tra quattro e
cinquecento* (Naples: Liguori, 1974), pp. 193-200.

[29] "And more than a month then the two lovers took pleasure in diversion.
Longer the woman did not see the youth, and she could not get her fill of him;
nor, in spite of always hanging from his neck, did she feel her desire for him
satisfied."

the cave in which Dido and Aeneas, seeking shelter from the rain, consummate their love (19.35.7-8). Although there seems to be no necessity to do so, the narrator refers to a couple more famous for its separation than its brief common pleasures. The restlessness of a narrative of desire imbues even the (probably) mutual love of Medoro and Angelica with its insatisfaction. Yet Ariosto's narrative of movement is also an emblem, I think, for the way we generally think of narrative, as the pursuit of a usually elusive goal, as the machine of desire, and of meaning as something that is not yet there.

*     *     *

In the following chapters I will concentrate on what resists this movement, and on what operates outside of this movement, in literature. For I am interested in the literary communication of *satisfaction*, and satisfaction not of desire, but a kind of intersubjective moral satisfaction *tout court*. I have studied mostly but not exclusively theoretical and literary works in the French and Italian sixteenth and seventeenth centuries. I am more interested in Aristotelian than Platonic strains in literary culture of the early modern period, for the following reasons. Aristotle's theory of friendship and its Ciceronian version distinguish clearly between erotic love and friendship, as do many Renaissance treatises and other works on this topic, whereas the confusion of erotic love and friendship is prominent in Plato, especially in the opening of the *Lysis*.

Another aspect of my focus on the Aristotelian tradition is my discounting of the rhetoric of inspiration. Montaigne's sublime formulations notwithstanding, friendship tends not to be ecstatic. I believe that the topoi of poetic and amorous "ravishment" or "furor" are largely irrelevant to the theoretical texts and also to the literature I will be discussing. Arguably, the melancholy inspiration of great men, found in the pseudo-Aristotelian *Problemata* (30.1), confirmed the Neoplatonic sympathies of many poets and philosophers, but on the whole the ethical writings of Aristotle, Cicero, and Seneca are resistant to a rhetoric of divine frenzy. I would also argue that much of narrative prose, even in writers whose knowledge of and sympathy with, say, Florentine Neoplatonism are in other respects evident, seems at least ambivalent about the efficacy and validity of inspiration and spiritual ravishment.

In the frequent Renaissance Neoplatonic dialogues about love and other matters inspiration is for the most part talked about, not shown. Characters discuss inspiration without being inspired. This is an important choice, for narrative as a form appears to invite representation, not just discussion, of the thing itself. In part the ambivalence toward inspiration is connected to the very nature of narrative, even relatively static narrative, which, as opposed to lyric poetry, resists representing the influx of an often incommunicable otherness. Narrative resists a turning-away from the characters' practical bonds with each other and with the surrounding world. Generally, too, narrative assumes the possibility of multiple perspectives, and the "ravishing" relationship between the lover and his beloved, the beautiful vessel of God's love, always risks being comic when seen through the eyes of others. That is perhaps why it is difficult to take entirely seriously the Neoplatonic ravishment of Pietro Bembo at the end of Castiglione's *Libro del cortegiano*. That is also why in Rabelais's books, even if vineous inspiration is a constant theme, the three-hour long ecstasy of the "Conseilliers et aultres Docteurs" at the conclusion of the judgment by Pantagruel of the Humevesne - Baisecul dispute (*Pantagruel*, 9) is truly comic. Moral philosophy, then, rather than solipsistic furor, has a more natural place in the literary worlds of narrative fiction, and it is that place which I focus on. Of course, we will see that moral relationships have their own problems in fictional worlds, and at times perfect friendship is reduced to an apodictic formula if not to an incommunicable feeling. But the relationship of "honest" friendship arises out of a tradition of discursive-rational theory, and out of its Christian modifications. When, at times, that relationship comes close to escaping representation entirely, it is largely because of particular logical and other intellectual developments that mark the Renaissance absorption of classical moral philosophy, not, I think, because of a shift to inspiration and the rejection of discursive-rational communication. In spite of a seemingly paroxysmal moment in Montaigne's *Essais*, friendship, then, is generally not ecstatic.

In that sense friendship may allow the modern reader more "identification" than, say, the highly stylized paths of neo-Petrarchan and Neoplatonist love. Friendship relationships lend themselves to this identification somewhat more than a love that is filtered through cosmological allegory, or through the conventional antitheses of the Petrarchists. Friendship relationships seem less buried in cultural historical specificity. However, as soon as one gets down to the particular problems or situations friendship involves - usefulness, motivation, identity, "otherness" - the need for contextual understanding becomes obvious. This understanding, I believe, enables rather than excludes an "ethical" criticism. By seeing what literature does to the moral-intellectual culture of which it is a product, the modern reader, if anything, understands better those choices made in the past that determine the choices he or she may find "natural" to make now.

# THEORETICAL CHALLENGES OF FRIENDSHIP

# CHAPTER I

# THE ETHICS OF FRIENDSHIP AND LITERARY MOTIVATION

Literature excludes ethics. Relationships that can be represented in literature cannot, by virtue of their representability, be considered to be perfectly ethical relationships. These statements are true if we understand "literature" in a certain way, and if we understand "ethics" in a sense most commonly associated with a Christian reading of Aristotle, but also deriving from an early modern reshuffling of that reading. For, to put it briefly, literature involves the establishment of a coherent fictional world in which human actions are made to appear motivated in various ways. On the other hand, the perfectly ethical relationship to another human being, in a tradition I will sketch out, is conceived of as an inclination towards the other for his own sake, that is, excluding motivation exceeding the pure fact of the individual himself. To the extent that the fictional world becomes "dense," worked-out, the less perfectly ethical human relationships necessarily appear. I will illustrate this "motivation imperative" first by looking at two examples of beginnings of relationships, one involving erotic love, the other male friendship.

## 1. Helisenne's Love, Tito and Gisippo's Friendship

At the beginning of Helisenne de Crenne's (Marguerite de Briet) novel *Les Angoysses douloureuses qui procedent d'amours* (first ed. 1538, revised ed. 1550), the narrator Helisenne falls in love with a young man, Guenelic, although she is apparently happily married. She has come to a city in which her husband is conducting a lawsuit concerning a piece of property, and spends her first day there "en toutes recreations, & voluptueux plaisirs" (Chap. 2).[1] On the morning of the next day she sees her future love, and relates the event in a relatively laconic way. The scene of first encounter functions as a (perhaps always partial) answer to the question, "Why did she fall in love?":

> Et le lendemain me levay assez matin (ce que n'estoit ma coustume) & en m'abillant vins ouvrir la fenestre, & en regardant à l'autre part de la rue, je vis un jeune homme, aussi regardant à la fenestre, lequel je prins à regarder ententivement. Il me sembla de tresbelle forme, & selon que je pouvois conjecturer à sa phisionomie, je l'estimois gracieux & amyable: il avoit le visage riant la chevelure crespe un petit blonde, & sans avoir barbe qui estoit manifeste demonstrance de sa gentile jeunesse. Il estoit assez honeste en son habit, toutesfoys sans user d'acoustremens superfluz. Et au moyen de la grande chaleur, n'avoit autre habillement, qu'un pourpoint de satin noir. (1.2)[2]

The meeting of glances (assuming their glances meet) is set up as something out of the ordinary: rising so early is not usual for her, just as the city is not her home. The advent of love as a transgression of normal affairs is obviously prepared for by the *dépaysement* of the narrator. Similarly, the reason for the couple's stay in the strange city, a "terre en litige" (a disputed property), announces the fight over and within Helisenne between Guenelic and her husband, as the wife is defined as the husband's property. The meeting of Helisenne's and

---

[1] I have used the 1560 edition of her *Oeuvres*, revised by Claude Colet (facs. repr. Geneva: Slatkine, 1977), no pagination.

[2] "And the next day I got up fairly early (which was not my custom) and in dressing I came to open the window, and in looking across the street, I saw a young man at a window, also looking, whom I began to look at attentively. He seemed to me of very beautiful appearance, and according to what I was able to conjecture, given his appearance, I deemed him to be gracious and friendly: his face was cheerful, his curly hair a bit blond, and he did not have a beard, which was an obvious sign of his pleasant youth. He was quite honorable in his clothes, without using excessive accoutrements. And, because of the great heat, he only wore a black satin doublet."

Guenelic's glances seems accidental, and accidentally reciprocal, for the usual situation would require the woman to be looking down from the window, and the man to be looking up from the street. This detail adds to the "out of the ordinary" aspect of the scene. The early morning situation, and the resulting half-dressed state of both the narrator and the young man, link the scene to amatory poetry, and its theme of "la Belle matineuse" (here, it is, however, *le Beau matineux*).[3]

Already the novel sets up the exchange of glances as an event disrupting the normal rhythm of life. What is suggested, then, is that the contextual conditions helped to determine the choice of Guenelic as object of love or desire. The presence of this information is not simply decorative: indeed one may ask if any circumstantial information can ever be "merely" decorative, and conversely, whether any such information is not always also decorative. The mention of circumstances inexorably *motivates* the choices or inclinations of the characters. Perhaps, had Helisenne seen Guenelic while, say, taking the Eucharist, or visiting a monastery, he might not have been chosen, although, given the constraints under which women of higher social classes were held, any meeting of a young married woman with a young man not her husband was charged with amatory possibilities. In fact, the narrator emphasizes that just any man would not do, for she has known many others: "J'avoys acoustumé de prendre les hommes, & ne me faisoys que rire d'eux, mais moymesmes miserablement je fus prise" (ibid.).[4]

The description of Guenelic confirms, then, the connotations of the circumstantial information, and inevitably says why Helisenne was "taken," although not completely so. The physical description of the young man, whose beauty is pointedly praised even by the husband in the following chapter, relies on commonplaces of love poetry, some of

---

[3] See the remarks on this theme in Yvonne Bellenger, *Le jour dans la poésie française au temps de la Renaissance* (Tübingen: Gunter Narr, 1979), pp. 148-152.

[4] "I was accustomed to take men, and only mock them, but I myself was taken miserably." A phrase which is simply taken from Boccaccio's *Elegia di madonna Fiammetta*: "credendo che la mia bellezza altrui pigliasse, avvenne che l'altrui me miseramente prese" (in *Decameron; Filocolo; Ameto; Fiammetta*, eds. Enrico Bianchi, Carlo Salinari, Natalino Sapegni, Milan, Riccardo Ricciardi, 1952, cap. 1, p. 1067).

which characterize the beautiful woman, as well (especially the "chevelure crespe un petit blonde"). The description also relies heavily on the description of Panfilo by Fiammetta in Boccaccio's *Fiammetta*.[5] This is, then, an eminently *desirable* young man, marked by his conventional description as an object of desire. It is also clear that the sight of Guenelic is sufficient to cause Helisenne to fall in love with him, since she has no opportunity to speak to him. It is also clear that what motivates the narrator to be attracted to the young man is *pleasure*:

> Et pour finale resolution, pour le moins, je vueil avoir le plaisir du regard delectable de mon amy.  Je nourray amours tacitement en mon cueur sans le divulguer à personne, tant soit il mon amy fidele.  Ainsi doncq' commençay du tout à chasser raison: parquoy la sensualité demoura superieure. (1.2)[6]

Helisenne's reasoning ("finale resolution") ends with a frank admission of physical pleasure as the motivating force behind her actions and feelings.  The narrative has set up the scene as a scene of sudden, unusual meeting, and has accumulated connotations of erotic pleasure in both the circumstances mentioned and the physical description of the character.  The narrative moves toward both the conclusion that Helisenne's feelings are "sensual" and that they will dominate her behavior.  Guenelic's function in the narrative is instrumental, in the sense that he is the means by which Helisenne's desire is either awakened or revealed.  The sight and physical possession of Guenelic by the narrator will be the cause of her "delectation suave" (1.3).  In other words, the information surrounding and concerning Guenelic functions

---

[5] "Egli era di forma bellissima, negli atti piacevolissimo e onestissimo nell'abito suo, e della sua giovanezza dava manifesto segnale crespa lanugine che pur mo' occupava le guancie sue. . ." (*Fiammetta*, cap. 1, p. 1067). See Mary J. Baker, "*Fiametta* and the *Angoysses douloureuses qui procèdent d'amours*," *Symposium* 27 (1973): 303-308.

[6] "And in conclusion, I wish at least to have the pleasure of the delightful gaze of my friend.  I will nourish my love silently in my heart without divulging it to anyone, may he be as much my loyal friend.  Thus I started to chase away reason, and my senses remained victorious."

as a revealing of desire, as a directionality of the story, the *telos* of which is for the moment the satisfaction of the narrator's physical desire.

The "instrumentality" of the information given to us about Guenelic is perhaps inherent in *any* information conveyed about a literary or fictional character. That is, if he had been old and ugly, or if he had been depicted doing his accounts, that information, since it was mentioned, is assumed to provide motivation for the relationship which constitutes the *telos* of the narrative. To the extent that other men can also be old and ugly, or do their accounts, Guenelic's *individuality* is not conveyed by the information. In fact, no amount of accumulated information about the person can place a fictional person into a category of which he would be the only possible member. If one can understand the attributes and events involving the person, one can imagine another person sharing those attributes and experiencing those events. Helisenne's choice of Guenelic, then, is by the very nature of his representation, motivated if not caused by the details mentioned in the representation. This sense of instrumentality of the person is heightened by the fact that literary writing in the Renaissance is profoundly generic, that is, it arises through channels provided by more or less rigid genres. In other words, Guenelic is not chosen "for his own sake"; nor is an attempt made to depict him as an individual "other" in relation to the narrator. Guenelic stands for the desirable youth in sentimental romance, any desirable youth.

In part, the status of Guenelic is determined by the fact that he is an object of desire, that he is depicted as an instrument to the "delectation" of the narrator. This is simply the understanding of sexual love for much of history. The love of the person "in himself" is secondary to the end for the sake of which he is loved, physical pleasure. The conveying of any information about him gives that information the status of a cause of pleasure, an explanation of the "why" of his choice by Helisenne. The suggestion is always that if the details mentioned (e.g., his curly blond hair) had been absent, he would not have been chosen (in fact, in relation to the fictional world of the sentimental romance, he would not exist). In other words, he in himself as separate from these attributes or circumstances would not have caused the physical pleasure described at the end of the chapter. Literary representation seems closely connected to physical desire by its teleological nature, by its very coherence.

If the beginning of Helisenne and Guenelic's relationship can serve as a version of an instrumental love, the beginning of the friendship between Guenelic and Quezinstra in the second book of Helisenne de Crenne's *Angoysses douloureuses* can serve as one example of explicitly non-instrumental love. This time the narrator is Guenelic, and he meets a young man with whom he will have a series of chivalric adventures in his search for the now emprisoned Helisenne:

> Mais je vous veulx exposer, dont procedoit la tresfidelle amytié, qui estoit observée entre nous: laquelle fut à l'occasion que le premier jour que je fuz surprins d'amours, comme je me pourmenois en un petit bois pres de nostre cité, nous nous rencontrames, & prismes cognoissance l'un à l'autre, en narrant chascun de nous les causes de nos anzietez. Et pource qu'il me fut advis qu'il precedoit tous autres (que jamais j'eusse veu) en discretion & prudence, je luy fis offre de tant petit de biens qu'en ma faculté j'avois, pour a sa volunté en povoir disposer, dont grandement me remercia. (2.2)[7]

Quezinstra is never described physically; the only information we have about him is that he excels in discretion and prudence. The circumstances of the meeting are telling: the walk outside the city induces reflection and philosophical discussion among friends or disciples. Pantagruel's encounter with Panurge in Rabelais's *Pantagruel* (chap. 9) is a similar event. The common walk is reflected in the mutuality of the pronouns ("nous nous rencontrasmes," "l'un à l'autre," "chascun de nous"). The most liberal gift of Guenelic's possessions to his newly-found friend partakes of the rhetoric of friendship and the *beneficium* (favor) that seals and demonstrates the relationship (see Cicero, *De amicitia*, 9.31, and Seneca's *De beneficiis*). The motivation for such a gift, and the corresponding relationship, still seems relatively

---

[7] "But I wish to explain to you how the very faithful friendship between us originated: this friendship started when, on the first day of having fallen in love, as I was walking in a small woods close to our city, we met each other, and got to know each other, by telling each other the causes of our troubles. And because it was obvious to me that he excelled all others that I had ever seen in discretion and prudence, I offered to him the little wealth that I had at my disposal, so that he may avail himself of it, for which he thanked me very much."

sparse, out of proportion with the fabulous exploits that the friends will accomplish together and for each other.

An even sparser beginning of male friendship is found in the tale of Gisippo and Tito (10.8), in Boccaccio's *Decameron* (probably finished in 1351). Their love for each other explicitly puts the other's happiness above the own. One of the two male protagonists sacrifices his future wife Sofronia to the other, whereas the other later on offers his life in order to save the first. These *beneficia* are even more radical than those of Quezinstra and Guenelic, but are typical in the tradition of writing about friendship.[8] Tito and Gisippo meet in Athens where they study under the (somewhat unlikely?) tutelage of Aristippus:

> E venendo i due giovani usando insieme, tanto si trovarono i costumi loro esser conformi, che una fratellanza ed un'amicizia sí grande ne nacque tra loro, che mai poi da altro caso che da morte non fu separata; e niun di loro aveva né ben né riposo se non tanto quanto erano insieme.[9]

---

[8] See, on the exchange of women, Constance Jordan, *Renaissance Feminism: Literary Texts and Political Models* (Ithaca: Cornell Univ. Press, 1990), *passim*, and specifically her discussion of Alberti's *Della famiglia*, pp. 47-54; for an example of self-sacrifice for the friend similar to some of the elements of the Tito-Gisippo story, see Cicero, *De amicitia*, 7.24, on Orestes and Pylades.

[9] "And when it came about that the two youths were together, they found that their habits were so similar, that a fraternity and a friendship so great was born between them, that never for any reason except death it was dissolved; and neither of the two had pleasure or rest except when they were together." Ed. Charles Singleton ([Bari]: Laterza, 1966), vol. 2, p. 276. On the medieval prehistory of the Tito-Gisippo story, see the insightful discussion in Barry L. Weller, "The Other Self: Aspects of the Classical Rhetoric of Friendship in the Renaissance" (Ph. D. Thesis, Yale University, 1974), pp. 111 and ff.; on the lack of individuality of friendship couples, see pp. 38-40. Also Victoria Kirkham, "The Classic Bond of Friendship in Boccaccio's Tito and Gisippo (*Decameron* 10.8)," in *The Classics in the Middle Ages*, eds. Aldo S. Bernardo, Saul Levin (Binghamton, NY: Center for Medieval & Early Renaissance Studies, 1990), "Medieval & Renaissance Texts & Studies, 69," pp. 223-235.

The circumstances of being sons of parents who were friends, and of studying philosophy together, contribute to their relationship, but really the only salient feature of the conditions for friendship seems to be the two youths' similarity to each other.[10] Their *costumi* were similar, they climb the heights of philosophy *con pari passo*, and when the father of Gisippo dies, Tito's mourning equals that of his friend. When Tito falls in love with Gisippo's future wife, he ends up being substituted for his friend in the bedchamber. At the same time that they are similar to each other (except for the fact that Tito is more desperately in love with the bride Sofronia than Gisippo), the uniqueness of the other is a theme of their relationship. Gisippo is willing to give up Sofronia, for, he explains, "[posso] io leggerissimamente altra moglie trovare ma non altro amico" (p. 280) (I can most easily find another wife but not another friend). One is tempted to say that, if indeed the friend is another self, it is immensely easier to find a different spouse than another I. The uniqueness of the other is here perhaps the uniqueness of a perfect replica. The uniqueness of the friend is, in addition, a proof of the uniqueness of the I.

The friendship between the two is demonstrated by the things they do for each other, the *beneficia*, but that does not explain *why* they are friends, just *that* they are friends. Their similarity seems to be the only motivation, which, since neither one is characterized in himself, is largely a way of avoiding motivating characterization. That similarity does not, however, lend itself to narrative development, in the sense that, say, Helisenne's pursuit of Guenelic does. The text presents their friendship in some ways as already having happened, *ab aeterno*, in a sort of perfect tense, as a panegyric.

---

[10] A similarity that is underlined in the versified version (based on Filippo Beroaldo's Latin translation of Boccaccio's story) by the French poet François Habert: "On vid en eux telle similitude, / De bonnes meurs, & desir de l'estude / Qu'en peu de temps une amytié louable / Accreut en eux ( . . . ) Tous deux suyvoient d'heureux commencement / Philosophie, & d'un avancement / Tous deux se sont poulsez au degré mesme / De hault sçavoir, meritant Diadesme, / Ayants tous deux un mesme entendement, / Et mesme don de riche jugement" (*L'Histoire de Titus, et Gesippus, et autres petiz oeuvres de Beroalde latin. . .*, Paris, Michel Fezandat & Robert Gran Ion, 1551, no pagination).

In part, the similarity of virtuous men is a requirement of classical perfect friendship,[11] and their common study of philosophy, albeit with Aristippus, is a perfect testing-ground for the similar pursuit of wisdom. On the other hand, the nature of their love for each other implies a certain representation, or rather lack of representation, of their motivation. We have seen in the case of Guenelic's description that any information motivates the desire of the narrator, just as any information to some extent instrumentalizes the person represented. In the case of the two friends, it is precisely the absence of motivation (other than their similarity to each other) that is striking. As I have suggested, the emphasis on similarity is a way of avoiding the characterization of one or the other, and, paradoxically, underlines their uniqueness. Nothing other than Tito himself motivates Gisippo's love, just as nothing other than Gisippo himself motivates Tito's love. Montaigne's "par ce que c'estoit luy; par ce que c'estoit moy" (1.28) is a celebrated variation on these themes.

## 2. Representation and the Ethical Calculus of Ends

We have noticed a certain motivational denseness in the beginning of Helisenne's love and a contrasting motivational sparseness in the beginning of Tito and Gisippo's friendship. In part, I have suggested, the semantic poverty of friendship is an incarnation of the love of someone else "for his own sake." Whereas my interpretation of these two examples has been based on an understanding of the fabric of literary worlds, and perhaps on the phenomenology of reading, I also believe that the moral philosophical issue involved is bound to a particular intellectual tradition. The mutual exclusion of literary representation and the communication of another person "in himself" or "for his own sake" assumes a view of the ideally ethical relationship, friendship, that leads inevitably to such an exclusion. The source of Renaissance and, for that matter, much of Western philosophical reflection on friendship is ultimately Aristotle's *Nicomachean Ethics*, although, as we will see in other chapters, the most important literary

---

[11] See the discussion of Antiochus and Séleucus in Corneille's *Rodogune*, Chapter VII.

influence is often Cicero's and Seneca's treatises and letters. The problematic element of the ethical relationship is the loving of another *propter se*, καθ' αὐτόν, "for his own sake." Perfect friendship indeed involves this sort of love, but in Aristotle it is necessarily connected to goodness, in the sense that the quality of goodness is part of the person loved "for his own sake." I love someone else for his or her own sake because we, as good persons, love each other in our quality of goodness:

> Perfect friendship is the friendship of men who are good, and alike in excellence; for these wish well alike to each other *qua* good, and they are good in themselves. Now those who wish well to their friends for their sake are most truly friends; for they do this by reason of their own nature and not incidentally; therefore their friendship lasts as long as they are good - and excellence is an enduring thing. (1156b 6-12)[12]

---

[12] This is characterized as the "amistié honeste" or "amistié parfaite" in the vernacular tradition, as opposed to the "amistiés delitables et utiles." See Nicole Oresme, *Le livre de ethiques d'Aristote* (ed. 1488), ed. Albert Douglas Menut (New York: G. E. Stechert, 1940), 8.5 (p. 419): "Mais l'amistié de ceuls qui sont bons et semblables en vertu, elle est parfaite; car telz amis veulent l'un a l'autre choses simplement bonnes et selon lesquelles il sont bons. Et il sont bons selon culz meïsme. Et pour ce sont il mesmement tres grandement ou tres bien amis. Car il veulent bien a leur amis pour la grace et pour le bien d'eulz [mistranslating from the Latin "bona amicis illorum gratia volunt"]; car pour leur amis meïsme aimment il, et sont ainsy disposéz non pas selon accident." Compare the Latin, in *Ethica Aristotelis Peripateticorum principis, Cum Ioannis Maioris Theologi Parisiensis Commentariis* (Paris: Iodocus Badius, Jehan Petit, 1530), f. 126r: "Bonorum autem amicitia, similiumque virtute: perfecta est amicitia. Hi namque mutuo sibi bona, similiter volunt, quo boni sunt. Boni vero sunt per seipsos. Atque ii maxime sunt amici qui bona amicis, illorum gratia volunt. Propter seipsos enim ita sese habent, & non per accidens." Major comments on these lines by enumerating six conditions of perfect friendship: "Prima est quod talis amicitia est per se amicitia. Secunda quod talis amicitia est maxime amicitia. Tertia quod est permansiva. Quarta quod talis amicitia in genere amicitiae est perfecta. Quinta quod talis amicitia est optima. Sexta conditio quod huiusmodi amicitia est rara inventu" (fs. 126v - 127r).

Perfect friends love each other not because of an interest - pleasure, utility - that is conferred to them by their love, but because they are who they are. "Who they are" is indeed a positive definition, for perfect friends are *good*. When the friend becomes bad, he is no longer a friend.[13] The fact that the love is not based on pleasure or usefulness does not mean that it is not without any external determination. Rather, there always is a ground or determination outside of the person loved, namely goodness.[14] In this sense also, goodness motivates friendship. In Cicero's treatise on friendship, virtue similarly provides a motivation for friendship, both starting and conserving friendships ("Virtus . . . et conciliat amicitias et conservat," *De amicitia*, 27.100). The Roman ethical tradition seems to render virtue more explicitly a *cause* of perfect friendship, and generally imposes a more clearly causal framework on discussions of ethical love.

This grounding of the ethical relationship in a quality outside of itself becomes the crux of a problem in the Christian reading of Aristotle, especially as *any* external grounding or determination of the relationship is felt to be a teleological constraint. For, in this reading, the most perfect relationship should be one in which the object loved is loved entirely for its own sake, that is, in the absence of any other end outside of itself. Although the Latin reception of Aristotle provides a language more obviously teleological than the original, Aristotle himself provides the impetus for this twist, in the first book of the *Nicomachean Ethics*:

---

[13] See chapter II on the problem of ending relationships when one of the friends no longer is worthy of the friendship.

[14] See Martha C. Nussbaum, *The Fragility of Goodness: Luck and Ethics in Greek Tragedy and Philosophy* (Cambridge: Cambridge University Press, 1986), p. 355 n: "Here it is important to distinguish three things: the *basis* or *ground* of the relationship (the thing 'through (*dia*) which' they love); its *object*; and its *goal* or *end*. Pleasure, advantage, and good character are three different bases or original grounds of *philia*; they are not the goal or final (intentional) end of the relationship. In other words, the two people are friends 'through' or 'on the basis of' these, but the goal they try to achieve in action will still be some sort of mutual benefit."

Now we call that which is in itself worthy of pursuit [τὸ καθ᾽ αὐτὸ διωκτὸν] more complete than that which is worthy of pursuit for the sake of something else, and that which is never desirable for the sake of something else more complete than the things that are desirable both in themselves and for the sake of that other thing, and therefore we call complete without qualification that which is always desirable in itself and never for the sake of something else [τὸ καθ᾽ αὐτὸ αἱρετὸν ἀεὶ καὶ μηδέποτε δι᾽ ἄλλο].[15]

The criterion proposed by Aristotle is the basis for the distinction explained by Saint Augustine between the love of the creature for God and the love a creature holds for other creatures, including itself. The love for God should be "enjoyment" (*fruitio*) whereas the love for another creature should be "use" (*usus*). Before Augustine proposes this distinction, in his *De doctrina christiana*, he introduces a more fundamental distinction concerning the possible objects of learning, things and signs. In the realm of things, two sorts of relationships prevail:

Res ergo aliae sunt quibus fruendum est, aliae quibus utendum, aliae quae fruuntur et utuntur. Illae quibus fruendum est, beatos nos faciunt. Istis quibus utendum est, tendentes ad beatitudinem adiuvamur, et quasi adminiculamur, ut ad illas quae nos beatos faciunt, pervenire, atque his inhaerere possimus. Nos vero qui fruimur et utimur, inter utrasque

---

[15] 1097a 30-35. Oresme's version is the following: "Or disons nous que la chose que l'en poursuit et quiert pour elle meïsme est plus parfaicte que n'est celle que l'en quiert pour un autre. Et la chose que l'en quiert et est eslisible pour elle et onques n'est eslisible pour autre, elle est plus parfaicte que ne sont celles qui sont eslisibles ou desirees pour elles ou pour autre" (p. 118). In St Thomas Aquinas's commentary on this and contiguous sections in Aristotle, this highest good and end, the "bonum perfectissimum," corresponds to the perfect first mover who is not moved by anything else, namely God. Man's highest good is his beatitude, which is God. See *In X. libros Ethicorum ad Nicomachum*, liber 1, lectiones 9-10.

> constituti, si eis quibus utendum est, frui voluerimus, impeditur cursus noster. . . .[16]

Following this distinction we find a lapidary distinction between enjoyment and use that will be used by all scholastic theologians commenting on this question:

> Frui enim est amore alicui rei inhaerere propter seipsam. Uti autem, quod in usum venerit ad id quod amas obtinendum referre, si tamen amandum est.[17]

These definitions will do a lot of work throughout the Middle Ages and the Renaissance, especially the words *propter seipsam* (for its own sake)

---

[16] "Some things are to be enjoyed, others to be used, and there are others which are enjoyed and used. Those things which are to be enjoyed make us blessed. Those things which are to be used help and, as it were, sustain us as we move toward blessedness in order that we may gain and cling to those things which make us blessed. If we who enjoy and use things, being placed in the midst of things of both kinds, wish to enjoy those things which should be used, our course will be impeded and sometimes deflected. . ." (1.3.3). I have modified slightly the translation by D. W. Robertson (*On Christian Doctrine*, Indianapolis, Bobbs-Merrill, 1958).

[17] "To enjoy something is to cling to it with love for its own sake. To use something, however, is to employ it in obtaining that which you love, provided that it is worthy of love." *On Christian Doctrine*, 1.4.4. See also his *De trinitate* 9.8.13. The distinction between *fruitio* and *usus* is the key to an analogy John Freccero makes between idolatry and autoreferentiality, in "The Fig Tree and the Laurel: Petrarch's Poetics," in David Quint, Patricia Parker, eds., *Literary Theory/Renaissance Texts* (Baltimore: Johns Hopkins University Press, 1986): 20-32. This is, I believe, a misreading of Augustine, who uses the distinction only to refer to things, as we have seen. According to Freccero "all things are signs" (p. 28), which is contradicted by Augustine: *non autem omnis res etiam signum est* (not every thing is also a sign) (1.2.2). For Augustine the realm of signs is by the nature of the sign a realm of use, in the sense that a sign inherently is the sign *of something else*, otherwise it would not be a sign. Speaking about verbal signs, Augustine states that *nemo enim utitur verbis, nisi aliquid significanda gratis* (no one indeed uses words, except to signify something) (ibid.).

and the final *si tamen amandum est* (provided that it is worthy of love).
The relationship of use always supposes a third term, a final end or
object external to the relationship between user and used.  Use in
Augustine is full of ethical connotations and problems, too, as these
sentences suggest.  Use as such is not bad, if the final object is worthy
of one's desire.  If, presumably, the final object of a relationship of use
is not worthy of one's efforts (say, money or physical pleasure), then,
given Augustine's formulation, one should not use objects (and especially
not persons) to obtain these other unworthy things.  But one should not,
strictly speaking, *enjoy* human beings, either, for they are to be loved as
a step toward God, not for themselves.[18]    Only God is to be
enjoyed.[19]  All human relationships, if not practiced in view of the final
object of love, God, are profoundly problematic; in fact, they can be
nothing *but* problematic, given the double bind imposed by the dialectic
between use and enjoyment on the one hand, and the exclusive definition
of the object worthy of love, on the other.

   The Augustinian distinction is the basis for an important analysis
in the beginning of Peter Lombard's *Sentences* (I dist 1 cap 1-3).  This
textbook, composed in the mid-twelfth century, had an enormous
influence in the shaping of medieval theology.  In the elaboration of the
enjoyment/use distinction Lombard essentially patches together quotes
from Augustine, but isolates several questions that will be debated for
the next four centuries.  What should be enjoyed and what should be
used?  (All things other than the Father, the Son, and the Holy Ghost
should be used only).  Should creatures enjoy or use each other? (Use).
Does God enjoy or use his creatures? (Use).  Should the virtues be

---

[18] "For it is commanded to us that we should love one another, but it is to
be asked whether man is to be loved by man for his own sake or for the sake
of something else.  If for his own sake, we enjoy him; if for the sake of
something else, we use him.  But I think that man is to be loved for the sake of
something else.  In that which is to be loved for its own sake the blessed life
resides; and if we do not have it for the present, the hope for it now consoles
us.  But 'cursed be the man that trusteth in man'" (1.22.20).

[19] "The things which are to be enjoyed are the Father, the Son, and the
Holy Spirit. . ." (1.5.5), since God is "thought of in such a way that the thought
seeks to attain something than which there is nothing better or more sublime"
(1.7.7).

enjoyed or used? (Used).[20]   Lombard maintains a strict difference between human love of God and human love of other creatures or qualities.

Ethical relationships are simply relegated to a status secondary to the relationship with God.  The virtues cannot be loved in the same way that we love God.  In a question that also forms the beginning of a long line of scholastic commentary, Lombard asks, "Utrum fruendum an utendum sit virtutibus" (Whether the virtues should be enjoyed or used).  The author, referring to Augustine, claims that we love the virtues not entirely in themselves but because of the highest good, beatitude. In this sense the virtues are always instruments to something else.[21]  Virtuous actions towards fellow creatures are also always secondary.   For example, in the *Summa contra gentiles* (3.34), Aquinas uses the Aristotelian analysis to show that "man's ultimate felicity does not lie in acts of the moral virtues," for moral virtues are always means to something else, never an end in themselves.  The highest end is God, who cannot except metaphorically be said to perform moral acts. Therefore moral virtues are necessarily instrumental, aligned in a teleological ladder the highest point of which is God.  The classical sense of the moral virtues as an integral part of the good life, not submitted to higher ends, has been lost.

In spite of this clearly anti-ethical bias of the sources of medieval theological reflection on love of the creature, in the commentaries on Lombard's first distinction we can observe a loosening of the categorical difference between instrumental human friendship and the non-instrumental love of God.  What this brings about, however, is not a

---

[20] "Quid sit frui et uti," "De rebus quibus fruendum est," "De rebus quibus utendum est" (I dist 1 cap. 2); "Utrum hominibus sit utendum vel fruendum," "Utrum Deus fruatur an utatur nobis," "Utrum fruendum an utendum sit virtutibus" (I dist 1 cap 3).  Quoted from *Sententiae in IV libris distinctae* (Grottoferrata: Collegium S. Bonaventurae, 1971), vol. 1, part 2, pp. 56-59.

[21] "Ideo Augustinus dicit quod eas [the virtues] diligimus propter solam beatitudinem, non quin eas propter se diligamus, sed quia id ipsum, quod eas diligimus, referimus ad illud summum bonum cui soli inhaerendum est; et in eo permanendum finisque laetitiae ponendus.  Quare virtutibus non est fruendum" (I dist 1 cap 3 (9), vol. 1 part 2, p. 60). See also the following section (10): "Utendum est ergo virtutibus, et per eas fruendum summo bono" (ibid.).

return to the conditional perfect friendship in goodness envisaged by
Aristotle in the eighth and ninth books of the *Nicomachean Ethics*, but
the possibility of conceiving of human relationships as ends in
themselves *irrespective* of their motivation through virtue or goodness,
and obviously independent of any other motivation or interest. In this
sense the ethically ideal relationship comes to be incompatible with
coherent representation.

We have already noted a theoretical separation, in scholasticism,
between pursuit of the moral virtues and the relationship with God. In
the elaboration of the definition of "enjoyment" (*fruitio*) we find both a
link to the ethical discourse of friendship and the consignment of the
pursuit of virtue to a certain category within the overall definition. This
makes possible a separation between the love of the creature for another
creature *per seipsam* and the love of a creature in virtue, or with virtue
as a condition. The other human being becomes an end in himself or
herself, just as virtue is an end. In other words, the individual human
being does not have to be virtuous in order to be treated as an end,
*propter seipsum*.

In his discussion of the question whether the object of enjoyment
for its own sake is the ultimate end ("Utrum obiectum fruitionis per se
sit finis ultimus") Duns Scotus (d. 1308) explicitly links enjoyment
understood in a large sense with "honest" love, as opposed to love born
out of usefulness or pleasure: "dico quod frui accipitur extensive, pro
amore honesti distincto contra amorem utilis et delectabilis."[22]  The
reference is clearly to Aristotle's tripartite definition of friendship, as it
was translated and used in commentaries in the Latin tradition.[23]
Enjoyment, when understood "extensively," is similar to "perfect"
friendship, as a mutual love for the other's own sake. Scotus is echoed
by later scholastics, who distinguish between *fruitio* broadly speaking
and *fruitio* strictly speaking. Pierre d'Ailly (d. 1420) uses the by then
standard terminology derived from William of Ockham and Gregory of

---

[22] *Ordinatio* I dist 1 pars 1 qu 1 [II.18], in *Opera omnia*, vol. 2, ed. P.
Carolus Balic (Vatican: Typis polyglottis vaticanis, 1950), p. 12.

[23] See *Nicomachean Ethics*, 1156a 6-21. Following Aquinas, John Major
comments: "Tres sunt amicitiae species ab invicem distinctae. Hanc probat,
quia tria sunt amabilia inter se distincta: scilicet honestum, utile & delectabile"
(*Ethica Aristotelis* [1530], f. 126v).

Rimini, identifying *fruitio* as a non-referring act (as it does not refer to any object other than the object loved), and describing it as an act of the will. He distinguishes between proper (strict) and improper (broad) usage of the term:

> [The way in which an act can be non-referring can be] vel sic quod obiectus acceptetur a voluntate tanquam summe diligendus ab ea. Et hoc est diligere aliquid tanquam finem ultimum. Et talis actus apud theologos proprie et stricte vocatur fruitio. ( . . . ) Vel aliter talis actus non referens fertur in obiectum absolute sic quod absolute acceptetur et assumatur in facultatem voluntatis nec ut summum nec ut non summum. Non tamen referendo in aliud tanquam in finem. Et talis actus improprie et large posset dici fruitio.[24]

This calculus of enjoyment sometimes filters into the language used to describe perfect friendship. In Johannes Altensteig's treatise on friendship we find a discussion of *amor amiciciae* that juxtaposes Gabriel Biel's definition of this concept with Aristotle's definition of friendship in the eighth book of the *Nicomachean Ethics*:

> Amor amiciciae (ut scribit Gabriel libro ii sententiarum, dist. i. q. v et dist. xxvii. q. unica li. iii) est amor quo volo alicui bonum propter ipsummet amatum sine relatione eius in aliud. ut si volo alicui sanitatem, scientiam, virtutes, gratiam, etc. quia sunt illi bonum praecise, non referendo illud in me vel in aliud et non attendendo quod is cui volo ulterius potest mihi vel

---

[24] "The way in which an act can be non-referring can be either such that the object is accepted by the will as to be most highly loved by it. And this is to love something as the ultimate end. And this act is called among theologians properly and strictly enjoyment. ( . . . ) Or on the other hand such a non-referring act is performed on an object absolutely, such that it is absolutely accepted and assumed into the faculty of the will neither as the highest thing nor as not the highest thing. Not however by referring to another thing as end. And this act can be called, improperly and broadly, enjoyment." *Quaestiones super libros sententiarum cum quibusdam in fine adjunctis* (Strasbourg, 1490, facs. repr. Frankfurt: Minerva, 1968), I dist 1 qu 2 B. In Johannes Altensteig's *Lexicon theologicum* (1517; rev, ed. Johannes Tytz, 1617; facs. repr. Hildesheim: G. Olms, 1974) we find a similar distinction (p. 351, under *frui*).

alteri proficere. Et dicitur amor ille amiciciae, quia secundum philosophum, viii Ethicorum ca. iii. Perfecta amicicia est quando volumus bona amicis illorum gratia propter seipsos amicos, et non secundum accidens et non propter aliquod quod sibi ex amicis perveniat delectabile vel utile etc.[25]

The goods we wish for our friends refer to nothing else, and they are given because of the friends themselves: this language of teleological "reference," derived from theological commentaries, and ultimately from Scotus, comes to characterize on occasion "perfect friendship" in spite of the restrictions placed on the human possibilities for enjoyment of creatures.

Sometimes the broad and "improper" sense of enjoyment, of an object other than the highest one, was thought of as an *actus medius*, neither use nor enjoyment.[26] The question of the love of the virtues was felt to be important, since Lombard had quoted Saint Ambrose as saying that the virtues are to be sought and loved for their own sake, and Lombard himself had seemed to allow the production of spiritual joy in those who possessed certain virtues.[27] The love of another creature or

---

[25] "The love of friendship . . . is the love by which I wish for someone else a good loved because of itself without any relation of this good to something else. So I wish for someone health, knowledge, virtues, grace, etc. for they are precisely [i.e., in themselves] a good, not referring this good to me or to something else and not expecting that he to whom I wish this good can do something for me or for someone else later. And this love is said to be of friendship, for it is according to the philosopher. . . Perfect friendship is when we wish good things for friends for their own sake because of the friends themselves, and not by accident, and not because of something pleasurable or useful that would come to us [from our action]." *Opusculum de amicicia. . .* (Hagenau: Henricus Gran, 1519), cap. 19, no pagination.

[26] As reported in William of Ockham, *Ordinatio* I dist 1 qu 1, in *Opera theologica*, vol. 2, ed. Gedeon Gál, Stephan Brown (St Bonaventure, N.Y.: Franciscan Institute, 1967), pp. 376-379, and Pierre d'Ailly, I dist 1 qu 2 D.

[27] Lombard quotes Ambrose's commentary on Gal 5:22 ("Fructus Spiritus autem est. . ."). Ambrose says that the use of *fructus* here indicates that the virtues (charity, etc.) enumerated are thus to be loved for their own sake. Lombard answers: "Virtutes propter se petendae et amandae sunt, et tamen

the love of the moral virtues fall, then, into the "broad" sense of enjoyment.[28] The secondary nature of this latter sense is, however, never questioned.

Another way of distinguishing among the senses of *fruitio* is perhaps more productive, as it introduces specific psychological criteria for the highest sense of enjoyment. William of Ockham provides a neat summary:

> Fruitio est duplex, scilicet ordinata et inordinata. Fruitio ordinata est illa quando aliquid summe diligendum summe diligitur. Fruitio inordinata est illa qua summe diligitur et propter se quod minus et propter aliud est diligendum. Sed fruitio ordinata est duplex, quia quaedam est quietans simpliciter voluntatem, qualis dicitur esse fruitio patriae; alia non simpliciter quietat, sed permittit secum, etiam naturaliter, anxietatem et tristitiam, qualis est fruitio viae.[29]

---

propter solam beatitudinem. Propter se quidem amandae sunt, quia delectant sui possessores sincera et sancta dilectione et in eis pariunt gaudium spirituale" (*Sentences* I dist 1 cap 3 (9), p. 60). This is also cited by later scholastics as Adam Wodeham's opinion, and is criticized by Augustinians such as Gregory of Rimini, in his *Lectura super primum et secundum sententiarum*, I dist 1 qu 3, ed. A. Damasus Trapp OSA, Venicio Marcolino (Berlin: Walter de Gruyter, 1981), pp. 251-253.

[28] See Johannes Eck, *In primum librum sententiarum annotiunculae* (ed. 1542), ed. Walter L. Moore, Jr. (Leiden, E. J. Brill, 1976), dist 1, p. 19: "Fruitio autem usurpatur bifariam. Primo large, et hoc modo frui est alicui inhaerere rei propter seipsam. Sic fruimur virtutibus, angelis, hominibus bonis."

[29] "Enjoyment is twofold, ordinate and inordinate. Ordinate enjoyment is when the object most worthy of love is loved in the most worthy way. Inordinate enjoyment is when an object is loved in the most worthy way and for its own sake, but which should be loved less and for the sake of something else. But ordinate enjoyment is twofold: when an object completely satisfies the will it is called the enjoyment of the blessed [*fruitio patriae*]; when an object does not satisfy completely, but permits along with it, also naturally, anxiety and sadness, it is called enjoyment of the way [*fruitio viae*, in the sense of the Christian wayfarer, the *viator*]." *Ordinatio* I dist 1 qu 4, p. 431.

Far from being mere exercises in hair-splitting jargon, these distinctions actually made way for an understanding of human relationships as ends in themselves. As in the case of *fruitio* "broadly speaking," the creature can love another creature for its own sake (*propter se*), without that object of love being *summe diligendum*, most worthy of love. This enjoyment is, however, distinct from the enjoyment of God (the object most worthy of love) by the wayfarer not yet in the presence of his object of love, the *fruitio viae*. It is also distinct from the highest type of enjoyment, which is that of the saved (the *beati*), the *fruitio patriae*. Enjoyment is above all conceived as a satisfaction of the will.[30] These precise distinctions are to be found in Renaissance dictionaries of theology (Johannes Altensteig in 1517, Erasmus Sarcerius in 1546) and in the commentaries of the University of Paris theologians (such as John Major in 1519).

As in the case of the previous distinction between a strict and a broad sense of *fruitio*, we find here a place for the love of another creature for its own sake, and this place is distinct from the love of virtue. The question becomes, then, whether there is any phenomenal difference between the love of the creature *propter seipsam*, and the love of God *propter seipsum*. In other words, is one love simply illicit, whereas the other is licit, or is the nature of the love really different (in the case of the creature, inferior)? Duns Scotus tried to show that the enjoyment of anything other than God himself could not entirely satisfy desire (the *appetitus materiae*); only the most perfect form and the object that includes all other objects can perfectly satisfy, as desire is as multiple as the multiplicity of material forms.[31] Ockham, however,

--------------------------------

[30] "Frui itaque est amore alicui inhaerere propter se, sed ad solam voluntatem pertinet alicui inhaerere per amorem," according to Johannes Altensteig (*Lexicon theologicum*, p. 351). In his definition Altensteig refers to Gabriel Biel.

[31] "Dico quod non quaecumque forma satiat appetitum materiae extensive, quia tot sunt appetitus materiae ad formas quot sunt formae receptibiles in materia; nulla igitur une forma potest satiare omnes appetitus eius, sed una satiat perfectissime, scilicet forma perfectissima; illa tamen non satiat omnes appetitus materiae nisi in illa une forma includerentur omnes aliae. Ad propositum dico

distinguishes between a rational demonstration of totally satisfying enjoyment (or its lack) and, on the other hand, *belief* that totally satisfying enjoyment can or cannot take place. In the domain of rational demonstration, we cannot know that enjoyment of the divine essence is possible, and, conversely, we cannot know that the enjoyment of something other than God cannot entirely satisfy the creature.[32] Enjoyment of God can be assumed only in the domain of belief and cannot be known through natural reason.[33] On the other hand, a created being could present itself to the will as if it were the total immediate cause of the satisfaction of the will's desire.[34] Ockham concludes:

> Et ita non potest probari quod voluntas est satiabilis et quietabilis fruitione quam de facto ponimus, nec quod non

---

quod unum obiectum potest includere omnia obiecta aliquo modo, et ideo solum illud obiectum perfecte quietat potentiam quantum potest quietari" (*Ordinatio* I dist 1 pars 1 qu 1, pp. 14-15).

[32] "Ideo dico . . . quod non potest naturaliter demonstrari quod talis fruitio divinae essentiae est nobis possibilis, quia istud est mere creditum; et ita non potest naturaliter demonstrari.  Secundo, dico quod non potest naturaliter demonstrari quod voluntas non potest satiari nec quietari in aliquo citra Deum" (*Ordinatio* I dist 1 qu 4 art 1, pp. 433-434). See also Gordon Leff, *William Ockham: The Metamorphosis of Scholastic Discourse* (Manchester: Manchester University Press, 1975), 518; Arthur S. McGrade, "Ockham on Enjoyment: Towards an Understanding of Fourteenth-Century Philosophy and Psychology," *Review of Metaphysics* 34 (1981): 706-728.  I am thankful to William J. Courtenay for directing me to this source, and for having pointed out the relevance of the use/enjoyment distinction.

[33] "Dico quod de facto talis fruitio est ponenda, sed hoc tantum est creditum et non per rationem naturalem notum" (*Ordinatio* I dist 1 qu 4 art 2, p. 439).

[34] "Ideo dico quod non potest naturaliter demonstrari quin voluntas possit recipere unum actum ab alio ente creato sicut a causa totali immediata qui satiet totum appetitum voluntatis, sicut non potest probari quod aliquod delectabile sensibile non potest quietare appetitum sensitivum quamdiu sensus retinet omnem dispositionem eandem praeviam illi delectationi" (*Ordinatio* I dist 1 qu 4 art 1, p. 435).

potest quietari aliqua alia respectu alicuius creaturae, nec potest
per quamcumque quietari. (*Ordinatio* I dist 1 qu 4 art 1, pp.
435-436)[35]

Ockham's *logical* possibility that a creature may satisfy another
creature's will finds echoes in scholastics following him, when they
debate Lombard's questions on use and enjoyment. John Major, in his
commentary on the first book of the *Sentences* of 1519, entertains as a
proposition to be debated, "qualibet re mundi voluntas potest frui: loquor
de potentia logica."[36] Before Major, Pierre d'Ailly seems to have come
closest to Ockham when he says, "dico . . . quod nihil aliud a deo potest
satiare voluntatem obiective. hoc autem solum fide creditur nec est
evidens."[37] Similarly, he invokes God's absolute power which could
oblige the creature to enjoy another creature, although, according to the
laws set down by God, such enjoyment is culpable.[38]

Ockham's unwillingness to exclude logically enjoyment of a
creature on the basis of phenomenal criteria (the entire satisfaction of the
will) is perhaps the result of his general retreat from the rational
certainties of earlier scholasticism, but it also indicates the consequences
for ethical thought which the Augustinian distinction seems to have
produced. For by establishing the Aristotelian criterion of the absence

---

[35] "And so it cannot be proven that the will is satisfiable and can be given
rest through the enjoyment which we are posing in fact, and it cannot be proven
that the will cannot be given rest in some other regard to another creature, and
that it cannot be given rest by any creature."

[36] "The will can enjoy any thing of this world: I am speaking about logical
ability," *In primum sententiarum* dist 1 qu 5, f. 21v.

[37] "I say that nothing other than God can satisfy the will objectively. This
is, however, only believed through faith and is not evident," *Quaestiones super
libros sententiarum* I dist 1 qu 2 P.

[38] "Patet quod omnis dilectio qua aliquid aliud a deo diligeretur super omnia
sive tanquam finis ultimus esset inordinata et culpabilis secundum leges statutas.
Et dico secundum leges statutas. Quia non videtur impossibile nec implicare
contradictionem quod deus posset absolute obligare creaturam ad utendum deo
et fruendum seipsa aut alio obiecto creato" (ibid., I dist 1 qu 2 N).

of other ends as the sole criterion for the highest sort of love, medieval Christian thought seems to have reduced human relationships to a reproduction of the teleological paradigm. *All* ethical relationships are instrumental and thus secondary, or, any ethical relationship with another creature that is not instrumental is by that very fact a deification of the other. The enjoyment of oneself is also the sort of deification of the self that is the basic characteristic of sin.[39] But conversely, this also means that the only possible way of conceiving of the perfect relationship is one that is devoid of ends other than the person himself. Which means that when Aristotle, in his description of "perfect" friendship, always subjects the ethical relationship to goodness, this no longer is *logically* the criterion for the most perfect relationship in Christian thought. God is not loved *because* of his goodness, but in himself. When Ockham concedes that we cannot rationally demonstrate that enjoyment of the other creature could not be as satisfying to the will as enjoyment of God, this opens the way for regarding the other "in himself," apart from the moral virtues due to which people become objects to be loved. Through the mediation and paradigm of divine love the ethical love for the creature has lost the conditions which had defined it in Antiquity.

This concentration on the individual other as an end in himself is obviously consonant with the epistemological nominalism for which Ockham and his followers are famous, although, as we have seen, the problem ultimately depends on Augustine's distinctions. For when categories are not inherent in the individual objects being categorized, but merely a product of convention, in the sense of a common decision, then goodness, for example, cannot partake of the object which is sought out in the absence of all other ends. If you love someone and he or she is good, that goodness is thought of as a mere appendage to the individual object of your love. For, if goodness really were an essential part of the individual, why would you not love someone else whose goodness was greater than the first person's? The object "in itself" will constitute itself by the negation of all categories which apply to more

---

[39] See Gregory of Rimini, who also repeats the Augustinian condemnation of the enjoyment of that which should only be used: "multi sunt peccatores se ipsos amantes et nonnisi propter se et etiam alia propter se, et per consequens se ipsis fruentes. Patet etiam, quia sicut aliquis amor est caritas, ita est aliquis qui est cupiditas" (*Lectura* I dist 1 qu 3 art 1, p. 245).

than itself. What this means is that ultimately the individual perfectly loved cannot be given any attributes by which he or she could be known to others as an individual. You cannot say, "I love the person who is good, generous, courageous," for the suggestion always is that those attributes constitute the person, who is, then, less of an individual and by the same token less perfectly loved. In other words, objects in their individuality can be pointed to, named (in the sense of a proper name), but not described: you can legitimately say "I love you," or "I love him," or "I love George," but that is about it. This brings us back to the problem of literary representation and motivation.

If the perfect ethical relationship relies on the love of another for his own sake, as an end beyond which there can be no other end, then literary representation can only do justice to such a relationship if somehow it deprives itself of motivation. For the other to be invoked as a radically individual end in himself or herself, the recourses are few: incoherence, the prevalence of referring over signifying, silence. This is what some writers of the early modern period have resorted to, when attempting to represent what was felt to be the ideal ethical relationship, friendship. The calculus of ends and means underlies in one way or another apparent inconsistencies and lapses of early modern literary worlds that deal with this relationship.

An interesting modern parallel to the problems I have been sketching out can be found in a recent collection of essays by the philosopher Martha C. Nussbaum. In an essay written against the usual style of philosophical argumentation, "Love and the Individual: Romantic Rightness and Platonic Aspiration," Nussbaum's protagonist contrasts a "romantic" love of another person as beyond any attributes with a "platonic" or perhaps more generally classical love of another person as constituted by his or her choices and commitments. The question becomes existentially acute when the person loved no longer is living, or has rejected the lover. If love of the other person involves in an important way the other person's choices or commitments, there is a sense in which the love can be repeated, since another person, with similar choices and commitments, can take the place of the lost object of love:

> Since these patterns of commitment are repeatable and not idiosyncratic, the [platonic] account implies that there might have been, at least at the beginning, more than one person of

the appropriate soul type who might have answered to the lover's inner needs. It is also plausible that a single life might (in the wake of a death or a departure) come to contain a plurality of similar loves.[40]

In the "romantic" view, not only can love not be repeated, but the very act of representation of that love is felt to be a betrayal of it:

> Nobody else will ever know his special perfectness. One cannot find such another character. ( . . . ) Could it be that to write about love, even to write humbly and responsively, is itself a device to control the topic, to trap and bind it like an animal - so, of necessity, an unloving act? And if I could set him down in writing, every movement and look and virtue translated into words, if I could do this without in fact ceasing to write, would I not have most perfectly, most finally controlled him and so banished the power of love? (p. 321)

Nussbaum's reflection on "romantic" love involves a series of moves, some philosophical, some historical, that lie at the center of the preceding and the following chapters. Among these suppositions the first is the conception of language as mimetic representation, that is, a written portrait of the object of love is a second presentation of the object itself. In that sense the portrait is *already* a "repetition" of the object, it has already betrayed the object which before its representation was utterly individual, non-repeatable. Not only is the object itself repeated through its representation, but the love for the object is rendered accessible in a way that violates the non-instrumentality of that love, that is, the constitution of the other person himself or herself as the highest possible end. This, we have seen at the beginning of this chapter, is less a feature of mimetic representation itself than of the motivatedness of literary worlds, as products of projected intentions. These two interwoven suppositions - representation as repetition and the person himself or herself as the highest end of perfect love - inform the suspicions of written or literary representation that constitute the "romantic" view of love. But they also are a product of historical shifts,

---

[40] *Love's Knowledge: Essays on Philosophy and Literature* (New York, Oxford: Oxford University Press, 1990), p. 325.

as we have seen, in the criteria and conceptions of "perfect" love, and
in its relationship with motivation.

I would argue that it is precisely in the early modern period that
these shifts become noticeable and are recorded in some of the most
moving works of literature. Indeed Boccaccio's Gisippo and Tito, in
their laconically perfect beginning, are not the only example of early
modern literature attempting to convey the highest ethical relationship.
When we ask why the Princesse de Clèves did not marry the Duc de
Nemours at the end of *La Princesse de Clèves*, why, in Rabelais's
books, Pantagruel chooses to be friends with his trickster companion
Panurge, why, in Marguerite de Navarre's *Heptaméron*, 10, Floride and
Amadour's relationship fails, and why Montaigne and La Boétie were
sublime friends, the answers involve in some way motivation for what
by its very nature is perceived as escaping motivation.

# CHAPTER II

# THE EMPTY OBJECT OF FRIENDSHIP: ANTOINE HOTMAN'S PARADOXES

In 1616 the widow of Matthieu Guillemot, a Parisian printer, published a volume of treatises all written by members of the Hotman family, François, a prominent legal scholar and Protestant pamphleteer, Jean, his son, and Antoine, his brother, an advocate at the Parlement of Paris.[1]   A good deal is known about François Hotman, whose *Francogallia* (1573) was an important theoretical text in Huguenot resistance to tyranny.[2]   His brother Antoine is much less known, although he left a number of curious treatises.  He was also a jurist by training.  Whereas François sided with the Huguenots, Antoine was in the service of the Cardinal of Bourbon and contributed to the cause of the ultra-conservative Catholic League by arguing in 1588 for the Cardinal's succession rights to the throne after Henri III.[3]  The Cardinal died in 1590, and Antoine proved to be willing to change.  According

---

[1] *Opuscules françoises des Hotmans* (Paris: Veuve M. Guillemot, 1616). There is another edition of this work in 1617, also with Guillemot.

[2] See Donald R. Kelley, *François Hotman: A Revolutionary's Ordeal* (Princeton, N.J.: Princeton Univ. Press, 1973).

[3] See his *Advertissement sur les lettres octroyées à M. le cardinal de Bourbon* (1588), *Lettres patentes du Roy déclaratives des droicts, privilèges et prérogatives de Mgr le cardinal de Bourbon. . . - Requeste faicte par maistre Antoine Hotman, advocat dudict seigneur* (Paris: F. Morel, 1588), and the *Traicté sur la déclaration du Roy pour les droits de prérogative de Mgr le cardinal de Bourbon* (Paris, 1588).  On these arguments, see Jacques-Auguste de Thou, *Historiarum sui temporis opera* (Frankfurt: P. Kopffius, 1621), Books 91 (p. 212D) and 97 (p. 329A); also Kelley, *François Hotman*, p. 301.

to the poet and writer Scevole (Ier) de Sainte-Marthe, he ended up arguing for Henri de Navarre, apparently at the risk of his own life, in the face of a hostile Parlement.[4]  The moderate Catholic historian Jacques-Auguste de Thou calls him a *vir doctrina praestans* (a man excelling in learning) and praises his legal arguments, although he disagrees with them.[5]  Hotman's various writings are witnesses to a deft mind: he left behind, among others, a treatise on the dissolution of marriage through impotence and frigidity of the man or the woman (1581), an erudite satirical eulogy of beards (1586), a treatise on the Salic laws, reaffirming the exclusion of women and descendants through the female line from the French throne (1593), and two writings on friendship and avarice, *Deux paradoxes de l'amitié et de l'avarice*, which apparently were composed in 1598 and which we know through their inclusion in the *Opuscules* of the Hotman family.

---

[4] "Mais pourois-je sans injustice oublier icy ce second ornement de la mesme Famille, Antoine Hotman frere de François? Puisque ce fut luy qui pendant la furieuse sedition de Paris se comporta si courageusement dans la charge d'Advocat General du Roy, où il avoit esté mis par ceux du party contraire, qu'apres avoir dissipé les conseils des factieux, il soustint avec ardeur a la face de tout le Parlement la puissance legitime du Roy, & l'Authorité de la Loy Salique.  Ce qu'il fit mesme au peril de sa vie, & avec tant de merite, que si d'abord il eust suivy le party de ce grand Monarque" (*Eloges des hommes illustres, qui depuis un siecle ont fleury en France dans la profession des Lettres*, trans. Guillaume Colletet, Paris, A. de Sommaville, Aug. Courbé, Fr. Langlois, 1644, pp. 403-404).  For a physical description of Hotman (who is made to resemble the "Silenes d'Alcibiade"), see Antoine Loisel, *Pasquier, ou Dialogue des advocats du parlement de Paris* (comp. 1602), in *Divers opuscules tirez des Memoires de M. Antoine Loisel advocat en parlement. . .*, ed. Claude Joly (Paris, Veuve J. Guillemot, J. Guignard, 1652), especially pp. 552-553, and the accompanying note by Joly, who asserts that the king gave Hotman 2000 livres as a reward for his services.  For a brief evocation of Hotman, see also the opening chapters of the hagiographical biography of his devout wife, by Jean Auvray (*Modele de la perfection religieuse en la vie de la venerable mere Jeanne Absolu dite de S. Sauveur*, Paris, Adrian Taupinart, 1640).

[5] *Historiarum sui temporis opera*, Book 9 (p. 212D ff.).

The "paradox" was a species of the mock encomium, and enjoyed a certain favor in the Renaissance.[6] It allowed its author to explore "silly" subjects, in order to demonstrate his rhetorical prowess in making a frivolous object of praise seem important, in transforming an object of blame into an object of praise, or in turning a commonplace object of praise into an object of blame. For example, in Ortensio Landi's *Paradossi*, we find attacks on Boccaccio, Aristotle, and Cicero, and a "paradox" showing that women are of greater excellence and worth than men.[7] The preface to Hotman's *Paradoxes* neatly summarizes the parameters of the genre:

> Cet Autheur a donné carriere à son bel esprit par ces deux Paradoxes pendant un loisir des champs, à l'exemple de plusieurs autres en tous les siecles, ou loüans des choses de neant, ou disputans contre l'opinion commune: non qu'il ait voulu dire absolument que l'Amitié est mauvaise, puis qu'elle est le vray ciment de la societé humaine [see *Nicomachean Ethics* 1155a 21-22]; que l'Avarice est bonne & louable, puis qu'au dire de S. Paul [1 Tim 10], elle est la racine de tous maux. . . . (preface not paginated)[8]

---

[6] See Annette Tomarken, *The Smile of Truth: The French Satirical Eulogy and Its Antecedents* (Princeton: Princeton University Press, 1990), pp. 102-166, and Rosalie L. Colie, *Paradoxia Epidemica: The Renaissance Tradition of Paradox* (Princeton: Princeton University Press, 1966). Neither Tomarken nor Colie discuss Hotman's paradox on friendship.

[7] I have consulted his *Paradossi. Cioè, sententie fuori del comun parere novellamente venute in luce* (Lyons: Gioanni Pullon da Trino, 1543). On Landi's reception in France, see Michel Simonin, "Autour du *Traicté paradoxique en dialogue* de Bénigne Poissenot: dialogue, foi et paradoxe dans les années 1580," in M. T. Jones-Davies, ed., *Le paradoxe à la Renaissance* (Paris: Jean Touzot, 1982), pp. 23-39.

[8] "This author gave course to his good wit with these two paradoxes which he made during a stay in the country, following the example of several others in all centuries, either praising things of no worth, or disputing against received opinion: not that he absolutely wanted to say that friendship is bad, since it is the true glue of human society, nor that avarice is good and praiseworthy, since, according to Saint Paul, it is the root of all evil. . . ."

The emphasis on pastoral leisure, and on the cultivation of "esprit" rather than, say, *doctrine* or learning, defuses objections to the potentially offensive material.   On the other hand, the "opinion commune" that Hotman is about to argue against is not argued *for*, and is presented as opinion rather than knowledge, as maxims rather than reasoned positions. Indeed, Hotman will reasonably and skillfully argue that friendship is an evil and avarice a good.  The genre of the mock encomium is here an important trying-out of ideas, and in a sense can be attached to a legal culture in which hypothetical argumentation is always good practice for the *advocat*.  For Charles Estienne the genre of the paradox itself was a kind of practice forensic "declamation."  We read in the preface to his translation of Landi's *Paradossi* not only that the truth is known more clearly when its opposite is held up against it, but also that lawyers should train themselves by arguing for extreme positions:

> Pour bien faire un advocat, apres qu'il a longuement escouté au barreau, il luy fault donner a debattre des causes que les plus exercitez refusent a soustenir: pour a l'advenir le rendre plus prompt & addroit aux communs plaidoyers & proces ordinaires.[9]

For Estienne, however, paradoxical argumentation is not meant to persuade the reader of any opinion other than the commonly held one.[10] For Pierre de Sainct Julien, the word "paradox" can also mean something contrary to commonly held opinion, but true nevertheless.[11]

---

[9] "In order to form a good trial lawyer, after he has listened for a long time at the bar, he should debate the causes the most experienced lawyers refuse to defend, so that he may be rendered quicker and more skillful in common pleadings and ordinary trials."

[10] "En quoy touteffois je ne vouldrois que tu [the reader] fusses tant offensé, que pour mon dire ou conclusion, tu en croye [sic] autre chose que le commun" (*Paradoxes*, preface).

[11] "On trouvera qu'il [the word "paradox"] ne signifie pas seulement chose contre la commune opinion: ains une proposition vraye, & qui neantmoins cause esbaïssement, comme contraire à ce qu'est communement creu: & de laquelle

The distinction between skillful hypothetical argumentation and baffling truths is indeed a murky one, as the reading of these texts demonstrates. For far from being inconsequential and merely "witty" exercises, Hotman's paradoxes contain seriously elaborated positions: the first pushes friendship to a sort of theoretical limit, working out rational-legal objections to friendship as a preferential relationship, and as a relationship with someone *propter seipsum*. The second constitutes a defense of material accumulation, perhaps in the line of a portion of Poggio Bracciolini's *De avaritia*, and of a domestic economy, somewhat in the spirit of Alberti's *Della famiglia*, although it is not clear that Hotman knew the Italian dialogues. The defense of avarice is implicitly connected to the blame of friendship, as the advocacy of interested relationships underlies both. Which is the opposite of the commonplace view of avarice and friendship: avarice, the most obviously interested of personal attributes, is to be banished because it prevents relationships of friendship, which in their perfect state exclude self-interest. In Poggio's dialogue Bartolomeo of Montepulciano expresses the conventional view: "Denudat [avaritia] illum virtute omni, spoliat amicitia, benivolentia, charitate" (Avarice deprives one of every virtue, removes friendship, goodwill, charity).[12] Hotman claims that avarice in fact *allows* the

---

on n'avoit encores ouy parler. Or pource que je maintien ces miens discours, intitulez Meslanges, estre vrays, & neaumoins [sic] non encores receuz pour veritables: ains contraires (pour la pluspart) aux opinions communes: je les ay qualifié Paradoxe, & declairé icelles mes Meslanges Paradoxalles" (*Meslanges historiques, et recueils de diverses matieres pour la pluspart Paradoxalles, & neantmoins vrayes* (Lyons: Benoist Rigaud, 1588), "Advertissement au Lecteur." Sainct-Julien criticizes Landi and his French translator Estienne for understanding paradox as an "exercice en la preuve du faulx" (ibid.).

[12] Quoted from the facsimile reprint of his *Opera* (Basel: Henricus Petrus, 1538), p. 4, in his *Opera omnia* (Torino: Bottega d'Erasmo, 1964), vol. 1. After a prolonged attack on avarice, Antonio Loschi defends it in part, by saying that without avarice there would be no trade, agriculture, arts (p. 11), and that the *appetitus pecuniae* is in our nature (p. 12). It is by no means evident that Antonio's position is Poggio's.

virtues,[13] and that, conversely, friendship is not a virtue, although goodwill and charity are. Hotman's analysis of friendship constitutes at the same time the most radical Renaissance rejection of the medieval scholastic synthesis of friendship and charity, and announces the modern Christian critique of friendship as a preferential relationship that we find in the writings of Kierkegaard.[14] In addition, Hotman's rationalistic examination of how the choice of an object of friendship is motivated prepares the way for Pascal's reduction, and destruction, of the *moi* as an object of love. In its dissection of motivation, too, Hotman's analysis can be connected to the paradoxes of literary representation of love and friendship that we encounter in Montaigne's essay and in Rabelais's books.

The impetus for a "paradoxical" treatment of friendship may well have been furnished also by a real friendship celebrated in the lawyer milieu of the 1580's and 1590's with which Hotman was familiar. His fellow jurists Antoine Loisel and Pierre Pithou were linked in friendship, and known to be so inseparable that they called each other brothers.[15]

---

[13] Thomas Aquinas argued, in the *Summa contra gentiles* (3.133.1), that external riches are necessary for the good of virtue, in order to support our own body and to give assistance to other people. Hotman's advocacy of avarice imitates certain scholastic arguments, but in his enthusiastic endorsement goes beyond the spirit of Aquinas.

[14] "Erotic love and friendship are preferential and the passion of preference" (Søren Kierkegaard, *Ways of Love*, "You Shall Love Your Neighbour," II B, in Michael Pakaluk, ed., *Other Selves: Philosophers on Friendship*, Indianapolis: Hackett Publishing Co., 1991, p. 240).

[15] See Claude Joly, in his preface to his edition of various works by Loisel, Pithou, and Baptiste Du Mesnil: "le nom le plus ordinaire qu'ils [Loisel and Pithou] se sont donnés [sic] estoit celuy de frere. . . . Aussi se trouve t'il quantité de grands Auteurs qui n'ont gueres parlé de celuy là, sans parler aussi de celuy cy; tant leurs maximes & inclinations, leurs emplois, & leurs estudes ont eu de rapport & de ressemblance" (*Divers opuscules de M. Antoine Loisel*, preface). Indeed, in an epistle to his friend from 1572, Pithou repeatedly calls Loisel "mi frater" (in *Petri Pithoei opera, sacra, iuridica, historica, miscellanea*, Paris, Sebastien Cramoisy, 1609, pp. 808-809). Attesting to the renown of this friendship, Jean Mercier, professor of law in Bourges, describes Loisel as "veterum eius [of Pithou] amicum & studiorum omnium communione

Loisel included a moving praise of his friend in his biography of Pithou composed after the latter's death in 1596.[16] The commonplaces of friendship theory, especially the resemblance of studious friends, appear in the descriptions of their relationship. Hotman's text, however, contains no explicit references to Pithou or Loisel; elsewhere Hotman heaps praise on Pithou.[17] It seems that his "paradoxical" condemnation of friendship is motivated mainly by a desire to "try out" arguments, to push the analysis of friendship to its limits.

## 1. Exclusive vs. Inclusive Love

Beginning his denunciation of friendship, Hotman first distinguishes two related affective relationships from *amitié*: love of God, and the "lien de Societé" by which we are well-disposed toward each other, love, help, and cherish each other "par la loy de nature" (p. 115). Love of God is love of an object worth loving, which is not the case with other human beings, as they do not possess what we desire from God (pp. 114-115).[18] The natural social "bind" is a combination of Aristotelian goodwill (*Nicomachean Ethics*, 1166b 30 - 1167a 20, *benevolentia* or *benivolence* in translations) and Christian charity ("tous les hommes se doivent aimer," p. 115). Friendship, in counterdistinction to these affects, is an exclusive relationship, compressing one's energy into a little space:

---

coniunctissimum Antonium Oiselum," a formula echoing Cicero's "omnium divinarum humanarumque rerum . . . consensio" (*De amicitia*, 6.20), in his *Vita* of Pithou written in 1597 (in Pithou's *Opera*, p. 825).

[16] In Joly, ed., *Divers opuscules tirez des Memoires de M. Antoine Loisel*, pp. 253-292. Loisel compares Pithou to Socrates (p. 275).

[17] In his *Observationum, quae ad veterem nuptiarum ritum pertinent* (Jean le Preux, 1585), p. 27: "Petrus Pitheus, vir singularis doctrinae ac praestantissimi ingenii" and p. 74: "doctissimus P. Pithoeus."

[18] This is the scholastic identification of God as the object *summe diligendum*, the object most worthy of love (see Johann Altensteig, *Lexicon theologicum*, p. 352, under *Fruitio Dei*).

> Ce que nous appellons amitié, consiste seulement, comme ceux qui en ont escrit confessent, en une affection que nous portons particulierement aux uns plustost qu'aux autres, & mesme quelques-uns, voire la pluspart disent, qu'une vraye & entiere amitié ne peut estre qu'entre deux ou trois, comme si de la societé, qui est infinie au genre humain, on avoit extrait toutes les forces, pour les assembler en un petit endroit, afin qu'estans pressees, elles ayent plus d'effect entre deux ou trois personnes. (p. 115)[19]

The sense of compression of affection that exclusive friendship represents is commented upon by Renaissance moral writers before Hotman: in Theodose Valentinian's (Nicolas Denisot?) awkward novel, *L'amant resuscité de la mort d'amour*, this compression is a proof of the "dignity" of love.[20] The exclusive nature of friendship was examined from a religious perspective by Hotman's contemporary Pierre de la Primaudaye, who acknowledged the obligation charity imposes on the Christian to love even enemies, but felt that a perfect relationship with only one other person was not incompatible with charity towards all.[21]

---

[19] "What we call friendship consists only, as those who have written about it admit, in an affection which we bring more particularly to some rather than others, and some, or rather all, even say that a true and entire friendship can only be between two or three, as if one had extracted all the forces from society, which is everywhere in human society, in order to assemble them in a small place, so that, being pressed together, they would have more effect between two or three persons."

[20] "Or combien soit grande la dignité de l'amour, il se peut facilement juger. Voires de ce seul, qu'en ceste infinie societé des hommes & des femmes, l'amour est reduite & rendue à telle rarité & angustie, qu'elle se treuve seulement entre deux personnes" (Repr. of the 1558 ed., The Hague, et al., Mouton, et al., 1971, p. 89).

[21] "Ce-pendant nous avons à noter, que mesurans icy l'amitié au nombre de deux, nous n'entendons pas en exclurre les autres: ains nous sçavons, que la vraye charité s'estend sur un chacun, & que nous devons mesmes aimer nos ennemis, & bien faire à tous: mais entre tous nous pouvons choisir un seul amy, pour l'aimer, & estre aimé de luy en perfection: Taschans au surplus par mille bons offices, de nous acquerir tous hommes bien-vueillans" (*Academie*

This theme is most famously developed by François de Sales, in his *Introduction à la vie dévote* (1609). Charity must extend to all human beings, but "spiritual" friendship is between two or three or several souls who, in Aristotelian fashion, fuse into one mind, "se rendent un seul esprit entre elles."[22] According to François de Sales, "Plusieurs vous diront peut estre qu'il ne faut avoir aucune sorte de particuliere affection et amitié, d'autant que cela occupe le coeur, distrait l'esprit, engendre les envies" (ibid.).[23] This is only true when the common good is clear, and any particular friendship would be unnecessary, as in the case of monasteries (p. 48).[24] But when people do not agree on the goal to attain, the good should band together in a "partialité sainte" which is founded on divine virtue and grace, and which above all excludes physical pleasure.

Hotman, however, excludes all particular friendships based on affection or inclination. The problem of such relationships is that they distract us from relationships with everyone else, and from our duty towards "le public." Whereas Cicero, for example, had seen friendship as an integral part of the civic life, where "private" affection is constantly a model for emulation, and the energy devoted to friendship is an energy devoted to virtue, Hotman, on the contrary, radically separates the domain of private affection from the domain of public good and rational action:

---

*francoise*, Paris, Guillaume Chaudiere, 1581, 1.4.13, f. 43v).

[22] 3.19 (ed. Charles Florisoone, Paris, Les Belles Lettres, 2nd ed. 1961), vol. 2, p. 47.

[23] "Several will tell you perhaps that one should have no particular affection and friendship, since that occupies the heart, distracts the mind, engenders envy."

[24] See, on the medieval antecedents to monastic friendship, Brian Patrick McGuire, *Friendship and Community: The Monastic Experience, 350-1250* (Kalamazoo, MI: Cistercian Publications, 1988). McGuire, in his pages on François de Sales (pp. 420-422), criticizes him for providing reasons for condemning particular friendships in monasteries.

> Rien ne nous distrait du devoir que nous devons au public,
> sinon l'amitié, & n'y a point de plus grand moyen de se
> contenir en une humeur sociable & accompagnable, qu'en
> chassant de nous ceste passion d'amitié, qui nous gehenne &
> nous lie brutalement en certaines affections particulieres, &
> nous faict perdre tout discours de raison, & oublier le devoir
> que nous devons au public. (p. 114)[25]

Hotman will go on to spend much time showing that the "passion d'amitié" is indeed a passion, and thus not a virtue. Furthermore, friendship is inherently incompatible with reason. It brutally constrains human beings in "particular" affections; inversely, reason is identified with free will and judgment.[26] Whereas much is made of the rational choice of the friend in classical moral philosophy (e.g., *Nicomachean Ethics*, 1157b 30),[27] for Hotman friendship and love (which he intentionally conflates) are passions which impose themselves on the friend or lover, depriving them of any choice, and thus depriving them of reason.[28]     Hotman insists on a complete antinomy between the

---

[25] "Nothing distracts us from the duty we owe to the public as much as friendship, and there is no better way of containing oneself in a sociable mood, than by chasing from us this passion of friendship, which emprisons and ties us brutally to certain particular affections, and makes us lose all reason, and forget the duty we owe to the public."

[26] "Nous parlons de la raison donnee à l'homme seul, à ce que comme par un liberal arbitre, il se gouverne par jugement, c'est à dire par un discours de plusieurs occurrences, pour les conferant les unes avec les autres, juger ce qui est bon ou mauvais" (p. 120).

[27] In scholastic translations and commentaries, friendship is a *habitus*, which allows for *electio*: "Amici autem amant sese mutuo cum electione. Electio vero ab habitu proficiscitur" (trans. John Major, in his *Ethica Aristotelis Peripateticorum principis*, Paris, Jehan Petit, 1530, f. 129r).

[28] "Car la chose aimee est la chose sensible, & de l'impression de la chose sensible en nostre fantasie, qui est un de nos sens, se fait l'amour qui est le sentiment. Et puisque la chose sensible agist en nos sens, le sentiment en nous n'est pas action, mais passion" (p. 118). "Et s'il est ainsi qu'amour soit un sentiment, il s'ensuit que nous n'aymons pas par raison, c'est à dire par un

private sphere of irrational, passive affections, and the public sphere of rational action and sociability.

It is the sense of connection between the individual's affection for another individual and an individual's affection for all those connected to the other individual that underlies the scholastic synthesis of friendship and charity, the most important theological attempt at combining classical virtue and Christian precepts. In Saint Thomas Aquinas's sections on friendship in the *Summa theologiae*, the question is asked, "Whether Charity Is Friendship?" (II-II qu 23). In his reply to the negative answer, Aquinas first allows a sense in which we can be friends with God, based on Christ's words to his disciples (Jn 15:15): "Vos autem dixi amicos" (I call you friends). Then he draws an analogy between friendship with another human being and friendship with God:

> Dicendum quod amicitia se extendit ad aliquem dupliciter. Uno modo, respectu sui ipsius; et sic amicitia est nisi ad amicum. Alio modo se extendit ad aliquem respectu alterius personae, sicut si aliquis habet amicitiam ad aliquem hominem, ratione cuius diligit omnes ad illum hominem pertinentes, sive filios sive servos sive qualitercumque ei attinentes. Et tanta potest esse dilectio amici quod propter amicum amentur hi qui ad ipsum pertinent etiam si nos offendant vel odiant. Et hoc modo amicitia caritatis se extendit etiam ad inimicos, quos diligimus ex caritate in ordine ad Deum, ad quem principaliter habetur amicitia caritatis. (II-II qu 23 art 1 ad 2)[29]

---

discours de ce qui se doit faire ou non, mais seulement par un instinct naturel qui est sensuel en nostre fantasie" (p. 120).

[29] "It should be said that friendship extends to a another person in two ways: first in respect of himself, and in this way friendship never extends but to one's friends: secondly, it extends to someone in respect of another, as, when someone has friendship for a certain man, for his sake he loves all belonging to him, be they children, servants, or connected with him in any way. Indeed, so great can the love of the friend be, that for his sake all who belong to him are loved, even if they hurt or hate us; so that, in this way, the friendship of charity extends even to our enemies, whom we love out of charity in relation to God, to Whom the friendship of charity is chiefly directed."

For Aquinas there is an important *inclusive* impulse to friendship that allows certain "private" sentiments to be generalized to persons contiguous to the friend; in this sense friendship reattaches particular affection to a domestic context and, by analogy, to a civic context. Since the "domestic" context of God is his creation, the relationship of friendship with God necessarily includes even our enemies, which means that charity and friendship (in the second sense) are structurally homologous. Aquinas's solution is, however, tenuous. In good scholastic fashion, he first distinguishes two "extensions" of friendship, one of which is exclusive, in which the other person is loved only in respect of himself. This is the "perfect" friendship, which Aquinas also discusses in his Aristotle commentary (*In X libros Ethicorum Aristotelis*, 9, lectio 12). That friendship cannot be charity, as none other than virtuous persons can be loved (see II-II qu 23 art 1 ad 3). Nor is, *stricto sensu*, the second sort of friendship, which is inclusive and extended, a relationship of charity, for the final object of one's friendship is a human being, not God. The purpose of Aquinas's argument is primarily to explain why the term *amicus* is used by Christ in the Gospels to designate God's creature, not to justify human friendships in themselves. Untenable as the Thomist synthesis of friendship and charity seems in the end, the basis for it is the sense that the friend is connected to the world, and that one's love for another can be transferred to the context in which the love is played out.

Although he does not discuss charity in the main body of his text (having excluded it at the beginning), Hotman does address the "contextual" aspect of friendship, and finds it to be particularly objectionable, as it clouds our "jugement de toutes choses." Hotman has a predilection for analogies with dogs, who pursue their desires as we do, in our unreasonable love (pp. 122-123), and the dog reappears in this argument against friendship:

> Ce n'est pas sans raison que l'on dit par un commun proverbe, que qui aime le maistre, aime le chien: car certainement l'amitié nous offusque de telle façon le jugement, que le chien de nostre amy, bien qu'il soit laid, & mal-plaisant, toutesfois nous sera bien agreable: la maison, le jardin, ou autres lieux qui luy appartiennent, nous paroistront tousjours les plus beaux . . . ( . . . ) Car mesme nous negligerons toutes autres personnes [than the one we love] . . . & ruinerions volontiers

le reste du monde pour enrichir un ou deux, à qui nous avons seulement esgard. (pp. 140-141)[30]

The argument presented here suggests that in fact, contrary to Aquinas, there is only one type of friendship, and that it is exclusive. For in the "contextual" scenario that forms the basis of Aquinas's synthesis of charity and friendship, the reason why one would love those attached to one's friend is not any quality they possess on their own, but only the accidental fact that they are attached to the person one loves. So the love of the friend is absolutely primary and determining. Hotman demonstrates this by showing that we find beautiful things that are not beautiful in themselves, just because they are owned by our friend. The clouding of one's judgment that is the result of friendship for Hotman is more convincing in this case, as the French writer has conflated love and friendship, whereas Aquinas is careful to distinguish beforehand concupiscence from friendship. Moreover, Aquinas would admit that the final cause of friendship is always the good of the friend, whereas in charity we love God through our love of other creatures. But what separates Hotman from the scholastic position is the emphasis on the disastrous results of preferential love. Loving someone else, and what is attached to him, means *not* loving all others, which leads to "envies, & mescontentemens" and to "dissensions & querelles" (p. 141). Friendship is, then, not that particular bind that leads to a greater, domestic and social bind, but instead the cause of the destruction of civic ties. It is judgment, that is, the exercise of reason, that enables us to live together.

---

[30] "It is not without reason that one says in a common proverb, that whoever loves the master, loves the dog: for certainly friendship clouds in such a way our judgment, that the dog of our friend, even though he is ugly and unpleasant, nevertheless will be very agreable to us: his house, his garden or other places that belong to him will always appear to be the most beautiful. . . ( . . . ) For we will even neglect all others . . . and would gladly ruin the rest of the world in order to enrich one or two to whom we only pay attention to."

## 2. The Person As Distinct From Personal Attributes

In his denunciation of erotic love and friendship as preferential and selfish relationships, as opposed to the law of charity, Kierkegaard insists on the *arbitrariness* of the former. Like Hotman, he conflates *eros* and *philia*, and he interprets the famous classical dictum, "a friend is another self" (*Nicomachean Ethics* 1166a 31-32), as a supreme form of self-love ("the I intoxicated in the other-I").[31] The "idolatry" of friendship and love is not based on external standards or laws, but derives from the choice itself of the friend, in counterdistinction to all others, in a gesture of essentially unjustifiable abandon and inclination:

> If passionate preference had no other selfishness about it, it still would have this, that consciously or unconsciously there is a wilfulness about it - unconsciously insofar as it is in the power of natural predispositions, consciously insofar as it utterly surrenders itself to this power and consents to it. However hidden, however unconscious this wilfulness is in its impassioned yielding to its "one and only," the arbitrariness is nevertheless there. (p. 242)

Kierkegaard's critique of friendship as willful is possible only when the classical sense of *philia* is deprived of virtue as its final cause. For Aristotle, Cicero, and Seneca the "reason" for friendship is always in some way external to the friends: the insistent exclusion of evil persons from perfect friendship (as opposed to friendships based on utility or pleasure) means that classical writers were careful to provide measures

---

[31] In *Works of Love* (You shall love your neighbour, II-B), p. 243. Kierkegaard's critique is more radical than Nietzsche's, who accuses erotic love of "wilde Habsucht und Ungerechtigkeit" and claims that it is the "unbefangenste Ausdruck des Egoismus." Friendship, however, is different: "Es gibt wohl hier und da auf Erden eine Art Fortsetzung der Liebe, bei der jenes habsüchtige Verlangen zweier Personen nacheinander einer neuen Begierde und Habsucht, einem *gemeinsamen* höheren Durste nach einem über ihnen stehenden Ideale, gewichen ist: aber wer kennt diese Liebe? wer hat sie erlebt? Ihr rechter Name ist *Freundschaft*" (*Die fröhliche Wissenschaft*, 14, in Friedrich Nietzsche, *Werke*, ed. Karl Schlechta, vol. 3, Munich, Carl Hanser, 1966, p. 48). This new, "higher" thirst is still, of course, a "covetousness."

*outside* the personal choice and abandonment that friendship represents.[32] Virtue and excellence are both conditions for, and results of, the association of friends.    In a paraphrase of Aristotle's *Nicomachean Ethics* translated by Daniel Heinsius, we read "virtutis enim causa sunt amici."[33] This should be understood in a strong sense: virtue stands to friendship as an efficient cause and at times seemingly even as a final cause.  Virtue and excellence are the product of a certain civic practice, and cannot be conceived of as qualities of an individual in isolation.  Aristotle's discussion of why good men need friends is an example of the way in which friendship is an eminently *social* quality.[34]

It is with some Renaissance reinterpretations of friendship, and perhaps most famously in Montaigne's essay on friendship, that such external measures are lost.  Virtue or any other quality becomes a constraint, or limitation, on the self being loved.  This sense of separation between an individual and the qualities he possesses or enacts is most clearly seen in Hotman's reworking of Aristotle's discussion of the ending of friendships.  In the case of friendships based on utility or pleasure it is evident that once utility or pleasure are no longer provided, the friendship will cease to exist.  The problem arises in the third type of friendship, of good men with each other *qua* their goodness.  This type is more durable, as it does not depend on pleasure or utility, but on the friends *themselves*:

> If these [pleasure or utility] be the objects of friendship it is dissolved when they do not get the things that formed the motives of their love; for each did not love the other person himself but the qualities he had, and these were not enduring; that is why the friendships also are transient.  But the love of

---

[32] See *Nicomachean Ethics* 1157a 16-19, *De amicitia* 5.18, and the judiciousness with which one must give *beneficia*, in Seneca's *De beneficiis*.

[33] "It is truly because of virtue that friends are [friends]" (*Aristotelis Ethicorum Nicomachiorum Paraphrasis, incerto auctore, antiquo & eximio peripatetico. . .*, ed. and trans. Daniel Heinsius [Lyons: 1607], 9.4, p. 428).

[34] See the opening discussion of the *Nicomachean Ethics*, Book 8, where the social advantages of friendship are listed.

characters, as has been said, endures because it is self-dependent. (*Nicomachean Ethics*, Book 9, 1164a 8-12)

In Latin translations of this passage, such as John Major's scholastic edition and commentary, the phrase "for each did not love the other person himself but the qualities he had, and these are not enduring" is rendered "Non enim se mutuo amabant, sed ea quae inerant, quae non permanent" (For they did not love each other, but those things that were in them, which do not endure). Aristotle's enduring "self-dependent love of characters [φιλία . . . τῶν ἠθῶν καθ' αὐτήν]" is translated as "morum vero amicitia, cum per se sit, permanet" (truly the love of moral manners, since it is for the sake of itself, endures).[35] The first French translation, by Nicole Oresme, says "amistié qui est selon bonnes meurs."[36] Both are relatively close to the Greek (which they may well not have known), but in a sense the translation of τὸ ἦθος (character) as *mores* or *virtutes* or *bonnes meurs* makes the goodness out of which perfect friendship arises more into attributes which one can possess and then not possess, without changing the "one" who possesses. In addition, the love of "characters" (τῶν ἠθῶν) in some sixteenth-century Greek editions of Aristotle is rendered as the love of "things expressing

---

[35] *Ethica Aristotelis Peripateticorum principis* (Paris: Jehan Petit, 1530), 9.1, f. 139v. In his commentary Major uses the phrase "virtutum amicitiae" (f. 140r). Other Latin translations differ little in these instances; the translation in Pier Vettori's commentary says, "non enim semetipsos amabant, sed quae in ipsis tunc erant, quae stabilia non sunt . . . amicitia autem, cuius solum, ac fundamentum sunt mores, cum per se sit, manet," in *Petri Victorii commentarii in X. Libros Aristotelis De Moribus ad Nicomachum* (Florence: Ex officina iunctarum, 1584), p. 496.

[36] Maistre Nicole Oresme, *Le Livre de Ethiques d'Aristote*, ed. Albert Douglas Menut (New York: Stechert, 1940), p. 452. Bernardo Segni's Italian translation avoids the difficulty, reading "l'Amicitia morale per se stessa" (*L'Ethica d'Aristotile tradotta in lingua vulgare fiorentina*, Vinegia, Bartholomeo detto l'Imperadore, 1551, f. 279r).

moral character" (τῶν ἠθικῶν). This is the case with Erasmus's editions of the Aldine text.[37]

The problem of identity and attributes is posed later in the same book of the *Nicomachean Ethics*, when Aristotle discusses the breaking off of friendships. If the good man and friend becomes bad, efforts should be made to correct him, but when all fails, since one cannot love what is bad, it will not be "strange" (ἄτοπον) to break off the friendship: "for it was not to a man of this sort (τοιούτῳ) that he was a friend; when his friend has changed, therefore, and he is unable to save him, he gives him up" (1165b 21-22).[38] There is a strong sense here that in the friendship of good men *qua* their goodness, when one of them becomes bad, there is a more fundamental transformation involved than the acquisition or loss of attributes. In becoming bad, one changes, which means that what one's friend loves changes, too. At a certain point it might not be important to speak of a person as independent of his goodness, since what constitutes him as a person is in part his goodness. Loving someone "for his own sake" does not mean, then, that one loves *him* as opposed to his goodness. The "person" tends to be conceived of as an enactment of choices, not as something separable from the behavior that manifests these choices.[39]

---

[37] I have consulted the 1550 edition (the text is a reprint, with some corrections, of the Aldine edition of 1495-1498), Αριστοτέλους ἅπαντα. *Aristotelis summi semper philosophi . . . opera . . . omnia* (Basel: Johannes Bebel, 1550), vol. 2, p. 46. In Vettori's commentary, however, the Greek excerpt reads τῶν ἠθῶν (p. 496).

[38] Major has "Non enim huic aut tali amicus erat: cum igitur mutatum ad priores mores redigere nequeat: sese ab illo seiungit" (f. 142v). Oresme does not translate this sentence.

[39] See A. W. Price, *Love and Friendship in Plato and Aristotle* (Oxford: Clarendon, 1989), pp. 108-109 for a good discussion of this topic in Aristotle. In a slightly different Ciceronian view, the individual possesses both a universal *persona*, which he has in common with all human beings, and a particular one. The universal *persona* allows a determination of *honestum* and *decorum* for all; the universal *persona* is always naturally a part of an individual's make-up. In this sense the connection to a supra-individual virtue is always already there, by the rationality that our universal *persona* gives us. The self is never radically

The classical sense of the person as constituted by his choices, as inseparable from a chosen behavior, can still be seen to function in the astute commentary on the *Nicomachean Ethics* by John Buridan. This fourteenth-century theologian anticipated the difficulty posed by the distinction between a person and his attributes: if in perfect friendship the other is loved for his moral goodness, "propter honestum," then he is not loved as a person, "non est persona amata" or he is not loved for his own sake, "secundum seipsum." The answer for Buridan was that virtuous behavior is in the power of the person to choose and to preserve, whereas things such as youth or beauty are not. In that sense the virtues are a part of the person "secundum seipsam" and when the friend loves the other's virtue, he loves the other for his own sake.[40] In Josse Clichtove's commentary on Jacques Lefèvre d'Etaples' "introduction" to Aristotle's ethics, the objection raised by Buridan is

---

prior to or outside of this connection to other human beings (see *De officiis*, 1.30.107 and ff.). For a stimulating general discussion of the difference between classical, Renaissance, and modern conceptions of the self, see Robert E. Proctor, *Education's Great Amnesia: Reconsidering the Humanities from Petrarch to Freud* (Bloomington: Indiana Univ. Press, 1988), parts 1 and 2.

[40] See *Questiones Joannis buridani super decem libros ethicorum aristotelis ad nicomachum* (Paris: Ponset le Preux, 1513), 8.4, f. 172r: "Sed dices quod ita argueretur de amicitia propter honestum. Obiectum ei per se talis amicitie non est persona amata. Sed eius virtutes quae nec sunt animate nec readamant ergo concluderetur quod illa non esset vere dicta amicitia quid est falsum. Ad hoc dicendum est quod virtutes dicuntur homini habenti eas inesse secundum seipsum. Per tanto quia in hominis potestate est fieri virtuosum et manere virtuosum: sic autem non convenit homini secundum seipsum quod sit alteri utilis vel delectabilis. Honestum enim est in potestate sua quod sit iuvenis et pulcher nec est in potestate sua quod sit dives aut potens alterius negocia procurare. Imo nec vita alterius est in sua potestate. Quam remota nec amplius erit sibi utilis nec delectabilis. Patet ergo quod amicitia propter utile vel delectabile non est secundum se ad personam amatam. Imo per accidens pure: sed amicitia propter honestum ad personam secundum seipsam: quia eius grata quid convenit homini secundum seipsum. Ut potest dici quod praemium honestum non est virtus nec opus virtutis imo ipsa persona."

rehearsed and refused, although Buridan's solution is not reproduced.[41] The possible separation between a person and his or her attributes has become a more commonplace difficulty in the early modern understanding of perfect friendship.

In some cases the contrast between friendship and charity produces a similar insistence on the distinction between attributes and the object of love: since charity obliges us to love sinners as well as virtuous persons, we love in sinners not their sin but the fact that they are creatures of God. In that sense the attribute of the person is irrelevant to the practice of charity. In perfect friendship, however, it is the person who is loved, not the creature of God. The presence of sinful attributes, if they are "his" (*res suae*), may prevent us from loving the person as a friend in virtue.[42] The friend as a person is distinct from the friend as a creature of God, and our love differs accordingly. In any

---

[41] "Quod siquis obiectet eadem ratione probari posse quod amicus studiosus magis virtutem quàm amicum studiosum diligat: quandoquidem propter virtutem ipsum diligat: non igitur ei vult aut facit bonum ipsius gratia, sed alterius, scilicet virtutis suae. Conceditur equidem quòd studiosus magis virtutem quam amicum diligat. Attamen negatur id quod deinceps subinfertur. Nam dicitur quis bonum velle aut facere cuiquam illius gratia, quando id agit gratia boni animae quod est in eo cui vult bonum aut facit, utpote virtutis. Tunc autem non suiipsius, sed alterius gratia, quando non ratione honesti, sed utilis aut delectabilis quod vel extrinsecum est, vel in corpore, ei bonum vult aut facit. Quare amicus studiosus alteri bonum vult aut facit, illius quidem gratia, utilis autem & delectabilis, gratia alterius" (*Moralis Iacobi Fabris Stapulensis in Ethicen introductio, Iudoci Clichtovei Neoportuensis familiari commentario elucidata*, Paris, Simon Colin, [1535?], f. 37r).

[42] This discussion of the difference between charity and friendship can be found in Johannes Altensteig's *Opusculum de amicicia. . .* (Hagenau: Henricus Gran, 1519), cap. 18: "Et nota quod quamvis amicicia honesti habeatur ad virtuosum, et charitas sit maxime amicicia fundata super re honesta, non obstat quod ex charitate diligamus etiam peccatores. Nam amicicia honesti habetur ad virtuosum sicut ad principalem personam, sed tamen respectu eius diliguntur etiam attinentes etsi sint peccatores, et etiam qui nos offenderent si attinerent ad amicum, et hoc non respectu ipsorum, sed respectu amici nostri ad quem illi pertinent ut res suae. Sic peccatores et inimicos debemus ex charitate diligere inquantum sunt creaturae ipsius dei, ad quem principaliter est amicicia charitatis."

case it is clear that theological considerations have seriously complicated the active, complete sense of the person inherited from classical moral philosophy.

For Hotman in particular the classical synthesis of person and chosen action no longer holds. While showing that "amitié" is contrary to reason, Hotman also discusses the termination of friendships, but in a way that both radicalizes friendship and separates a "person" from his attributes. In both cases he transforms the classical, Aristotelian discussion, and points to a rationalistic calculus of the self:

> Si l'amitié estoit chose bonne & raisonnable, nous ne la laisserions jamais pour quelque accident qui advint. . . . Aussi celuy qui aime un autre pour la vertu qu'il cognoist en luy, il n'aime pas la personne, mais la vertu qui luy plaist. Car s'il aymoit la personne, pour quelque changement qui advint il ne laisseroit de l'aimer. Mais ce n'est pas en ces choses que consiste l'amitié. Aimer la vertu procede bien du discours de raison, car c'est aimer Dieu: Mais ceux qui ont parlé d'amitié, ont entendu parler de l'affection portée à certaine personne, c'est à dire, pour vouloir du bien à la personne mesme, non à sa qualité. . . . (pp. 128-129)[43]

Hotman goes on to give examples, namely that fathers love sons, a brother his brother, etc., without regard to the faults that might arise in the other's body or mind. For Hotman, loving virtue is indeed a reasonable thing to do, but it is not friendship, which is desiring good for the other person, not for his qualities. Virtue has become a pleasing attribute such as beauty or wealth, and can be removed from the person without endangering the person's identity. Loving the "person" has become, then, essentially *unjustifiable*, unless the loved one happens to

---

[43] "If friendship were a good and reasonable thing, we would never abandon it for whatever accidental thing that happened to it. . . . So he who loves another because of the virtue he knows is in the person does not love the person but the virtue that he likes. For if he loved the person, he would not stop loving him whatever changes may happen. But it is not in this that friendship consists. To love virtue derives from reason, for it is to love God; but those who have spoken of friendship have meant an affection concentrated on a certain person, that is, in order to wish good to the person himself, not to his attribute.
. . ."

be a relative or a spouse, in which case the law provides a category for the person, and a motivation for the love. If, however, "natural" ties such as familial or conjugal relations are either absent or thought of as a constraint, then the "person" loved is both ineffable and empty, as he must be separated entirely from attributes he may possess. Hotman's conception of personal identity is that of a collection of attributes possessed by a sort of vanishing point or center which itself is always without attributes, thus indescribable. The "person" becomes indescribable precisely because the "discours de raison" requires the person to remain the same, in counterdistinction to his changing attributes.[44]

Hotman's rationalistic reduction of the "person" to the absence of attributes can be seen in the light of Kierkegaard's accusation of "wilfulness" against friendship. If loving another "for his own sake" is no longer compatible with loving another through virtue, and for virtue, then the choice of another is necessarily an arbitrary one, in the sense that it is unjustifiable and inaccessible. The exercise of the will is in this case not constrained by any knowledge that can be conveyed to another. As we have seen, this incompatibility represents a movement away from the classical sense of the person loved in a relationship of *philia*. Hotman is not alone in his critique; he foreshadows, with Montaigne, Blaise Pascal's fragmentary analysis of the *moi* as an object of love.

In what came to be called the *Pensées*, Pascal begins a fragment by asking what the self is: "Qu'est-ce que le moi?"[45] The movement of the argument soon turns to love: if someone loves someone else because of his beauty, does he love *him*? As many theoreticians of

---

[44] This goes further, it seems to me, than the Stoic insistence on detachment from "external" qualities. The exercise of virtue impels even the Stoic sage to friendship, which is praised, for example, by Hotman's contemporary, and *Politique* parliamentarian, Guillaume Du Vair, in his *La Philosophie morale des Stoïques* (1585): it is a "mouvement que nous donne la vertu" and can be broken off gently if, in the Aristotelian fashion, our friends abandon reason and philosophy, and all our efforts to bring them back have failed (ed. G. Michaut, Paris, Vrin, 1946, pp. 105-106). Friendship is, however, the last on the scale of affections, the first of which is the love of God.

[45] *Pensées sur la religion et quelques autres sujets*, ed. Louis Lafuma (Paris: Editions du Luxembourg, 1952), vol. 1, #688 (p. 395).

friendship Pascal answers in the negative, and he separates the attribute from the person in a way reminiscent of his predecessor Hotman: "Non: car la petite vérole, qui tuera la beauté sans tuer la personne, fera qu'il ne l'aimera plus."[46] However, Pascal goes from a relationship of erotic love or of friendship for pleasure to what seems more like the "honest" friendship conceived of by classical authors, although the perspective is very different:

> Et si on m'aime pour mon jugement, pour ma mémoire, m'aime-t-on? *moi*? Non, car je puis perdre ces qualités sans me perdre moi-même. Où est donc ce *moi*, s'il n'est ni dans le corps, ni dans l'âme? et comment aimer le corps ou l'âme, sinon pour ces qualités, qui ne seront point ce qui fait le moi, puisqu'elles sont périssables? car aimerait-on la substance de l'âme d'une personne, abstraitement, et quelques qualités qui y fussent? Cela ne se peut, et serait injuste. On n'aime donc jamais personne, mais seulement des qualités. (#688, p. 395)[47]

In Pascal's scenario of identity the person is composed of the body, the soul, and something that is loved, or is under the illusion that it is loved, the *moi* or self, distinct from body and soul, but possessing no attributes. In the consideration of the soul Pascal differs from his predecessor, as he does when he simply says that no one ever loves a *person* (playing on the ambiguity of the word "personne"), only attributes. But Hotman's calculus of friendship is the starting point, and it is taken to its logical end, as Pascal points out the resulting real impoverishment of the self. In the rhetorical fashioning of his argument, Pascal has turned away from an objective perspective to a subjective one: why does someone

---

[46] "No: for smallpox, which will kill the person's beauty without killing the person himself, will cause him to be loved no longer."

[47] "And if one loves me for my judgment, for my memory, does one love me? *myself*? No, for I can lose these qualities without losing myself. So where is this *self*, if it is neither in the body nor in the soul? and how can one love the body or the soul, unless it is for these qualities, which do not constitute the self, because they can perish? For would one love the substance of the soul of a person, abstractly, and any attributes that may be there? That is not possible, and would be unjust. So one never loves a person, but only attributes."

love *me*? (and not: why do friends love each other?).  This subjective presentation is a final move away from the picture of the person enacting choices in an interpersonal environment that dominates the discussion in Aristotle.  For Pascal the *moi* has the feeling that it can remain the same despite the loss of memory or judgment, but for a classical author, seen from the outside, or in an interpersonal situation, it is not clear that the "person" would indeed remain the same.  The scenario of identity is skewed, then, *a priori* to prepare the way for a radically interiorized, yet evanescent and arbitrary (for Pascal, presumptuous) self.

When the relationship of *philia* seeks out the friend "for his own sake," *propter seipsum* or καθ᾽ αὐτόν, this very gesture is, in classical moral philosophy, an exercise in virtue, and it demonstrates the *civic* or *social* foundation for personal happiness.  This sort of secular tending to the other is at times deprived in early modern moral thought of all justification, as it becomes either an arbitrary gesture, or one that is deluded.

# FRIENDSHIPS IN LITERARY WORLDS

# CHAPTER III

# THE SINGULAR OTHER:
# RABELAIS'S PANTAGRUEL AND PANURGE

The two linked gestures that constitute the core of the present chapter, an offer of classical friendship and the refusal to come to the friend's aid, constitute a provocation to the ethical and theological codes through which human relationships are understood in the early sixteenth century. The resulting imaginative reordering of human love makes way for a kind of freedom of literary representation that borders on the incoherent, and that prepares a perception of the object of love as above any external measure or end.

## 1. Panurge Disappoints Pantagruel

At the conclusion of the war against the Dipsodes and the giants, the hero of Rabelais's book *Pantagruel* (1532) faces his evil Mohammedan counterpart, Loupgarou, the wolf-man, the incarnation of Plautus's phrase, *homo homini lupus* (man is a wolf to man), the figure of hatred and cruelty among men.[1] Pantagruel, the good Christian humanist giant, finds himself in dire straits, his weapon, a ship mast, having been shattered by Loupgarou's enchanted mace. In desperation he calls out to his friend, "Ha, Panurge, où es-tu?", in an appeal reminiscent of Christ's words, "My God, my God, why have you

---

[1] Plautus's phrase is from his *Asinaria* (l. 495) and is reproduced by Erasmus in his *Adagia* (1.1.70), as a pendant to the phrase 'man is a god to man.' On the significance of Loupgarou as an antithesis of charity, see Edwin M. Duval, *The Design of Rabelais's Pantagruel* (New Haven: Yale University Press, 1991), 36-40.

deserted me?" (Mk 15:34).[2] Pantagruel's cry for help is in fact doubly reminiscent of Christ's words (pronounced in Aramaic, *lama sabachthani*), as the Hebrew *lamah hazabthani* is used earlier in the book by a lady friend of Pantagruel. The giant left her abruptly to go off to war, and she sends him a ring containing a false diamond and the engraved Hebrew phrase. Wily and polyglot, Panurge translates the phrase and finds the solution to the rebus: "Dy, amant faulx, pourquoy me as tu laissée?"[3] The phrase indicates the insufficiency of love between men and women: men are always ready to embark on epic voyages and desert their ladies. In this earlier episode Pantagruel certainly was no *homo homini deus*, no god to his fellow creature.

When Pantagruel cries out, "Ha, Panurge, où es-tu?," he is showing, rather understandably, evidence of anxiety or sadness (*anxietas* or *tristitia*). Given the echoes of Christ that surround the characterization and the words of the giant, the fact that anxiety is present at all is a problem.[4] The fact that the words are directed to a human being, not to God, is no less of a difficulty. But Panurge is no ordinary creature, he has been chosen by Pantagruel as his companion.

Pantagruel and Panurge are friends, in counterdistinction to lovers, and the mark of friendship would surely be the sacrifice of one for the other. Rabelais is careful to set up their relationship as friendship: when they first meet, the humanist giant announces to Panurge "par ma foy, je vous ay jà prins en amour si grande, que, si vous condescendez à mon vouloir, vous ne bougerez jamais de ma

---

[2] Jerusalem Bible. All quotations from *Pantagruel* are taken from the edition by V. L. Saulnier (Geneva: Droz, 1965), chap. 19 [29], p. 156. The numbers in brackets indicate the chapter numbers from the revised 1542 edition. Unless indicated otherwise, all translations are my own.

[3] "Say, false lover, why have you abandoned me?" (*Pantagruel*, chap. 15 [24], p. 129). See Duval, *Design*, pp. 13-14.

[4] There is a tradition of allowing anxiety or sadness in Christ, following Scotus, to whom Ockham refers when he says, "quamvis forte de potentia Dei absoluta posset compati secum tristitiam et anxietatem, sicut fuit in Christo secundum aliquos" (*Ordinatio* I dist 1 qu 4, pp. 446-447). See also Pierre d'Ailly, *Quaestiones super libros sententiarum*, I dist 1 qu 2 Q (Strasbourg, 1490, repr. Frankfurt: Minerva, 1968), who copies Ockham.

compagnie, et vous et moy ferons ung nouveau per d'amytié, telle que fut entre Enée et Achates."[5] Epic friends prove their friendship in battle; when one cries out for help the other rushes to stand by his side. In addition to Aeneas and Achates and Achilles and Patroclus, Virgil's Euryalus and Nisus (*Aeneid* 9.176-445) and Statius's Hopleus and Dymas (*Thebaid* 10.347-448) provide models for epic friends' behavior. Emulation and surpassing of models is part of the epideictic rhetoric of friendship, most famously in Montaigne's praise of his friendship with La Boétie, but in lesser writers, as well.[6] Lucian's *Toxaris*, a dialogue compiling examples of Greek and Scythian friends and their self-sacrifice in peace and war, was among the sixteenth-century sourcebooks for epic friendship, and Rabelais was an avid reader of Lucian.

Another avid reader of Lucian was Erasmus. In the opening section of his *Adagia* we find, among a series of phrases on friendship, the two adages most relevant to Pantagruel's desperate situation: on the one hand, "man is a wolf to man" (1.1.70), on the other, "man is a god to man" (1.1.69). Since Loupgarou, as we have seen, is obviously the former, should Panurge not be the latter? In his commentary on *homo homini deus* Erasmus catalogues instances in which the ancients have

---

[5] "By my faith, I have already conceived such a love for you that, if you agree, you will never leave my company, and you and I will be a new pair of friends, such as Aeneas and Achates" (*Pantagruel*, chap. 9, p. 54). On this meeting, see most recently the suggestive study by Timothy Hampton, "'Turkish Dogs': Rabelais, Erasmus, and the Rhetoric of Alterity," *Representations* 41 (1993), pp. 58-82. François Rigolot has studied the patristic notion of *condescendance* (*sygkatabasis*) to illuminate the relationship between Pantagruel and Panurge, in "Quand le géant se fait homme: Rabelais et la théorie de la *condescendance*," *Etudes rabelaisiennes* 39 (1993): 7-23.

[6] See, for example, the version of Boccaccio's Tito-Gisippo story by François Habert, in which Gisippo praises hyperbolically their friendship: "Et croy que j'ay vers toy plus d'amytié, / Et bon vouloir, voire de la moytié, ( . . . ) Que n'eut Enée oncques vers Achates, / Ou Pilades vers son amy Oreste, / Et desormais de t'aymer je proteste, / Plus que n'ont faict les susdictes, voire plus / Qu'aymé ne fut d'Achilles Patroclus, / Ou de Glaucus le vaillant Diomede. / Tous ces amys de fermeté j'excede / En ton endroict. . ." (*L'Histoire de Titus, et Gisippus, et autres petiz oeuvres de Beroalde latin. . .*, Paris, Michel Fezandat & Robert Gran Ion, 1551).

conferred the name of "god" on someone or something that preserved them "in desperate and involved situations, or in deadly peril."[7] Erasmus condemns as disgusting flattery the use of "God" by Christians to designate other mortal men, even in jest, and allows its use only when it is clear that the term is part of a saying carefully attributed to the Greeks ("but I might almost say, as the Greeks do," etc.).

In fact, Pantagruel never gets to use the adage, even under the guise of Erasmus's prudent presentation, since Panurge fails to help his friend in his moment of greatest need. Upon hearing Pantagruel's plea Panurge makes what would be easy to interpret as an ironic remark: "Par Dieu! ilz se feront mal, qui ne les despartira" (p. 156).[8] He does not attempt to intervene, however, and it is Carpalim, another of Pantagruel's companions, but not his chosen friend, who wants to get up and help his master, the Christian giant.

It is clear that Panurge is in no mood to provide the sort of sacrifice that the rhetoric of friendship would demand of him. On this point the moral imperative cannot be clearer; the Ciceronian and Ovidian commonplace, *amicus certus in re incerta cernitur* (the true friend is discerned in times of trouble), is ever-present in Renaissance moral

---

[7] Erasmus, *Adagia*, in *Collected Works of Erasmus*, vol. 31, trans. Margaret Mann Phillips (Toronto: University of Toronto Press, 1982), 113. See also Henri Estienne's similar comment on the proverb "L'homme à l'homme un dieu peut estre" in his *Les premices, ou le I livre des proverbes epigrammatizez, ou, des epigrammes proverbializez* (repr. of the 1593 ed., Geneva: Slatkine, 1968), p. 145. See also Louise Labé, "Débat de Folie et d'Amour," in ed. François Rigolot, *Oeuvres complètes* (Paris: Flammarion, 1986), pp. 69-70; finally, a prudent summary by Pierre Boaistuau, who makes this theme into a rather narcissistic trait of the Ancients: "Bref, il se treuve des choses si fantasticques et estranges en l'homme, que plusieurs anciens après avoir consideré l'essence de toutes choses, et ne trouvans rien qui se peust egaller à la merveilleuse providence, et exquise industrie de l'homme, se sont voulu faire appeler Dieux, et reverer, et honorer comme quelque deité" (*Bref discours de l'excellence et dignité de l'homme (1558)*, ed. Michel Simonin, Geneva, Droz, 1982, p. 72).

[8] "By God! they will hurt each other if one doesn't separate them."

philosophy.[9] Henri Estienne provides the French counterpart, *Au besoin congnoist-on l'ami*, in his *Precellence du langage françois* (1579).[10] This particular failing of Panurge as friend, manifestly set up in the novel, announces the cowardly and indecisive character traits that Panurge will show especially in later books, the *Tiers livre* and the *Quart livre*, and confirms some suspicions the reader may have had about Panurge all along.

Pantagruel, however, does not have these suspicions. His choice of Panurge as friend for eternity is never in doubt; his generosity toward his friend is in no proportion to the (lack of) merit Panurge continues to prove. He subverts the epic pretensions of the war against the Dipsodes in *Pantagruel*, even though he resuscitates a character from death. He is a thief, he is cruel, he is spiteful. In the *Tiers livre* he has squandered the enormous revenue assigned to him from the domain of Salmigondin (which clearly meets Pantagruel's disapproval); when he wonders about getting married, he cannot make up his mind. During the sea voyage of the *Quart livre* he proves himself to be the most cowardly of the crew. Although the trickster and polyglot Panurge is often useful to the giant, especially in the first book *Pantagruel*, he is essentially a *voyou*, a good-

---

[9] Cicero, *De amicitia* 17.64 (Cicero is quoting Ennius). See also Ovid, *Tristia*, 1.9.24. Among the many commentators on this commonplace, see Petrarch, *De remediis utriusque fortunae. . .* (Cremona: Bernardinus Misinta & Caesar of Parma, 1492), Book 1, Dialogue 50, "De amicorum abundantia," where the figure of Reason uses this line (which the edition misprints, however, as "in re certa"!). Alberti quotes it in the 4th book of the *Libri della famiglia*. We find in florilegia such as the *Flores poetarum de virtutibus et viciis* (Cologne(?), 1490) a category entitled, "De amico non derelinquendo in diversis" (Book 2, chap. 42), and so forth. Distinguishing between good will and friendship Johannes Lonicer says that the friend helps in deed, not just in words and intention: "Benevolus voluntatem non egreditur, amicus benevolentiam non verbis tantum et voluntate, verum etiam opere & ope testatur" (*Librorum Aristotelis . . . compendium*, Marburg, Christian Egenolph, 1540, f. 125v). In Theodor Zwinger's voluminous compendium of examples of moral philosophy, we find a section on friends proving their fidelity to each other "defendendo, non deserendo" (*Theatrum humanae vitae*, Vol. 18, liber 2).

[10] Ed. Léon Feugère (Paris: Jules Delalain, 1850), p. 232. He includes a whole list of proverbs treating friendship on pp. 213-215.

for-nothing out for cheap thrills. Panurge, however, enjoys the giant's unfailing financial and emotional support. Pantagruel's friendship with Panurge presents, then, a real problem, which the epic combat with Loupgarou only highlights. Their relationship is also paradigmatic, in the sense that unequal literary friendships such as those of Don Quixote and Sancho Panza, Dom Juan and Sganarelle in Molière's *Dom Juan*, Jacques and his Master in Diderot's *Jacques le fataliste*, relate in some way to the problem of Pantagruel and Panurge.

The issue is not merely a matter of literary types. It is also not a matter of the internal esthetic coherence of the fiction in which it occurs. Friendship couples, as we have seen, can function and be represented in various ways. It does not seem clear that the decision to make Panurge into what he is and Pantagruel's love for him into what it is somehow arose out of an esthetic necessity. Even if we were able to see this necessity retroactively, it is even less clear that it would have been obvious to Rabelais or to any of his readers. Representations of fictional relationships are not divorced from the intellectual and generally cultural climate in which they are conceived. The issue of Pantagruel and Panurge involves, then, the ways in which a culture conceives of its members' relationships with each other, and specifically the way in which a relationship can be explained or motivated. It also involves the question of whether one *ought* to motivate, provide reasons for, the love of one human being for another. In Rabelais's time these questions involve competing discourses which are, finally, inadequate to the literary representation of Pantagruel's friendship. Rabelais's representation unwittingly offers an anti-theoretical move beyond the disputes concerning friendship dividing humanism and scholasticism in the early sixteenth century.

*     *     *

What are the possibilities for understanding Pantagruel's excessive love for Panurge?

Before delving into the intellectual discourses available to Rabelais, a first solution might be to locate the giant's generosity in the social relationship implied by Pantagruel's status as the sovereign and Panurge as his vassal, or simply as his inferior. In this sense Pantagruel's *liberalitas* is simply the product of nostalgia for feudal ways: the generosity of the lord is a natural feature of his social status, and is exercised irrespective of friendship toward anyone in particular. As the very exclusivity and excess of the friendship between Pantagruel and his vassal suggest, however, the feudal bond is insufficient to motivate their attachment. In addition, in the instance cited above, the vassal has failed to perform the essential feudal function of military succor to his lord, and so is less than deserving of his generosity. Clearly more is at play.

## 2. Charity

The selflessness with which Pantagruel apparently loves an undeserving companion seems to link him to a discourse of charity that was familiar to the evangelical humanist Rabelais. This discourse constituted a key element of the Christian humanist reaction to the perceived irrelevance of scholastic theology. In a famous annotation of 1 Tim. 1:6-7 (on *vaniloquium*), Erasmus enumerates scurrilous distinctions and questions debated by the scholastics and in a typical and dramatic way dismisses centuries of scholastic theology. He concludes:

> Breve tempus est, & arduum est negotium agere vere Christianum. Quin igitur omissis rebus supervacaneis, ea potissimum spectamus, quae Christus nos scire voluit, quae prodiderunt Apostoli, quae proprie ad charitatem faciunt, de corde puro, & conscientia bona, & fide non ficta, quam unam Paulus appellat [in 1 Tim. 1:5] finem & perfectionem totius Legis.[11]

---

[11] "Life is short; and to lead a Christian life is an arduous task. Putting trifles aside, then, let us concentrate most of all on those matters which Christ wanted us to know, which the apostles proclaimed, which emphasize charity, a pure heart, a good conscience, and a faith not vain; which Paul calls the sole end and consummation of the entire Law." In *Opera omnia*, vol. 6 (Loudun: P. Vander Aa, 1705), 926D n. 13. The translation is by Craig R. Thompson, in "Better Teachers than Scotus or Aquinas," in *Medieval and Renaissance Studies*, Proceedings of the Southeastern Institute of Medieval and Renaissance Studies, vol. 2, ed. John L. Lievsay (Durham, NC: Duke University Press, 1968), 144 n. 58.

Charity is at the heart of the urgent tasks in a Christian life, and scholastic quibbling will only take time away from those tasks. The relationship of charity ("Dilige proximum tuum sicut teipsum") is indeed one of gratuitous love, in the sense that no return is expected from the gift of love. Commenting on this precept in his *Paraphrases* on the New Testament, Erasmus emphasizes the gratuitousness of charity. When you love yourself you do not require a return.[12] Since, according to the New Testament commandment, you should love another as yourself, you cannot require a return of your love; in fact, loving someone only if he loves you back is against the spirit of charity that commands love of friends and enemies alike.[13] The inclusiveness of charity poses a problem for the understanding of Pantagruel's love, however, since the latter is exclusive. In his commentary on the adage *homo homini deus* Erasmus points out the inclusiveness of Pauline charity: "Paul, though, places the height of virtue in charity; but charity which consists in doing the greatest good to the greatest number" (p. 114).[14] Commenting on a different version of the adage, "Chaqu'homme est l'un à l'autre un dieu," Henri Estienne exhorts Christians not to be exclusive in their affection:

> Il [the proverb] ne dit pas tan-seulement
> L'ami à l'ami, le parent
> Au parent mais l'affection
> Entre nous, sans exception,
> Il dit reciproquement pouvoir:

---

[12] "Unusquisque sibi charus est, nec aliquod a seipso praemium amoris exigit," on Luke 6:31; quoted from *Paraphrases in novum testamentum*, vol. 7 of his *Opera omnia*, 347E. Erasmus is borrowing this idea from Cicero (*De amicitia*, 21.80). On the economic implications of self-love and love of the other, in respect to usury, see Chapter V, 2.

[13] "Qui redamat amantem, non amaturus nisi redametur, is multum abest ab Evangelica charitate quae amicos pariter & inimicos complectitur" (ibid.).

[14] "Porro Paulus virtutem summam ad caritatem refert: caritatem autem in eo sitam, ut de quamplurimis quamoptime mereamur," in *Opera omnia*, vol. 2, 55A.

Et tel estre nostre devoir.[15]

If Christians cannot do the act of the Samaritan, Estienne goes on to say, they are worse than pagans, from whom we have received the proverb. In addition to its inclusivity, however, charity is always exercised toward fellow creatures as a step toward God, the ultimate object of the creature's love.[16] In his extensive treatise on friendship the Tübingen theologian Johannes Altensteig simply says that whereas friendship is towards friends, the law of charity obliges us to love of our enemies.[17] Although he discusses both friendship and charity in great detail, there is a major difference between the two, "quia amicicia fundatur super honestatem virtutum et charitas super bonitate divina" (Cap. 18).[18]

In addition, it is unclear to what extent charity is ultimately gratuitous, given that charity toward other creatures can reap great benefits from God. Erasmus expresses this underlying, discreet calculus in commenting on Luke 6:35 ("Date mutuum nihil inde sperantes" [Lend not hoping for a return]):

> Benefacite etiam his, qui vel non referunt beneficium, vel beneficium maleficio pensabunt. Et dato mutuum hoc animo, ut etiam si nihil sit ad te rediturum, tamen gaudeas opitulari

---

[15] "It does not only say friend to friend, relative to relative, but it says that we can show affection to each other without exception; and such is our duty" (*Les premices*, epigram 14 on "l'homme," pp. 146-147). See also epigram 12: "Je ne scay comment tu l'entens, / N'aidant qu'aux amis & parens: / C'est te monstrer presque inhumain / Vers le reste du genre humain" (p. 144).

[16] See on this question Erasmus's *Enchiridion militis christiani* (1518), 4th canon.

[17] *Opusculum de amicicia. . .* (Hagenau: Henricus Gran, 1519), cap. 12, no pagination.

[18] "For friendship is based on the [moral] goodness of the virtues, and charity on the goodness of God."

proximo.  Nec est periculum, ne vobis pereat merces vestra,
siquidem hoc copiosus praemium rependet deus. . . .[19]

In spite of a rhetoric of gratuitousness, evangelical charity institutes
human relationships that point to God as the ultimate motivation, the true
end and reward.


## 3. Classical Friendship

The exclusive generosity of the giant's love takes us away from
charity and brings us closer to classical discourse on friendship, a
discourse that pervaded moral philosophy in early modern Europe, and
provided many commonplaces for humanist epideictic rhetoric.[20]
Charity and friendship - at least the terms - are associated already in
Roman moral philosophical sources: Cicero uses *caritas* and *amicitia*
together (as in "hominum caritas et amicitia gratuita est," *De natura
deorum*, 1.44.122).  Charity and friendship are compared during the

---

[19] "Do good also to those who will not do you good in return, or will pay
for good with evil.  If your loan is given in this spirit, even if nothing should
be given back to you, nevertheless you will enjoy helping your neighbor.  And
there is no danger that your goods should be lost to you, since God will most
richly pay back a reward" (*Paraphrases*, 348).  See also Henri Estienne, *Les
premices*, pp. 90-91, epigram 117: "Quiconque du sien donne, / Le Seigneur
apres luy redonne" (Estienne points out that this means giving to the poor).

[20] Among the abundant literature, see, on classical friendship, Jean-Claude
Fraisse, *Philia: la notion d'amitié dans la philosophie antique* (Paris: Vrin,
1984); see also Marie Aquinas McNamara, *L'amitié chez Saint Augustin* (Paris:
P. Lethielleux, 1961); on medieval friendship between kings, the interesting
piece by C. Stephen Jaeger, "L'amour des rois: structure sociale d'une forme
de sensibilité aristocratique," *Annales: Economies, Sociétés, Civilisations* no. 3
(May-June 1991): 547-571; Barry L. Weller, "The Rhetoric of Friendship in
Montaigne's *Essais*," *New Literary History* 9 (1977-78): 503-523; Ronald A.
Sharp, *Friendship and Literature: Spirit and Form* (Durham: Duke University
Press, 1986).  On Montaigne's essay on friendship, see also my *Divine and
Poetic Freedom in the Renaissance: Nominalist Theology and Literature in
France and Italy* (Princeton: Princeton University Press, 1990), 182-190.

Middle Ages, by St Thomas Aquinas as well as by Ethelred of Rievaulx and Pierre de Blois, and the humanists follow suit.[21] Erasmus himself likens the Christian precept of charity to classical friendship, in his adage *Amicitia aequalitas. Amicus alter ipse* (1.1.2), as does an early translator into French of Cicero's treatise on friendship, Jean Collin.[22] Compilers and commentators on Aristotle, too, note the similarity of charity and friendship.[23] Treatises of moral philosophy are no exception: "toutes

---

[21] See, for a comprehensive and useful overview of different medieval conceptions of love, Rüdiger Schnell, *Causa amoris: Liebeskonzeption und Liebesdarstellung in der mittelalterlichen Literatur* (Bern: Francke, 1985), especially 53-76.

[22] In the preface to his *Livre de amytie de Ciceron* . . . (Paris: V. Sertenas, 1537): "Laquelle chose [my translation] jay entreprise dautant plus voluntiers, pource que la matiere de ce livre est conjoincte a la loy Evangelique, laquelle est toute acomplie par dilection & amytie. . ." (a translation which I have undertaken all the more willingly, since the matter of this book is connected to the evangelical law, which is accomplished by love and friendship) [no pagination].

[23] For example Lonicer in his *Librorum Aristotelis* . . . *compendium* (1540), who adduces the theological example of Christ's friendship with his disciples: "Satis quidem est divinum auxilium, verum in humana societate, de qua hic philosophus [Aristotle, in the *Nicomachean Ethics*] loquitur, infelix est vita, omnis amiciciae expers. Quod si Theologice loqui velimus, Et Christus amicos habuit apostolos, hodieque charos habet omnes in se fidentes. Quin etiam apostoli & omnes pii, bonorum societate gaudent, quod quid est aliud, quàm piorum etiam summam esse animorum coniunctionem, summam amiciciam, maximumque caritatis vinculum?" (f. 128v). For Josse Clichtove charity is superior even to perfect friendship of the "men of letters": "Et cum dei in homines syncera dilectio, charitas dicatur: ut mutuus sit amor, debet homo fervente itidem charitate ferri in deum, quae ad hanc virtutem reducitur: imò vero est supra amicitiam studiosam" (*Moralis Iacobi Fabris Stapulensis in Ethicen introductio, Iudoci Clichtovi Neoportuensis familiari commentario elucidata*, Paris, Simon Colin [1535?], f. 33v). See also Jacques Lefèvre d'Etaples' commentary on the *Nicomachean Ethics*, 8.1, where charity is the highest form of friendship (*Decem librorum Moralium Aristotelis, tres conversiones: Prima Argyropyli Byzantii, secunda Leonardi Aretini, tertia vero Antiqua*, Paris, Simon Colin, 1535, bound with the preceding, f. 78r).

parfaites amitiés doivent estre conjointes du lien de charité, & referées à luy [Dieu] comme au souverain bien & premier amy," says Jean des Caurres, claiming Socrates as his authority.[24]  Generally but not always felt to be compatible with the precept of charity, friendship and its commonplace literature was in a way the site of humanist nostalgia for the times when men were true friends, when interest and ulterior motives did not cloud human relationships.

Although the variety of sources makes for a rather heterogeneous picture, there is a broad consensus in this literature: in spite of doubts here and there (especially in Plato), friendship generally requires a resemblance in the friends.  Friendship generally is impossible among the unjust.  Friendship generally has as its aim the exercise of virtue, especially in the civic sphere.  On the surface not one of these conditions is fulfilled by the friendship between Pantagruel and Panurge.  The giant is very different from his unreliable friend; Panurge is rather uncharitable even though he seems to require charity from Pantagruel; finally, Panurge, even given his friendship with Pantagruel, hardly excels in providing examples of virtuous civic involvement, proposing, for instance, the building of walls around the city of Paris with female genitalia and monks' erect penises.

There is, however, at the heart of friendship "theory" a reflection on the gratuitousness of human relationships that will lead closer to their literary representation.  This is the notion of the *beneficium*, the service or favor one performs for a friend.  Seneca provides the most extensive analysis of these services, and insists that a true favor is one which is performed without hope of a return or of interest: *demus beneficia, non feneremus* (let us give favors and not lend with interest).[25]  The most virtuous favor is one in which neither "interest" nor principal is expected in return.[26]  In fact, the scandalous behavior of Panurge is the best

---

[24] "All perfect friendships must be conjoined by the bind of charity, and referred to God as the highest good and the first friend" (*Oeuvres morales et diversifiées* [rev. ed. Paris: Guillaume Chaudiere, 1584], f. 92v).

[25] *De beneficiis*, 1.1.9.

[26] "Nunc est virtus dare beneficia non utique reditura" (*De beneficiis*, 1.1.12). See also Lactantius: "Si vertu ne demande remuneration, si pour elle mesmes (comme tu [Cicero] dis) lon la doit desirer, estime doncq justice

guarantee of the *beneficium* offered through Pantagruel's love, as the giant can assume that his favors will not be returned. This logical reduction of the virtuous favor points to a profound incompatibility between the economic analysis of friendship and the civic and ethical intentions that motivate its praise. The most generous act is also the one which is least likely to produce ethical results. Seneca senses the dangers of what we may call sophistic analysis, and requires in the *beneficium* a proportionality: the favor has to be adapted to the character of the person who performs it, who receives it, and to the circumstances and intentions surrounding it.[27] It is important to exclude prodigality, *largitio*; generosity must be neither absent nor excessive.[28] In the evolution of Rabelais's books, this sense of measure is progressively lost: generosity is practiced on a literally gigantic scale, by both Gargantua and his son. Pantagruel assigns to his friend Panurge the revenue of the (fictive) domain of Salmigondin, which amounts to fantastic annual sums, and which his friend proceeds to squander on banquets and prostitutes, prompting a dispute between the friends at the beginning of the *Tiers livre* (1546). Although through the analysis of the *beneficium* the classical account of friendship comes close to providing a model for the literary unequal pair, more yet is still at play.[29]

---

princesse & mere de vertuz, par son pris & non selon ton proffit, & donne principalement à celluy duquel tu ne espereras aucune recompense" (*Lactance Firmian des Divines institutions, contre les Gentilz & Idolatres*, trad. René Fame, Paris, Galliot du Pré, 1543, 6.11, f. 136r).

[27] *De beneficiis*, 2.16.1.

[28] "[Liberalitatem] nec deesse oportet nec superfluere" (*De beneficiis*, 1.4.2).

[29] In my hasty overview of Renaissance intellectual discourses I am neglecting two important currents in early sixteenth-century culture: Neoplatonism (Marsilio Ficino, Leone Ebreo) and the mystical tradition (e.g., Nicholas of Cusa). Neoplatonism reproduces in this instance classical accounts of friendship; in Leone Ebreo's *Dialoghi d'amore* (1535) it goes something like this: if love is a desire for perfection, how can one explain the love of the more perfect for the less perfect? The answer assumes the superiority of giving over receiving: those who give favors love more perfectly than those who receive

## 4. Pantagruel's *Fruitio* (Enjoyment)

We can also understand the Rabelaisian giant's unreasonableness, his gratuitousness, in light of the (nominalist) late scholastic tradition, given that we find among many late scholastics an emphasis on the willful-conventional aspect of human and divine relations. The relationship between Pantagruel and Panurge involves in many ways theological paradigms; the insistence, especially in the later books, on the exercise of the will in contingent matters seems to reproduce questions about human and divine agency that one finds in scholastic treatises and commentaries. The vicissitudes of the two characters' interaction are a kind of intellectual and cultural playground in which Rabelais confronts some of the most interesting and refined conceptualizations of the passage from will to action. These conceptualizations are primarily theological, and fundamentally scholastic, as I have shown in a previous study.[30]

The problem of the Rabelaisian pair of friends brings us back once again to theological paradigms, this time involving not will but love. Pantagruel's love for Panurge seems unconditional in a profound sense: neither virtue nor pleasure nor even usefulness are motivations for his friendship; in fact, Rabelais appears to make certain that we exclude these motivations. The exclusion of all ends external to the person who is the object of love forms part of the scholastic concept of the love of God, although the history of this particular notion goes back much

---

them. The inferior depends on the superior as the effect on the cause, or the son on the father. When the superior loves the inferior, he would like to remove the latter's imperfection so that he himself may be more perfect, so that they may resemble each other in their perfection. The mystical tradition, although it touches on the problem of the gratuitous through its cultivation of paradoxes, is in the end a cultivation of a trans-logical, silent contemplation of God, which is, I think, antithetical to the practice-oriented, thoroughly verbal and communicative fictional universe of the novel.

[30] See my *Divine and Poetic Freedom in the Renaissance: Nominalist Theology and Literature in France and Italy* (Princeton: Princeton University Press, 1990), pp. 126-148. See also Schnell, *Causa amoris*, p. 71.

further, as I have shown in greater detail earlier in this book.[31] Since this concept is crucial to understanding the exceptional nature of Pantagruel's love, I will briefly recall its outlines. It derives from a reading of Aristotle, whose definition of the highest good implies the absence of any other good desired beyond it. The concept is transmitted to medieval theology through Augustine's *De doctrina christiana* and the first distinction of the *Sentences* of Peter Lombard.[32] Augustine distinguishes between signs and things; signs are always, by their nature as signs, used in relation to something else (that which they signify or refer to). Things either are used in relation to something else (*usus*) or for their own sake (*fruitio*, enjoyment). Briefly, use of an object or person means that the object or person is desired with another end in mind, whereas enjoyment of an object or person entails the absence of any other end. When we "enjoy" something or someone, we enjoy the object or person "for its own sake." We should only enjoy God, as he is the highest possible object, and thus *summe diligendus* (to be loved in the greatest way). We should use creatures in view of God, or with God as a final end. There is a question, as we have seen, as to whether human beings *can* enjoy something other than God completely. In a marked shift away from classical views of friendship, virtue as an ever-present condition of love "for its own sake" seems to be conceived of as another end, distinct from the object desired, and subordinated to God who, properly speaking, does not possess moral virtues and is certainly not constrained by them. The Augustinian distinction between use and enjoyment (without, albeit, its various scholastic subdistinctions) is found in humanist writings as well, from Lorenzo Valla to Erasmus himself.[33]

---

[31] See Chapter I.2, for a more extensive discussion of the Aristotelian concept and its Augustinian and scholastic transformations.

[32] See Chapter I.2 for a more elaborate discussion of the history and features of the distinction.

[33] In Valla's *De vero bono* (1433) and his *Dialecticae disputationes*. See, on this particular point, Charles Trinkaus, *In Our Image and Likeness: Humanity and Divinity in Italian Humanist Thought*, vol. 1 (London: Constable, 1970), 114-116, 138-140. Erasmus uses the distinction in his *Enchiridion militis christiani* (1504), 4th canon (see the trans. by A. J. Festugière, Paris, Vrin, 1971, 64 [p. 137]). See also Mario Equicola, *Libro di natura d'amore* (rev. ed.

By the very form of their commentaries, a sort of trying-out of positions for and against a thesis, the scholastics, however, push to logical extremes the love of God: they begin to provide paradigms for a way in which human relationships can be conceived of in the same light.

For what does it mean to love someone absolutely (*summe diligere*) for his own sake (*propter seipsum*)? The conceptual paradoxes of this sort of love are revealed especially when God is the object of love. For how can the creature love God for his own sake? In fact, loving God because of the rewards he may be capable of giving, such as salvation, is not acceptable, for in that case one would be using him:

> Dicimus nos ea re frui quam diligimus propter se, sicut est Deus [diligendus]. Unde Deus non est diligendus propter beneficia vel propter beatitudinem, sed propter se. (Altensteig, *Lexicon theologicum*, p. 351)[34]

Altensteig has made explicit and succinct what is present in many commentaries on the first distinction of Lombard, namely that God cannot be thought of as an instrument to the gratification of self-love.[35]

---

Vinegia: Gioanniantonio & Fratelli de Sabio, 1526), f. 99v: "Il primo [God] è segno & fisso termine, alquale l'anima aspira: l'altro [the creature] è grado & mezzo, di pervenire al fine."

[34] "We say that we enjoy something that we love for its own sake, such as God is to be loved. For God is not to be loved because of benefits or salvation, but for his own sake."

[35] See, for example, Gregory of Rimini, *Lectura super primum et secundum Sententiarum*, ed. A. Damasus Trapp OSA, Venicio Marcolino (Berlin: Walter de Gruyter, 1981), vol. 1, p. 259: "dico quod omnis actus, quo quis diligit deum propter se ipsum diligentem vel propter aliquid aliud a deo, est illicitus et abusus" (I dist 1 qu 3). Similarly, for the early 16th-century Paris theologian Jacques Almain, the "actus spei" (act of hope) may be caused by the love of God or the love of self. In the first case, the "act of charity" is prior to the act of hope. In the second, "iste actus videtur esse malus: quia amo deum propter me" (*Moralia acutissimi et clarissimi Doctoris theologi magistri Jacobi Almain . . .*, Paris, Claude Chevallon, 1520, f. 51r). The problem of the completely gratuitous love of God by the creature does not really pose itself for the

Saint Bernard, in his *De diligendo deo* (7.17), would like to have it both ways: on the one hand you must love God freely, not in a mercenary way, on the other hand charity cannot be empty, and God is not loved without a reward.

It is indeed obvious that God is the object most worthy of love; however, that very worthiness makes it difficult to conceive of the proper way of loving him, except in negative terms. For his worthiness as object of love is constituted precisely by the creature's conceiving of his all-goodness and promise of salvation, which, however, cannot be the basis of the creature's love for him. Empirically speaking, the demonstration of God's *lack* of reward for the creature's love seems the best measure of that love, for then it is not exercised as a relationship of use. It is in the very "unreasonableness" and gratuitousness of the creature's love that this love proves itself enjoyment.

*   *   *

God is, of course, *summe diligendus*, the one to be loved in the highest way, and, for humanists and scholastics alike, reliable and good. Yet the negative conditions for the highest sort of love prepare the way for the relationship between human beings who are not *summe diligendi*, but, by the very fact of their imperfection, objects to be loved for their own sake. This seems to be the case with the heroes in *Pantagruel*, who in their inequality and difference from each other are a constant demonstration of a relationship that must derive from something other than use. The most obvious instance is the scene I evoked at the beginning of this chapter, in which Panurge fails to come to the aid of his giant friend, and which, in spite of the friend's failing, does not diminish their friendship. In this sense their relationship in the moments of its use*less*ness is an enactment of enjoyment of the other, and an implicit divinisation of the other, in the very love "for his own sake."

Yet theoretically this should not be the case. Evangelical humanism is clear about condemning what does not have God as its final cause: we remember that Erasmus clearly admonished Christians not to use the saying *homo homini deus*. He also recommends, in the

---

Ancients; for Cicero, the gods obviously care for human beings, for why would we otherwise pray to them? (*De natura deorum*, 1.44.122).

*Enchiridion*, relationships of use in the dealings of men with each other; these relationships should all have God as their end.[36] Scholasticism, on the other hand, by introducing those "sophistic" subtleties and questions (or *quaestiunculae*, to use Erasmus's dismissive term) we have just rehearsed, allows greater freedom of intellectual movement in the understanding of human relationships.   The scholastics introduce distinctions concerning enjoyment that gradually make it impossible to rationally demonstrate that human love for another human being could not reproduce the enjoyment of God.  Although theoretically enjoyment of an object other than the worthiest (*fruitio inordinata*) is always inferior to enjoyment of the highest object (*fruitio ordinata*), the subjective and practical criteria of enjoyment are such that the will may be completely satisfied by love of an object other than God.  In this sense it may be difficult to distinguish between the two kinds of enjoyment on subjective grounds.  This is the import of what Ockham appears to be saying, when he concludes that one cannot rationally demonstrate that the will *cannot* be entirely satisfied by an object other than God ("Dico quod non potest naturaliter demonstrari quod voluntas non potest satiari nec quietari in aliquo citra Deum").[37]  A love *propter se*, for his own sake, of another creature - that is, an object inherently imperfect - cannot be *excluded*.  This concession is, of course, far from saying that human beings should enjoy each other, nor is the statement in Ockham a product of, say, empirical psychological observation.  Rather, its formulation of rational uncertainty is part of the nominalist emphasis on the covenantal, freely willed order that God has established in his relationship with his creatures.  This emphasis underlines the contingent over against the necessary nature of the created world, and thus reduces possibilities in some non-theological areas for rational demonstration.   The concession, on the part of Ockham, of the possibility of entire enjoyment of another creature, was part of what

---

[36] See his *Enchiridion militis christiani* (1504), 4th canon.

[37] *Ordinatio* I qu 4 art 1, p. 434.  See also Gordon Leff, *William Ockham: The Metamorphosis of Scholastic Discourse* (Manchester: Manchester University Press, 1975), 518; Arthur S. McGrade, "Ockham on Enjoyment: Towards an Understanding of Fourteenth-Century Philosophy and Psychology," *Review of Metaphysics* 34 (1981): 706-728.

Christian humanists tended to find abhorrent in and symptomatic of the scholastics' sinful "curiosity."[38]

Within the radical formula *propter seipsum*, for his own sake, we find at the same time the condition for individuality and the possibilities for its representation.  When Pantagruel loves Panurge for the sake of Panurge, *what* does he love?  We have seen that in the deliberate absence of coherent motivation the question can no longer be posed, as any answer to the question is a deformation of his love.  Similarly, asking what one loves when one loves God, in the terms set up, cannot have a coherent answer, as the answer would return the lover to a relationship of use.  So Panurge as an individual object of love is individual precisely because there are no prior constraints on his character or behavior: in spite of aspects of his personality that have literary antecedents he is *not* a coherent, virtuous or non-virtuous *persona* in the classical sense.

We have here, it seems to me, hints of the relational calculus of ends and means coming to its logical endpoint, and producing in this endpoint a representation of the individual as simply that which *is*, prior

---

[38] On this theme of humanist polemics, see the work of Gérard Defaux on Rabelais, especially *Pantagruel et les sophistes: Contribution à l'histoire de l'humanisme chrétien au XVIe siècle* (The Hague: M. Nijhoff, 1973) and *Le curieux, le glorieux, et la sagesse du monde: L'exemple de Panurge (Ulysse, Démosthène, Empédocle)* (Lexington, KY: French Forum, 1985).  See also André Godin, "Erasme: 'Pia/impia curiositas'," in *La curiosité à la Renaissance*, ed. Jean Céard (Paris: SEDES, 1986), pp. 25-36.  Mikhail Bakhtin's work, often brilliant as imaginative criticism, is no longer a reliable guide to the intellectual context and import of Rabelais's novels.  Among the large amount of work on the relationship between humanism and scholasticism, see Trinkaus, *In Our Image and Likeness*; John F. D'Amico, "Humanism and Pre-Reformation Theology" in *Renaissance Humanism: Foundations, Forms, and Legacy*, vol. 3, ed. Albert Rabil, Jr. (Philadelphia: Univ. of Pennsylvania Press, 1988), 349-379; Alan Perreiah, "Humanistic Critiques of Scholastic Dialectic," *The Sixteenth Century Journal* 13 (1982): 3-22.  The accusation of "curiosity" levelled against theologians by ecclesiastical reformers is not unique to the humanists, as we see in Gerson's *Contra curiositatem studentium* of 1402.  For an overview of the meanings of curiosity in the Renaissance, see Françoise Charpentier, Jean Céard, Gisèle Mathieu-Castellani, "Préliminaires," in *La curiosité à la Renaissance*, pp. 7-23.

to its signification. This issue of individuality returns us to the Augustinian distinction between things and signs which precedes the explanation of use and enjoyment in the *De doctrina christiana* (1.2.2). Signs are always signs *of* something, otherwise they would not be signs. Things can be signs of something else, or they could just be things. Things as "mere" things, and thus not as signs of something else, are more apt to be enjoyed, in the sense that the very relationship of enjoyment supposes its end in the thing itself, not in that to which it points, refers, leads. Seen from this perspective, the relationship of one creature to another *propter seipsum* is the assumption that the creature loved is loved not as a sign but as a thing, and in this sense a radically *individual* thing. A sign, by contrast, is always there *propter aliquid*, for the sake of something else, that which it signifies.

The enjoyment that is friendship leads, then, to the issue of individuality, and this both in a nominalist logical sense (our categorization of things is not inherent to the things themselves), and in an ethical sense (the most god-like relationship to another is as a radical individual, not as a member of a group, or as producing our own interest). Rabelais's novels are the ground on which "thingness" in the sense described can be displayed. Precisely and perhaps paradoxically because Panurge is not a consistent sign of something else Pantagruel can love him for his own sake. The "thingness" of Panurge is the very stuff of his literary representation, and, in its resistance to use and motivation, this literary representation is also the basis for an ethic incarnated by Pantagruel, and only imperfectly given in intellectual discourses of Rabelais's time.

## 5. Humanists Are No Friends Of Scholastics

For, in concluding, we cannot avoid the historical issue that arises out of the polemical nature of the intellectual context and the overt intentions of the author himself. Rabelais's text is overtly anti-scholastic, Erasmian Christian comedy. A small but representative instance of Rabelais's attitude towards scholasticism should suffice. In Erasmus's note to the "idle speculation" (*vaniloquium*) of the doctors of the law (1 Tim 1:6-7) he scornfully associates scholastic *theologia* with the Greek *mataiologia*, foolish, idle talk. Rabelais, in one of numerous instances of anti-scholastic satire, takes up the same joke in *Gargantua*.

The child Gargantua has spent his time being tutored by dusty scholastics, Thubal Holoferne and Jobelin Bridé. His father does not see any progress in his child; a friend of Gargantua's father proposes a disputation between Gargantua and one of his pages, Eudemon, an angelic little boy with a perfect Ciceronian humanist education. The terms he chooses recall Erasmus's mockery and indicate Rabelais's dismissal of scholastic theology as silly and anachronistic talk: "voyons, si bon vous semble, quelle difference y a entre le sçavoir de vos resveurs mateologiens du temps jadis et les jeunes gens de maintenant."[39] Indeed, the humanist youth goes on to trounce Gargantua, who ends up "weeping like a cow." The contrast could not be more stark between the unwieldy, stupid scholastic, and the graceful, angelic humanist. Nevertheless a character resembling the perfect Eudemon is not chosen by Pantagruel as his life-long friend, although it seems clear that he, and not the proto-scholastic, sophistic Panurge, would be more like the enlightened giant Pantagruel. However, this and many other negative presentations of scholastics and scholasticism in Rabelais's works leave no doubt as to the overt intentions of their author.

As we have seen, though, it is paradoxically scholasticism that provides the most intricate reading of human gratuitous love, and it is that reading that most closely accounts for this central feature of Rabelais's own literary world. Theoretical polemics have clouded an understanding of human individuality that is emerging in imaginative accounts of human experience in the early modern period. Our own tendency to focus on the ideological polarities of the Renaissance is perhaps a reenactment of the humanists' blindness to their imaginative practice. Which is not to say that this practice is independent of conscious intellectual choices and programs, but that the practice is at the same time more synthetic and more daring than the antithetical structure of much intellectual life in the early modern period seems to allow.

The force of this polemical atmosphere, and the sense of frustration it engendered, are captured by a simile drawn from an episode of the *Odyssey*, Ulysses' perilous navigation between the

---

[39] "Let us see, if you wish, what difference there is between the knowledge of your crazy dreamers of yesteryear and the young people of today" (quoted from *Gargantua*, 1534?, ed. M.A. Screech, Ruth Calder [Geneva: Droz, 1970], chap. 14, p. 100). See also the note by Screech on this passage.

monster Scylla and the whirlpool of Charybdis. The simile is used in
the mean-spirited debates of the 1520's among Erasmus, Luther, and the
University of Paris theologian Noël Béda, concerning the creature's
possibility for salvation.[40]  At issue is man's ability (or inability) to
achieve salvation by himself, with Luther arguing the negative. Erasmus
responds to Luther's radical denial of human merit by attempting to steer
a middle course between the "Scylla of arrogance" and the "Charybdis
of despair or indolence" ("Scylla arrogantiae . . . Charybdi[s]
desperationis aut socordiae").[41] Although the theological questions are,
of course, extremely complex, the choice of this metaphor indicates the
degree to which intellectual positions have been hardened into opposing
sides, and the increasing difficulty of a flexible course.  In Luther's
response to his Ulysses-like adversary he characterizes Erasmus's
solution as "evasive and equivocal" ("lubricus et flexiloquus"), and
denies that there can be a middle course at all.[42]   Luther responds to
Erasmus with the proverbial "Those who try to avoid Charybdis fall into
Scylla."[43]  In his rebuttal Erasmus tries hard to maintain the possibility
of a neither-nor solution: "And he does not sail unhappily, who holds a
middle course between two opposite evils."[44]  When Erasmus and his
fellow humanist Jacques Lefèvre d'Etaples are subsequently attacked by

---

[40]   See, on the debate between Erasmus and Luther, Marjorie O'Rourke
Boyle, *Rhetoric and Reform: Erasmus' Civil Dispute with Luther* (Cambridge:
Harvard Univ. Press, 1983); on Erasmian prudence here, see Victoria Kahn,
"*Stultitia* and *Diatribe*: Erasmus' Praise of Prudence," *German Quarterly* 55
(1982): 349-369.

[41] *De libero arbitrio diatribe* (1524); translation from *Luther and Erasmus:
Free Will and Salvation*, trans., ed. E. Gordon Rupp, A. N. Marlow, P. S.
Watson, B. Drewery (Philadelphia: The Westminster Press, 1969), p. 96.

[42] In his *De servo arbitrio* (1525); see *Luther and Erasmus*, pp. 103, 115.

[43] *Luther and Erasmus*, p. 311.  Erasmus cites and comments upon this
proverb in his *Adagia* (1.5.4).

[44]   "Nec infeliciter navigat, qui inter duo diversa mala medium cursum
tenet" (*Hyperaspistes*, Book 1, in *Opera omnia*, vol. 10, 1258A; my
translation).

the scholastic theologian Noël Béda, Erasmus once again uses the simile, and once again prefers a middle course, although he inverts the terms of the opposition: if you cannot navigate between them, the Scylla of Luther (i.e., total reliance on God's grace) is preferable to the Charybdis of the scholastics (i.e., efficaciousness of human merit).[45] Béda, in turn, wonders whether one should call the ability of the creature to save itself, aided by God's grace, of all things a *Charybdis!*[46] It is indeed ironic that two doctrines concerning human salvation should be figured in terms of two mortal dangers. It is, however, similarly ironic that the image of the middle course, conveying human effort and resourcefulness, should be invoked by an Erasmus who, when faced with scholastic censures, would rather throw himself into the Scylla of Luther than concede the merit, however limited, that scholastics accorded to human effort.

The sometimes confusing attacks and counter-attacks in this polemic demonstrate the way in which intellectual discourse touching upon theological matters was clouded by polarities. Some late scholastics, in their theological refinement of Lombard's questions, and some humanists, in their scholarly practice, had arrived at a sense of human effort and relations as somehow independent of religious teleology. But these hints are submerged in the adversary rhetoric of the time. This should, I think, make us suspicious of analyses of culture based on intellectual polarities. It should also make us take imaginative and theoretical expressions of culture seriously, in themselves, and not simply as the reproduction of social or ideological interests. The literary world of the humanist Rabelais does intellectual work that is connected in a profound way to work done by the enemies of humanism, even

---

[45] In his *Supputatio errorum in censuris Natalis Bedae* (1527) in *Opera omnia*, vol. 9, 568C: "Qui medium cursum tenet, incolumis est, sed si deflectendum est, tutius est incidere in Scyllam Lutheranicam, quam in Beddae Charybdim."

[46] In his *Apologia Natalis Bedae, theologi, adversus clandestinos lutheranos* (Paris: J. Badius, 1529), f. 62v: "Perpende lector, an Charybdis debeat dici hominibus contestari quod ad aeternam felicitatem nemo adultus perveniet, nisi per opera iustitiae quae humanis suis viribus dei gratia adiutis ipse fecerit." Béda, however, typically goes on to equate Erasmus's solution to Luther's Scylla.

though, on the surface, everything seems to tell us that Rabelais's interests are incompatible with those of his apparent adversaries.

When Pantagruel chooses Panurge as his eternal friend, and Panurge refuses, several chapters later, to help his friend in the moment of greatest need, that moment constitutes a realization of the human being in its thingness, as an object to be enjoyed, to be desired non-instrumentally.   It also goes beyond the impasse of Renaissance friendship, the impasse of resemblance and of repetition we can see in writers such as Boccaccio and Montaigne.  It goes beyond the impasse of representation, or the conflict between the teleological (and thus the representable) and the non-teleological imperative that friendship has become.   For now *whatever* Panurge does or is seems to characterize someone who is not by the fact of those attributes an instrument to something else.   There is nothing else, as it were, which means that Panurge the πανούργος, the one ready to do anything, can truly be *everything* and still be himself.

# CHAPTER IV

# FLORIDE'S FAILED "HONEST" FRIENDSHIP: MARGUERITE DE NAVARRE'S *HEPTAMERON*, 10

Whether we read classical moral treatises or their Renaissance versions, true friendships are always thought to be extremely rare, and the examples of good friends generally involve two males, Orestes and Pylades, Laelius and Scipio, Achilles and Patroclus, Aeneas and Achates, the brothers Castor and Pollux, Damon and Phintias, and so forth. In part, the exclusively male nature of exemplary friendship is derived from their essentially martial character: the true test of friendship involves physical help in battle or other life-threatening situations, and revenge for the friend's death is carried out through individual combat. Friendship is also at the heart of ancient moral philosophy, in a theoretical and a practical sense. In theory friendship is the paradigm of a virtuous relationship, and it is a fulcrum of the network of duties that constitute a civic life. In a practical sense the very act of philosophizing is a demonstration of a basic level of male friendship: Socrates' discussions with his disciples or adversaries and Laelius' conversation with Scaevola and Fannius in Cicero assume a society of men. Perhaps most obviously, in Lucian's *Toxaris*, the Greek and Scythian adversaries debating in their friendship contest end up becoming fast friends. In addition, the relationship of friendship is often presented in gradations, according to its motivation: motivations of pleasure and usefulness are secondary to love of the other "for his own sake." In male-female relationships, and particularly in the oft-cited conjugal relationship, pleasure and usefulness play a great part, which seems to exclude them from the very start.[1] This does not mean that desire as such disqualifies friends, in classical discussions of friendship: in Plato's *Lysis* the discussion of friendship begins as blushing Hippothales admits his love for the beautiful Lysis. But in moving away from Plato to Aristotle, Cicero, and Plutarch, desire plays a less significant role. In all these ways moral philosophy, and at its center *philia* or *amicitia*, seem a predominantly male enterprise.

There are some exceptions. Theodor Zwinger cites an example of female friendship (involving Egyptian virgin women priests) culled from Marullus, in his *Theatrum humanae vitae*.[2] A somewhat laconic example of a female epic couple is found in Christine de Pisan's *Livre de la cité des dames* (comp. 1404-1407). Two Amazon "pucelles," Manalippe and Ypollite, go into combat against Hercules and Theseus. They throw the men off their horses but are vanquished nevertheless. Theseus falls in love with Ypollite. However, there is no discussion of the women's relationship.[3] The romance generally is more open to female friendship, partly because one romance commonplace is the disguising of women warriors as men, which encourages a sort of female-female contact that begins in a vaguely erotic way and develops into female friendship. This happens in the *Amadis de Gaule* when in the 9th book Alastraxerée disguises herself as a male knight and becomes the champion of Silvie (chap. 27).[4] When Silvie discovers her real identity, she is "toute troublée & honteuse" (f. 127r), but in a later chapter, their relationship is described as one of "bonne amytié & familiarité" (chap. 29, f. 133r). A similar scenario is evoked in the 20th book, between Orontie, disguised as a male knight, and various women

---

[1] On male friendship (in Alberti's *Della famiglia*), see Constance Jordan, *Renaissance Feminism: Literary Texts and Political Models* (Ithaca: Cornell Univ. Press, 1990), pp. 49-50.

[2] Basel: Frobenius, 1565, Liber 17, p. 1108.

[3] Ed. Maureen Cheney Curnow (Thesis, Vanderbilt Univ., 1975), 1.18.

[4] I have consulted *Le neufiesme livre d'Amadis de Gaule*, trans. Claude Colet (Paris: Jean Longis, 1557).

characters.[5]  Shakespeare's *A Midsummer Night's Dream* contains two
female characters who use the rhetoric of friendship, Helena and Hermia
(especially 3.2.195-219), and his *As You Like It* also features a female
pair of friends, Rosalind and Celia.  But exemplary female friendship in
French and Italian literature before the seventeenth century and in moral
philosophy is highly infrequent.

Apart from conjugal love, which was intermittently conceived as
a relationship of friendship, there are also few examples of the rhetoric
of *amicitia* being deployed in the service of male-female relationships.
Among the rare examples that come to mind in the French Renaissance
are Helisenne de Crenne's *Epistres familieres*, in one of which she
addresses the friend of her lover Guenelic, Quezinstra, as *trescher amy*,
and cites Cicero's definition of friendship, and the commonplace that one
speak to a friend as to oneself.[6]  Marie de Gournay, the "fille
d'alliance" of Montaigne, speaks of her relationship to her "father" in
terms that closely recall Montaigne's own and classical rhetoric on
friendship.[7]

In novellas 10 and 21 of the *Heptaméron* (published in varying
versions after her death in 1549), Marguerite de Navarre has, however,
contributed female figures of friendship to the line of male exemplars,
although her heroines' male choices are not up to the demands of the
relationship.  Both novellas involve noble women; in the case of
Rolandine (novella 21) the two partners contract a clandestine marriage

---

[5] *Le vingtiesme livre d'Amadis de Gaule*, trans. Jean Boyron (Lyons:
Antoine Tardif, 1582), chaps. 49, 50, 67.  See on this aspect of the *Amadis*
Winfried Schleiner, "Le feu caché: Homosocial Bonds Between Women in a
Renaissance Romance," *Renaissance Quarterly* 45 (1992): 293-311.

[6] "Mais amytié est une grande convenance & consentement de toutes choses
divines & humaines, avecq' benevolence & charité. ( . . . ) Lon peult seurement
declarer le tout comme a soymesme," etc. (*Epistres familieres*, 12, 1st ed. 1539,
repr. Geneva, Slatkine, 1977, no pagination).

[7] See Marie de Gournay, "Préface à l'édition des *Essais* de Montaigne
(1595)," ed. François Rigolot, *Montaigne Studies* 1 (1989), especially pp. 47,
51-52.  On these textual echoes, see Rigolot, "L'amitié intertextuelle: Gournay,
La Boétie et Montaigne," in *L'esprit et la lettre: Mélanges offerts à Jules Brody*,
ed. Louis van Delft (Tübingen: Gunter Narr, 1991), pp. 57-68.

based on virtue and mutual understanding; in the tenth novella the two friends are each married to someone else.   Here the friendship is obviously not conceived as a prelude to marriage, and it is described in its evolution and difficulties, as a narrative of the interweaving of moral philosophical ideals and psychological, sexual, and social pressures.

## 1. The Meanings of "Ami"

When considering female-male relationships of affection in the Romance literatures and cultures, we confront a linguistic problem, the overlapping of terms of desire and terms of affection.   The general tenuousness (if not insufficiency) of the language of heterosexual relations is nowhere more evident.   The proximity of *amor* and *amicitia* was already pointed out by Cicero: "Amor enim (ex quo amicitia est nominata) princeps est ad benevolentiam coniungendam" (For it is love (*amor*), from which the word "friendship" (*amicitia*) is derived, that leads to the establishing of goodwill) (*De amicitia*, p. 487 [8.26]).[8] Once we enter the domain of the French vernacular, "ami," "amant," "amour," "amitié" often seem interchangeable, signifying relationships of affection whose degree is determined by the context of their use.   In the tenth and longest novella of Marguerite de Navarre's *Heptaméron*, a tale of tragic misunderstanding and brutal (male) passion, the language of love is highly varied.   Justifying the male protagonist's strategy of deception and attempts at rape, Saffredent, one of the male *devisants*, speaks about the transformation of courtly "servants" into "masters":

> Quant nous sommes à part, où amour seul est juge de noz contenances, nous sçavons très bien qu'elles sont femmes et nous hommes; et à l'heure, le nom de *maistresse* est converti en *amye*, et le nom de *serviteur* en *amy*.   C'est là où le

---

[8] I have used Cicero, *Opera philosophica*, vol. 4 of *Opera omnia* (Venice: Luca Antonius Iunta, 1536).   The *De amicitia* is on pp. 482-499.   Translations are my own.

> commung proverbe dist: "De bien servir et loyal estre, / De
> serviteur l'on devient maistre." (p. 84)[9]

The "servant," performing his courtly romance service to his lady
master, becomes, once a more intimate situation is achieved, her
"friend," just as she becomes his "friend." Here "amy" obviously means
"sexual lover," and the equality implied by the terms "amye"-"amy" is
false, as in fact the sexual situation reestablishes the man as master of
the woman. The use of "amy" by Saffredent is clearly the sexual
counterpoint to "serviteur," and is determined by that conventional
context.

In the introductory discussion of the tenth novella, however, we
encounter a different use of "amy" by the represented narrator of the
story of Floride and Amadour, Parlamente. She will tell this story as an
example of female virtue and conquest of love; although she herself did
not witness its events, it is a true story nonetheless, as it was told to her
by "ung de mes plus grands et entiers amys, à la louange de l'homme
qu'il avoit le plus aymé" (p. 54).[10] Not only does Parlamente turn
around the point of the story, which goes from a praise of the man to a
praise of the woman, but she also emphasizes that the original teller of
the story was one of her best *friends*. The use of "amy" here is
obviously not sexual, as Parlamente would not be announcing to the
assembly of nobles that she has many lovers.[11] In the context of

---

[9] "When we are alone together, when only love is judge of our behavior,
we know very well that they are women and we are men; and at that moment
the name of 'mistress' is converted to 'friend,' and the name of 'servant' to
'friend'. That is why the well-known proverb says, 'Through serving well and
being loyal, from servant one becomes master'." All quotations from
Marguerite de Navarre, *L'Heptaméron*, ed. Michel François (Paris: Garnier,
1967).

[10] "One of my greatest and most complete friends, praising the man he had
loved the most."

[11] I do not think that these differing meanings given to "amy" produce
difference, and that women's language is somehow incomprehensible to men,
and vice-versa. The male *devisants* understand very well what Parlamente
means, and the women understand very well what Saffredent means. It is not

"grand et entier" the word means "friend" in a decidedly non-sexual way. Presenting a similar story of female-male friendship, the story of Rolandine (novella 21), Parlamente also emphasizes that women can seek friends who are not lovers: "il y a des dames qui en leurs amityez n'ont cherché nulle fin que l'honnesteté" (p. 158).[12]

## 2. Floride's "Honest" Friendship

In the tenth novella itself the language of "amitié" recurs frequently, as the central relationship is a complex interweaving of desire, goodwill, and familiarity. Amadour loves Floride, but, owing to his inferior status (he is not the first-born son), he cannot hope to marry her. Becoming her friend and confidant, he marries another woman and friend of Floride, Avanturade, in order to be close to his love. From the very beginning Amadour hides his true feelings of desire from Floride,[13] and even takes a lover, Poline. In the first long conversation between Amadour and Floride, the former recalls to her his long "service" to her, claims to want only "virtuous" pleasure from her

---

that they *misunderstand* each other, it is that what is understood is not agreeable to the other. In spite of critics' tendencies to view many of the interpersonal and gender conflicts in the collection as somehow linguistic, it is more a matter of actual or intended behavior. See, most recently, Patricia F. Cholakian (*Rape and Writing in the* Heptaméron *of Marguerite de Navarre*, Carbondale, Southern Illinois Univ. Press, 1991) who, while correctly pointing out the ambiguity inherent in terms such as "honest friendship," goes on to generalize about the "inability [of male and female protagonists] to agree on the meanings of words connected to sexuality and gender relations" (p. 23). While this is true, what is vastly more important is the behavior that is reflected by their differing usage of words.

[12] "There are ladies who in their friendships have sought out no goal except honesty [moral goodness]."

[13] The narrator speaks about Amadour's almost military strategy in assuring himself the familiarity of Floride, and of his "feu caché en son coeur" which he finds difficult to continue to conceal while Floride speaks to him privately, "comme celle qui n'y pensoit en nul mal" (p. 61).

("ne bien ne plaisir autre que vertueux," p. 63), and asks her to accept him as "hers" ("pour du tout vostre," ibid.). Amadour does not, strictly speaking, challenge Floride's real love for another man, the son of the Infant Fortuné, for the latter has taken possession of her heart ("celluy qui en a pris la possession," p. 62).[14]

So what, then, does he want? In spite of his use of a "courtly" word such as *service*, Amadour's speech and his behavior are not in line with what one may expect of a courtly lover, for he has already broken a cardinal rule of "courtly love," the chastity a lover must maintain in respect to all women other than the one he loves, and he does not offer to sacrifice this physical pleasure.[15] In the chivalric romance, also, the perfect lover usually abstains from pleasure with women other than his lady. In the *Amadis de Gaule*, Amadis is faithful to Oriane, although the romance contains examples of knights who freely indulge in sexual pleasure, and Amadis and Oriane make love well before they are married. Amadis's chastity in respect to other women is part of what makes him more perfect than the other lovers. Similarly, in Helisenne de Crenne's *Les angoisses douloureuses qui procedent d'amours* (1538), the lover Guenelic affirms, concerning the sin of *luxure* (lasciviousness): "pour crainte d'irriter sa treschere Dame, de toutes autres se preservera."[16] Amadour's lack of chastity poses less of a problem in the case of Neoplatonic love, if his physical pleasure does not detract

---

[14] Amadour uses "propos d'amityé" here in order to refer to Floride's lover's amorous conversations with her.

[15] See Andreas Capellanus, *De amore libri tres*, Book 1, Chap. 4: "Est et aliud quiddam in amore non brevi sermone laudandum, quia amor reddit hominem castitatis quasi virtute decoratum, quia vix posset de alterius etiam formosae cogitare amplexu, qui unius radio fulget amoris. Est enim suae menti, dum de amore suo plenarie cogitat, mulieris cuiuslibet horridus et incultus aspectus" (Ed. E. Trojel, München, W. Fink, 1972, p. 10). See also, among the twelve rules of love for noble lovers, the second: "Castitatem servare debes amanti" (p. 106).

[16] "For fear of angering his dear Lady, he will preserve himself [from pleasure] with all other [women]." In her *Oeuvres* (1560) revised by Claude Colet (3.2). The sentence quoted differs insignificantly from the 1538 text, edited by Harry R. Secor, Jr. (Ph. D. Thesis, Yale University, 1957, p. 334).

from his special love of Floride, or if he succeeds in convincing her of his profound attachment to her in spite of contrary appearances.[17] But this assumes that the love of Floride for him is like the love she feels for the son of the Infant fortuné, which it is not, as Floride emphasizes. Amadour affirms that Floride's virtue is more important than any pleasure he might have, and that all honorable and virtuous deeds he performs are out of love for her ("toutes les choses honnestes et vertueuses que je feray seront faictes seullement pour l'amour de vous," p. 63). He also asks her to have full faith in his "seurté" (ibid.), meaning undoubtedly both his discretion and his constancy and reliability. Although the reader knows that Amadour is acting out of frustrated passion, his dissimulating words are what Floride wants to hear. They are also very close to an offer of true friendship, in the sense of Cicero's *vera amicitia*. The emphasis on virtue as the principle of friendship, with its attendant stability and fidelity, is a Ciceronian commonplace: "virtus virtus inquam . . . & conciliat amicitias, & conservat. In ea est enim convenientia rerum, in ea stabilitas, in ea constantia" (*De amicitia*, p. 499 [27.100]).[18]

---

[17] On the refusal of the "perfect (woman) friend" to be jealous, in Neoplatonic love, see Antoine Héroet, *La parfaicte amye* (1542), Book 1, vv. 395-452, in his *Oeuvres poétiques*, ed. Ferdinand Gohin (Paris: Droz, 1943), pp. 22-25. However, in an earlier poem Héroet's female narrator is less self-abdicating; if the *amye* gets the impression that her *amy* loves another woman as she loves him, it is time to end their relationship: "Mais s'il en ayme une sans fiction / Et qu'il l'aymast comme je veulx aymer, / Le seul penser m'en semble tant amer, / Qu'il me vault myeulx conclure mon affaire, / Qu'en denyant mon malheur me desplaire" ("Complaincte d'une dame surprinse nouvellement d'amour," p. 106, 292-296). Floride never endeavors to learn whether or not Amadour loves anyone else. Although she feels unaccustomed tinges of jealousy when Amadour has an affair with Poline, she requests no explanation of his behavior.

[18] "Virtue, I say, both establishes and maintains friendships. For in virtue there is harmony of things, in her is stability, in her constancy." Cicero speaks elsewhere of the "stabilitas amicitiae" (e.g., 22.82). See also the speech of Raison in the *Roman de la Rose*, who defines "Amytié" along Ciceronian lines. In the version attributed to Clément Marot, we read: "L'homme ne peult estre amyable / S'il n'est si ferme et si estable / Que pour fortune ne se meuve" (in Jean de Meung, *Le Roman de la Rose*, ed. Silvio F. Baridon, vol. 2, Milano,

Floride's response to Amadour's speech shows a beginning awareness of his duplicity, in that she wonders if there is some "malice cachée" underneath his "honnestes propos," his honorable words (p. 64). But Floride chooses to take his words literally, as an offer of "honneste amityé" (ibid.). She is also willing to listen to him, responding to his question, "lequel vault mieulx parler ou mourir?" by taking the alternative in a literal and "honest" way: "Je conseilleray tousjours à mes amys de parler, et non de morir" (p. 62).[19] The simplicity of her response demonstrates the equality of honest friendship, and her refusal of a Neoplatonic, or courtly, hierarchy of lover and beloved. In her reply to Amadour's long speech she repeats a theme that Amadour himself had addressed, the faith she could have in him ("je me suis plus fyée en vous, que en tous les hommes du monde," ibid.). Amadour, in his reply, underlines the necessity of a certain and stable foundation ("seur et ferme fondement") of their relationship. When Floride uses the term *honneste amityé*, she seems then to be referring to a friendship based on virtue, as opposed to friendships based on pleasure (excluded by Amadour himself) or on utility, although Amadour's service to her can indeed be useful.[20]

---

Istituto Editoriale Cisalpino, 1957, p. 27, ll. 4821-4823). I am grateful to Jan Miernowski for having reminded me of the discussion of friendship in Jean de Meung. See most recently Douglas Kelly, "Amour comme amitié: De Jean de Meung à Christine de Pisan," forthcoming in *Anteros*, eds. Jan Miernowski, Ullrich Langer (Orléans: Editions Paradigme, 1994).

[19] "I will always advise my friends to speak and not to die."

[20] The fact that Floride, too, can come to feel desire for Amadour ("[elle] commencea en son cueur à sentir quelque chose plus qu'elle n'avoit accoustumé," p. 65) does not in any way invalidate the premise of their relationship: she is demonstrating the rational-moral character of their friendship precisely by never giving in to that desire. To see Floride as primarily a victim of a "masculine definition of desire" is to privilege the sexual component of the relationship in a way that anachronistically discounts the force of ethical discourse in the world of the *Heptaméron*, and that neglects the "empowering" value of a moral tradition which, though defined by men, in fact is used successfully by women as well. This anachronistic view is held most recently by Lawrence D. Kritzman in *The Rhetoric of Sexuality and the Literature of the French Renaissance* (Cambridge: Cambridge Univ. Press, 1991), pp. 45-56, and

In speaking of *honneste amityé*, she is also echoing - perhaps unwittingly - the way in which Aristotle's "perfect" friendship tended to be formulated in Latin and vernacular languages,[21] and the way in which Ciceronian friendship was glossed in the Renaissance.[22] The

---

especially p. 51. On the presence of a discourse of *amicitia* in the *Heptaméron*, see also the concluding remarks in Axel Schönberger, *Die Darstellung von Lust und Liebe im 'Heptaméron' der Königin Margarete von Navarra* (Frankfurt am Main: Domus Editoria Europaea, 1993), pp. 432-435.

[21] Already in St Thomas Aquinas's commentary (on Aristotle, 1155b 16-19) we find the term *honestum*: there are "tres species amicitiae, aequales numero amabilibus. Quarum una est amicitia propter honestum, quod est bonum simpliciter. Alia propter delectabile. Et tertia, propter utile" (*In X. Libros Ethicorum ad Nicomachum*, Liber 8, Lectio 3, in *Opera omnia*, 1852-1873, repr. New York, Musurgia, 1949, vol. 21, p. 267). "Tres sunt amicitiae species abinvicem distinctae. Hanc probat, quia tria sunt amabilia inter se distincta: scilicet honestum, utile & delectabile," says John Major in his commentary on the *Nicomachean Ethics* (*Ethica Aristotelis Peripateticorum principis*, Paris, Jehan Petit, 1530, f. 126v). Nicole Oresme translates the relevant lines from Aristotle: "Ces choses amables dessus dites qui sont honestes, delitables et utiles, different ensemble en espece. Et les amacions de elles different aussi. Et donques les amistiés qui sont selon elles different en espece" (*Le livre de ethiques d'Aristote*, ed. Albert Douglas Menut, New York, G. E. Stechert, 1940, p. 417). Oresme's translation was completed in 1370 and published by Antoine Vérard in Paris in 1488. In Boccaccio's *Filocolo*, the three types of love are spoken of: the most perfect one is the "amore onesto" which binds God and his creatures; the others are the "amore per diletto" and the "amore per utilità" (in Boccaccio, *Tutte le opere*, vol. 1, ed. Vittore Branca, Verona, Mondadori, 4.44, p. 424). In the early 15th century, Leon-Battista Alberti speaks of the three "ties" ("vincoli") of friendship: "o iocundi e voluttuosi, o utili e con emolumento, o lodati, onesti e pieni di virtù" (*Della famiglia*, Book 4, p. 306, in his *Opere volgari*, vol. 1, ed. Cecil Grayson, Bari, Laterza, 1960).

[22] On the various meanings of "honneste" in the *Heptaméron*, see Nicole Cazauran, "'Honneste,' 'honnesteté' et 'honnestement' dans le langage de Marguerite de Navarre," in *La Catégorie de l'Honneste dans la culture du XVIe siècle*, Actes du colloque international de Sommières, 2 (Saint Etienne: Institut d'études de la Renaissance et de l'âge classique, 1985), pp. 149-164, and 161-162 on the tenth novella. Cazauran does not investigate the linkages to

Aristotelian distinction between the loves based on pleasure, usefulness, and virtue is present in the twenty-first novella of the *Heptaméron*, in a neat speech by the female protagonist Rolandine to her enemy, a malicious queen. The speech stands as a model for the description of a voluntary, rational, and virtuous relationship aristocratic women were mostly prevented from considering. The protagonist, having been prevented from marrying by the queen, has decided to take matters in her own hands (a dangerous thing to do). She has a chaste relationship with a male friend, called "le Bâtard," who is correspondingly without hope for advancement on his own. They perform a clandestine marriage for themselves (not a good idea in aristocratic culture); they are spied upon and persecuted by the queen when they arouse suspicion. In a dramatic confrontation, Rolandine justifies her conduct to the furious queen:

> Et, par le conseil de la raison que Dieu m'a donnée, me voyant vielle et hors d'espoir de trouver party selon ma maison, me suis deliberée d'en espouser ung à ma volunté, non poinct pour satisfaire à la concupiscence des oeilz, car vous sçavez qu'il n'est pas beau, ny à celle de chair, car il n'y a poinct eu de consommation charnelle, ny à l'orgueil, ny à l'ambition de ceste vie, car il est pauvre et peu advancé; mais j'ay regardé purement et simplement à la vertu [the Claude Gruget edition adds "honnesteté et bonne grace"] qui est en luy, dont tout le monde est contrainct de luy donner louange; à la grande amour aussy qu'il m' a portée, qui me faict esperer de trouver avecq luy repoz et bon traictement" (pp. 168-169).[23]

---

[23] "And, by the counsel of reason which God has given to me, seeing that I am old and without hope of finding a husband according to my standing, I have decided to marry one according to my own will, not in order to satisfy the concupiscence of the eyes, for you know that he is not handsome, nor of the flesh, for there has been no carnal consummation, nor pride or ambition, for he is poor and little-advanced, but I considered purely and simply the virtue that is in him, for which everyone is obliged to praise him, also the great love he has brought to me, which makes me hope to receive with him calm and good treatment."

Rolandine's justification of her conduct never implies anything other than a conscious choice ("me suis deliberée," "à ma volunté"). She is not impelled by a love against which she has no defense. She distinguishes various "reasons" for her choice - the teleological language is striking: "pour satisfaire à. . ." in answer to the implied question "pourquoi l'avez-vous choisi?" She distinguishes reasons of pleasure (beauty and sexual pleasure), reasons of usefulness (material wealth or social advancement) and eliminates those. Instead, she "purely and simply" looks at the Bâtard's virtue, his honesty (which is more or less "moral goodness" rather than sincerity in the sixteenth century), and at the fact that he seemed to love her (making it possible to envisage a relationship of mutual love). The way Rolandine sets up the justification for her choice of the Bâtard tightly reproduces the rhetoric of classical friendship, and is, above all, persuasive: the queen, seeing her constancy and the truth of her speech, cannot respond "par raison" (by reason), and instead becomes angry and cries, admitting her moral inferiority. The *Heptaméron* itself provides evidence both of the functioning of the rhetoric of *amicitia* and of a female character adopting it persuasively, although, as in the case of Floride and Amadour, the male character, though not as driven by physical desire as Amadour, is not equal to the demands of an "honneste amytié": the Bâtard ends up pursuing other women when it is clear that he cannot have his marriage to Rolandine recognized.[24]

But the discourse of friendship is present as well in the cultural milieu around the sister of François Ier. Marguerite de Navarre herself sponsored the translation of Plato's principal dialogue on friendship, the *Lysis*, by Bonaventure des Périers, and at least one French translation of

---

[24] Another instance of the use of friendship commonplaces is the 47th novella, where the perfect union of two (male) friends turns out to be less than perfect, because of the intervention of jealousy and desire. At the beginning, however, "[i]lz vesquirent long temps, continuans ceste parfaicte amityé, sans que jamays il y eut entre eulx deux une volunté ou parolle où l'on peut veoir difference de personnes, tant ilz vivoient non seulement comme deux freres, mais comme ung homme tout seul" (pp. 311-312).

Cicero's *De amicitia* was available in 1537.[25]  In her circle of poet friends there appears to have been discussion of Ciceronian friendship: one example is the religious poet Nicolas Denisot, who edited and translated the verses of three English princesses composed at the death of Marguerite de Navarre in 1549.[26]  We find in what is most likely Denisot's pseudonymous sentimental novel, *L'amant resuscité de la mort d'amour*, in the second book, a long monologue by the countess Marguerite (Seymour) on "la vraye & parfaicte amour" which turns out to be explicitly Ciceronian friendship as the basis for marriage.[27]  The countess insists on virtue as the "mother" of the perfect relationship: "[Vertu] certes est comme la propre mere de l'amitié de laquelle je parle.  C'est elle qui la produit & engendre.  Et n'est possible que sans vertu, se puissent trouver aucune amitié bonne & honneste."[28]  Above

---

[25] Des Périers' translation was published in his collected works in Lyons in 1544 (reprinted in his *Oeuvres françoises*, vol. 1, ed. Louis Lacour, Paris: P. Jannet, 1866, pp. 1-54).  Jean Collin's translation of Cicero was published by Vincent Sertenas in Paris in 1537, and was reprinted several times along with Cicero's other moral writings.

[26] See l'abbé Clément Jugé, *Nicolas Denisot du Mans (1515-1559): Essai sur sa vie et ses oeuvres* (Le Mans: A. Bienaimé-Leguicheux, 1907), pp. 59-70.

[27] See Margaret A. Harris, *A Study of Théodose Valentinian's 'Amant resuscité de la mort d'amour': A Religious Novel of Sentiment and Its Possible Connexions with Nicolas Denisot du Mans* (Geneva: Droz, 1966), pp. 41-55. A (now lost) first version of the novel was published in 1538; it apparently did not contain the speech on friendship.  The complete version was first published in 1555.  I find her arguments for Denisot's authorship entirely convincing.

[28] "Virtue is assuredly like the own mother of the friendship I am speaking about.  It is she who engenders and produces friendship.  And it is not possible to find any good and honest friendship without virtue," Theodose Valentinian Françoys, *L'amant resuscité de la mort d'amour*, ed. Margaret A. Harris (1558; repr. The Hague, et al., Mouton, et al., 1971), p. 50.  See also p. 93: "De l'amour honneste, & bien reglée, demeure à chacun son asseurée, stable, & certaine possession.  En ceste amour n'y a faute de chose quelconque digne d'estre souhaitée & desirée.  L'honnesteté y est, gloire & honneur, repos & tranquilité d'esprit, une joye, une lyesse perpetuelle, en maniere qu'avec tant de biens, il est impossible que la vie ne soit heureuse."  Cicero's *De amicitia*

all, this formerly "male" friendship is now conceived as the perfect conjugal relationship, that is, between a woman and a man.[29] The countess sums up her argument:

---

is indicated in the margin here as frequently elsewhere during the long discourse on friendship.

[29] One should note that there is a strong tradition of advocating friendship as the basis for the conjugal relationship, deriving from the scholastics but not limited to them. Aquinas, in the *Summa contra gentiles* (3.123.6), sees the conjugal relationship as the most perfect friendship, combining usefulness (the domestic economy) and physical pleasure with love. See also his commentary on the *Nicomachean Ethics*: "hujusmodi amicitia [conjugalis] potest esse et propter virtutem, et propter utile et propter delectabile" (*In X. Libros Ethicorum ad Nicomachum*, Liber 8, Lectio 12, in his *Opera omnia*, ed. 1852-1873, repr. New York, Musurgia, 1949, vol. 21, p. 290). See Erik Kooper, "Loving the Unequal Equal: Medieval Theologians and Marital Affection," in *The Olde Daunce: Love, Friendship, Sex, and Marriage in the Medieval World*, eds. Robert R. Edwards, Stephen Spector (Albany, NY: State University of New York Press, 1991), pp. 44-56. See also Michael Pakaluk, ed., *Other Selves: Philosophers on Friendship* (Indianapolis: Hackett Publishing Co., 1991), xiii, on the relative absence of concern with domestic relationships of classical philosophers dealing with friendship. In spite of his sublime depiction of his friendship with La Boétie, and his exclusion of sexual relationships from perfect friendship in *Essais* 1.28, Montaigne warmly praises a conjugal relationship that takes on the forms of friendship: "Ung bon mariage, s'il en est, refuse la compaignie et conditions de l'amour. Il tache à representer celles de l'amitié. C'est une douce societé de vie, pleine de constance, de fiance et d'un nombre infiny d'utiles et solides offices et obligations mutuelles" (3.5, p. 851). Montaigne does hedge his bets ("s'il en est"). The language here is very much in the Latin moral tradition, and is used as well by Montaigne's contemporary Pierre de la Primaudaye: "Or le fondement de tous les devoirs par nous icy mentionnez du mary envers la femme & tous autres que la communication ordinaire peult requerir, est ceste vraye, & non feinte amytié, qui doit estre le lien indissoluble de tout bon mariage" (*L'Academie francoise*, Paris, Guillaume Chaudiere, 1581, 1.12.47, f. 153v). See also Estienne Pasquier, who in *Le Monophile* advocates marriage based on friendship as the foundation for political harmony (in *Oeuvres complètes* [1723], vol. 2, repr. Geneva, Slatkine, 1971, 711C-D).

> Quelle dirons nous devoir estre l'amitié honneste & saincte de
> mary à femme & de femme à mary? comme ceux, qui à jamais
> ont à estre devant les yeux, & au costez l'un de l'autre? Ce
> n'est certes autre chose de ceste amour, de laquelle il y a ja
> long temps que je parle, qu'un merveilleux acord &
> consentement entre l'homme & la femme de toutes choses
> divines & humaines, avec grande bienveuillance. (p. 88)[30]

Marguerite Seymour has transposed onto heterosexual love the celebrated maxim of Cicero, *omnium divinarum humanarumque rerum cum benevolentia et caritate consensio* (*De amicitia* 6.20), and in her speech adds Christian faith to the qualifications perfect lovers must have.

The language connected to "honneste amityé" is taken up later in Marguerite de Navarre's novella, first in contrast to "serviteur": "elle estoit presque toute gaingnée de le recepvoir, non à serviteur, mais à seur et parfaict amy" (p. 71).[31] The contrast to the courtly lover again underlines the sense of friendship that dominates at least Floride's conscious perception of their relationship. When Amadour's blind passion, his "folle amour," surfaces, and he first attempts to seduce her, Floride reprimands him for not following his own virtuous counsel, and says that she had intended to found their friendship on the virtue she had known in him ("fondant ceste amityé sur la vertu que j'ay tant congneue en vous," p. 74). She continues by elaborating on the metaphor of the stable foundation:

> Sur ceste pierre d'honnesteté, j'estois venue icy, deliberée de
> y prendre ung très seur fondement; mais, Amadour, en un
> moment, vous m'avez monstré que en lieu d'une pierre necte

---

[30] "What should be the honest and holy friendship of husband to wife and wife to husband, as those who forever will be in front of each other's eyes, and beside each other? This love is none other than that of which I have been talking for a long time, the wondrous agreement and consensus between husband and wife on all matters divine and human, with great goodwill."

[31] "She was almost completely persuaded to receive him not as servant but as a reliable and perfect friend."

et pure, le fondement de cest ediffice seroit sur sablon legier ou
sur la fange infame. (p. 74)[32]

Whereas the idea expressed recalls Cicero's *stabilitas* and *constantia*, the
Biblical allusion is unmistakable.[33] The wise man who hears God's
words and acts accordingly builds his house on rock, whereas the foolish
man hears God's words without acting accordingly, and builds his house
on sand. The words "fondement" and "ediffice" recall the Biblical
*fundata* and *aedificavit* of the verses in Matthew:

> Omnis igitur qui audit ex me sermones hos, & facit eos,
> assimilabo illum viro prudenti, qui aedificavit domum suam
> super petram.  Et descendit imber, & venerunt flumina, &
> flaverunt venti, & irruerunt in domum illam, & non est
> prostrata: fundata erat super petram.  Et omnis qui audit a me
> sermones hos, & non facit eos, assimilabitur viro fatuo, qui
> aedificavit domum suam super arenam.[34]

---

[32] "I had come here, intending to find a very stable foundation on this rock
of honorableness; but, Amadour, in one moment you have shown to me that
instead of on a clean and pure rock, the foundation of this edifice would be on
light sand or on impure mud."

[33] For a similar metaphor, see also *L'amant resuscité de la mort d'amour*,
p. 51: "Le fondement [virtue in two similar persons] faict & constitué, faisons
maintenant provision de pierres, & autres matieres, lesquelles nous voulons
asseoir & mettre sur iceluy, pour le bastiment de nostre amour."

[34] "Therefore, everyone who listens to these words of mine and acts on
them will be like a sensible man who built his house on rock.  Rain came down,
floods rose, gales blew and hurled themselves against that house, and it did not
fall: it was founded on rock.  But everyone who listens to these words of mine
and does not act on them will be like a stupid man who built his house on sand
(Jerusalem Bible)," Mt 7:24-26. The Latin version is from Erasmus, *Novum
testamentum juxta graecorum lectionem* in *Opera omnia*, vol. 6 (Loudun: P.
Vander Aa, 1705), 42C. The language of foundation and edifice is frequent in
the Pauline epistles (e.g., "Dei aedificatio estis," 1 Cor 3:9), and is used
extensively by Guillaume Briçonnet in his correspondance with Marguerite de
Navarre, especially in his letter of July 6, 1524, where he reflects on the

It is important, however, to measure the extent to which Marguerite de Navarre has modified the context of the Biblical passage, and the extent to which Floride's description of her relationship goes beyond the evangelical interpretation of the verses in Matthew. Floride does exactly what Erasmus, for example, says one should *not* do. In his commentary and paraphrase of Matthew, Erasmus interprets the foundation on rock as a "sincerus affectus" directed to the glory of God, to the exclusion of the "worthless things of this world."[35] He contrasts concern for the external (fasts, alms, prayer, poor clothing, miracles) and desire for the praise of men, with an *affectus* that is based on the Gospels, and which expects reward from God alone (*Paraphrases*, 47B). In this sense *any* relationship with men that seeks a stable foundation in their hearts is inappropriate, for the "edifice" of affection is firm only in God. Seen through the lenses of evangelical commentary, Floride, unbeknownst to herself, attempted to make Amadour into a god-like object of friendship.

The mixture of Christian and moral philosophical language is especially significant in Floride's analogy because it recalls a distinction encountered in Marguerite de Navarre's religious poetry, and in evangelical language of her contemporaries, between fickle and stable

---

creation of woman, on carnal marriage and marriage with Christ. In the following passage these themes mingle with the founding of the church (Mt 16:18) and an allusion to the passage (Mt 7:24-26) echoed in Marguerite de Navarre: "Il dict avoir ediffié la coste de Adam en femme, qui est la roche immobile, sur laquelle est l'edifice de l'Eglise, construict et basty. . . . La solidité de l'edifice est la coste convertye en femme. C'est la divinité obumbrant et solidant l'Eglise, son espouze, que ventz, pluyes, torrens, tribulations, ne peuvent delocher ne faire dementir: les pierres dudict edifice sont vifves, leur subministrant la roche vive et les vivifiant. C'est le fondement fidelle, sur lequel chascun croist en temple de Dieu et tabernacle du Sainct Esprit. . ." (Guillaume Briçonnet, Marguerite d'Angoulême, *Correspondance (1521-1524)*, vol. 2, eds. Christine Martineau, Michel Veissière, Geneva, Droz, 1979, pp. 199-200).

[35] "Qui meum hauserit Spiritum, hoc est, sincerum affectum, non alio spectantem quam ad Dei gloriam, is est arbor bonae radicis. Ita qui non inititur inanibus hujus mundi rebus, sed veris animi bonis, atque in his constanter perseverat, is sapienter aedificat aedificium nunquam ruiturum" (*Paraphrases in Novum Testamentum* in *Opera omnia*, vol. 7, 46E-F).

love, *Eros* (Cupido) and *Anteros* (Amor virtutis).[36]   In one of her *Chansons spirituelles*, Marguerite de Navarre asks why "afection folle," fickle, blind love plays its role so well, whereas stable affection finds no place in hearts:

> L'amitié qui est estable,
> Ferme, seure et véritable,
> Sans dommaige ne danger
> Mais utile et profitable,
> Nul cueur ne la veult loger.
> La responce est véritable:
> Chacun ayme son semblable
> Et à luy se veult ranger;
> Dieu ferme au cueur immuable,
> Dieu vollant à cueur léger.[37]

The success of the "Dieu vollant" is based on the notion that resemblance is the basis for attraction, and, since the world is corrupt and fickle, the world is attracted only to the fickle God of desire, and vice-versa. The most obvious Biblical subtext here is Paul's epistle to Titus: "Omnia quidem munda mundis. iis autem qui inquinati sunt / &

---

[36] This distinction is found in Alciati's emblems, and the evangelical commonplace of "ferme amour" in much of Clément Marot's oeuvre and in the writings of evangelical poets at the time. *Anteros* can also mean "mutual love" in the 16th century. See on this question the introduction by Gérard Defaux to his edition of Marot's *Oeuvres poétiques*, vol. 1 (Paris: Bordas, 1990), "Classiques Garnier," pp. xxxvi-l, and his "Les deux amours de Clément Marot," *Rivista di letterature moderne e comparate* 46 (1993): 1-30.

[37] "Friendship that is stable, firm, trustworthy and true, without damage nor danger, but useful and profitable: no heart wants to accept it. The response is true: everyone loves someone like himself and wants to join him; firm God with an unchanging heart, fickle God with a fickle heart," *Chansons spirituelles*, ed. Georges Dottin (Geneva: Droz, 1971), p. 110, ll. 11-20 [Chanson 39].

infideles: nichil mundum est/ sed inquinantur eorum    & mens & conscientia" (Tit 1:15).[38]

The resemblance of friends is, however, also a subject of classical moral philosophy,[39] and the formulation "Chacun ayme son semblable" (Like loves like) recalls the (unresolved) disputes in Plato's *Lysis*, and specifically a passage in the translation by Bonaventure Des Périers. He inserted several verses alluding to Robin and Marion, replacing a quotation from Homer (*Odyssey*, 17.218): "Toujours Dieu mène et addresse / Le pareil à son semblable, / Dont après mainte caresse / Naist amitié perdurable," etc.[40] Having cited these lines, Socrates adds that the sages say that "toute chose, necessairement, ayme son semblable," that every thing, necessarily, loves what resembles itself (ibid.). In the verse dedication to Marguerite de Navarre, entitled "Queste d'amytié," Des Périers summarizes some of the themes of the *Lysis*, including the notion of resemblance:

> Les semblables
> Accointables
> L'ont, possible, en leurs quartiers:
> Tels, ce semble,
> Sont ensemble
> Amys loyaulx et entiers. (p. 48)[41]

---

[38] "To all who are pure themselves, everything is pure: but to those who have been corrupted and lack faith, nothing can be pure - the corruption is both in their minds and in their consciences (Jerusalem Bible)." I have quoted Jacques Lefèvre d'Etaples' Latin translation, in *Epistolae Beatissimi Pauli, adiecta intelligentia ex Graeco, cum commentariis Jacobi Fabri Stapulensis* (Paris: H. Estienne, 1512), f. 56r.

[39] See Oresme's translation of the *Nicomachean Ethics*, p. 419 [1156b 6-9]: "Mais l'amistié de ceuls qui sont bons et semblables en vertu, elle est parfaite."

[40] "God always leads like to like, from which after many caresses is born enduring friendship" *Oeuvres françoises*, vol. 1, p. 27.

[41] "Like people who are with each other possible have it [Amytié]; such people are, it seems, together loyal and complete friends."

The friendship of the similar in virtue is revised, then, by Marguerite de Navarre, in an evangelical spirit, in her religious poetry. When Floride speaks of "honneste amityé," in the *Heptaméron*, those connotations obviously resonate in her language. This seems to be especially true when we consider the ending of the story: having been disappointed by human love, Floride chooses to love God more than anything else. Her friendship with Amadour can be seen as a step towards divine love.

It is important to recall, nonetheless, that this Christian version of friendship is neither charity (which is not an exclusive relationship with another, as was Floride and Amadour's), nor Neoplatonic love. There is no gradual ascension through corporeal beauty to spiritual beauty and divine love; Amadour is not improved by his love of Floride - the contrary seems to be true - and Floride needs to be "delivered" from her love for Amadour in order to fully love God.[42] Her love of Amadour is not, I think, a way-station to the love of God. One love has to be replaced by another.

This very human relationship navigates, as we have seen, through the polyvalent language of "amitié," but it also can be characterized through typical *behavior*, and it is that behavior that links Floride's affection toward Amadour with friendship. It is also the discourse on friendship that accounts for the protagonists' failure.

When Amadour introduces himself into the household of Floride's family, he becomes so familiar that he is looked upon as a *woman* and as someone who can give good counsel:

> Après qu'il fut maryé, print telle hardiesse et privaulté en la maison de la contesse d'Arande, que l'on ne se gardoit de luy non plus que d'une femme. Et combien que à l'heure il n'eust que vingt deux ans, il estoit si saige que la contesse d'Arande

---

[42] Floride takes as her husband and friend "Celuy [God] qui l'avoit delivrée d'une amour si vehemente que celle d'Amadour, et d'un ennuy si grand que de la compagnye d'un tel mary" (p. 83). See on this question Philippe de Lajarte, who writes very perceptively, "la conversion de l'amour humain en amour divin y [in the *Heptaméron*] est la conséquence d'un *échec* de l'amour humain" (p. 345), in "L'*Heptaméron* et le ficinisme: Rapports d'un texte et d'une idéologie," *Revue des sciences humaines* (1972): 339-371, who sees the writing of the *Heptaméron* as inherently open and dialogic, and thus not compatible with Neoplatonic ideology.

luy communicquoit tous ses affaires, et commandoit à son fils et à sa fille de l'entretenir et croire ce qu'il leur conseilleroit. (p. 60)[43]

The mother of Floride finds Amadour trustworthy enough to invite him to participate in the affairs of the family, and he takes on the role of counselor, which is precisely what the good friend/courtier is supposed to do.[44] Not only does he fulfill his pedagogic function, but Amadour also comes to be regarded as someone entirely innocuous and *familiar*, that is, someone so closely resembling the members of the family that Floride loves him as though he were her own brother: "elle l'aymoit comme s'il eust été son propre frere" (p. 60). This is reinforced by the countess herself, who orders "qu'il fut traicté comme son propre fils," that he be treated as her own son (p. 61).[45] Amadour is thus so skillful that he sets himself up as someone not different from, alien to Floride, which enables her to develop her sororal or "fraternal" friendship with him.[46]

This sibling-like and feminine status of Amadour is not incompatible with his martial valor outside the family context, which is underlined at several points (e.g., "il alloit chercher la guerre aux lieux

---

[43] "After he was married, he became so audacious and intimate in the house of the countess of Arande that one did not pay more attention to him than to a woman. And even though at that time he was only twenty-two years old, he was so wise that the countess of Arande talked to him about all of her dealings and affairs, and ordered her son and her daughter to listen to him and believe what he counseled them to do."

[44] Frank counsel is essential to being a good friend: "consilium verum dare gaudeamus ["audeamus" in other versions] libere" (Cicero, *De amicitia*, p. 490 [13.44]).

[45] Amadour later tells Floride, "je suys en ceste maison tenu non comme serviteur, mais comme enffant" (p. 63).

[46] See Cicero, *De amicitia* 14.50: "[Addimus] nihil esse quod ad se rem ullam tam illiciat et tam trahat quam ad amicitiam similitudo."

estranges, où il estoit aymé et estimé d'amys et d'ennemys" p. 56).[47]
In Marguerite de Navarre's play called by the modern editor "La
comédie du parfait amant," the *amytié parfaicte* is exemplified by a
couple each of whose members want to attribute to the other the title of
perfect lover. The woman says while praising the man, "ung humble
cueur, magnanime, sans mal, / Pas ne se doybt appeller martial, / Mais
par ses faictz et son lointain renom / Il doybt avoir de Mars mesmes le
nom."[48]    Amadour's friendship with Floride is, if anything,
strengthened by his noble exploits in foreign lands.

     The relationship between Floride and Amadour causes the latter
to continue to shine in battle, but also causes Floride to perform good
and virtuous deeds: "elle se mect à faire toutes choses si bonnes et
vertueuses, qu'elle esperoit par cella actaindre le bruict des plus
parfaictes dames, et d'estre reputée digne d'avoir un tel serviteur que
Amadour" (p. 67).[49]    In doing so she is also imitating her friend's
virtuous actions: "toutes les choses honnestes et vertueuses que je feray
seront faictes seullement pour l'amour de vous" says Amadour (p.
63).[50]    The emulation of friends in virtuous deeds is a pervasive theme
in classical moral philosophy. Cicero's Laelius loved Scipio not because
he needed him but out of admiration for his virtue ("admiratione quadam
virtutis eius," 9.30).    When men are friends in virtue, they associate

---

[47] "He went looking for war in foreign countries, where he was loved and
respected by friends and enemies."

[48] "A humble heart, magnanimous, without evil, should not just be called
martial, but by his deeds and his reputation should carry the name of Mars
himself," *Théâtre profane*, ed. Verdun-L. Saulnier (Geneva: Droz, 1963), p.
338, ll. 153-156.

[49] "She began to do good and virtuous things, through which she hoped to
gain the reputation of the most perfect ladies, and to be considered worthy of
having a 'servant' such as Amadour."

[50] "All honorable and virtuous things that I will do will be done only out of
love for you."

with each other in order to be equal in love and in order to merit rather than demand, and so that between them there may be an honorable competition ("ut . . . sintque pares in amore et aequales propensioresque ad bene merendum quam ad reposcendum, atque haec inter eos sit honesta certatio," 9.32). The *honesta certatio* of Floride and Amadour, sign of a friendship generated from pedagogic and sibling-like love, is, however, between a man and a woman, and is from the very beginning corrupted by Amadour's unavowed desire. When Amadour attempts to seduce her while feigning to be ill, he destroys the "pierre d'honnesteté" on which Floride had hoped to build their love. In doing so Amadour has violated in his own way the first law of friendship, to ask of friends only what is honorable and to do for them only what is honorable ("Haec igitur prima lex amicitiae sanciatur, ut ab amicis honesta petamus, amicorum causa honesta faciamus," Cicero, *De amicitia*, p. 490 [13.44]).[51]

Sexual desire is not, however, the only element in the failure of Floride's classic friendship, although it is perhaps the first cause. Marguerite de Navarre plays up the extent to which deception characterizes especially Amadour's actions.[52] If he had admitted his desire from the very beginning, there would have been no story at all, for he would have been banished by Floride. The narrative rests on the elaboration of Amadour's deception, on his less and less concealed sexual desire, and, to a lesser degree, on the evolution of Floride's emotional attachment to him. He marries Avanturade so that their marriage may be a "couverture et moyen de hanter le lieu où son esprit demoroit incessamment" (p. 60)[53]; he has trouble suppressing the sparks from the hidden fire in his heart ("le feu caché en son cueur" [p. 61]); even Floride suspects some "malice cachée" in her friend (p. 64); he dissimulates, taking on "le plus fainct visage qu'il peut prendre" (p.

---

[51] See also Clément Marot's version of the *Roman de la Rose*, p. 28, ll. 4865-4871, for a paraphrase of Cicero on this point.

[52] See Nicole Cazauran, *"L'Heptaméron" de Marguerite de Navarre* (Paris: Société d'Edition d'Enseignement Supérieur, 1976), III, chap. 2.

[53] "Cover and means of frequenting the place where his mind remained incessantly."

75). Floride, on the other hand, "estoit si privée de luy, qu'elle ne luy dissimuloit chose qu'elle pensast": she deliberately dissimulates nothing to her close friend (p. 60). The discrepancy in their respective honesty toward each other makes a true friendship impossible, for friends do not simulate feelings to each other ("primum, ne quid fictum sit, ne ve simulatum," *De amicitia*, p. 493 [18.65]). A perfect friendship entails, according to Seneca, total confidence in the other: "Sed si aliquem amicum existimas cui non tantundem credis quantum tibi, vehementer erras, & non satis nosti vim verae amicitiae."[54] This entails the total lack of secrets between friends, once you have decided to accept someone as a friend: "toto illum pectore admitte, tam audacter cum illo loquere quam tecum" (ibid.).[55] Seneca's exhortation is echoed in Petrarch's letters: "Nemo igitur exigat ab amico quod a se non exigit: alioquin non sic cum amico loquitur ut secum."[56]

## 2. Female Economy, Male Economy

The difference between Floride and Amadour is also expressed in economic terms that derive in part from the "courtly love" tradition. Amadour often refers to the *recompense* (his *guerredon*, in medieval French) of his *travail* and especially his *service*. First he claims not to

---

[54] "But if you consider someone a friend whom you do not trust as much as you trust yourself, you err greatly, and you do not know the strength of true friendship," *Epistolae ad Lucilium*, 3, in *Lucii Annaei Senecae sanctissimi philosophi lucubrationes omnes. . .* (Basel: Johannes Frobenius, 1515), p. 194 [3.2].


[55] "Let that person into your soul; speak as boldly with him as with yourself."


[56] "Thus no one should ask of the friend what he does not ask of himself: otherwise he does not talk to the friend as to himself," *Epistolae de rebus familiaribus et variae*, vol. 2 (Florence: Le Monnier, 1862), 18.8, p. 488. Petrarch is, however, only speaking about the choice of familiar style in letters to friends.

want a "recompense au deshonneur des dames" (p. 63), but wishes as "la fin et recompense de mon service" that Floride remain loyal and maintain her confidence in him (ibid.). When Amadour becomes more desperate, he decides to seduce her, in order to "se payer en une heure du bien qu'il pensoit avoir merité" (p. 72).[57] To Floride's dismay and shock he only replies "Ung si long service merite-il recompense de telle cruaulté?" (p. 73).[58]   Before Amadour's attempt to rape her, he similarly announces, "le fruict de mon labeur ne me sera poinct osté par vos scrupules" (p. 78).[59] The language of finality and payment comes to its logical end in his acknowledgment that the possibility of his own death will not deter him, and that he will be satisfied even if he possesses only the bones of Floride (p. 79). Death is the final payment anyway, as it were. This economy of exchange and investment underlies Amadour's deceptive strategy: if he will only invest years of service, he will "merit" a prize as great as the possession of Floride, which, in turn, is the only thing valuable enough to pay him for such immense service.

The economic language of investment and return is one-sided, for Floride avoids formulating her relationship with Amadour in those terms. We have seen that Biblical and moral philosophical language dominate her formulations. When it is clear to her that Amadour will pursue his "payment," Floride decides to love him in a way that takes her out of the economy of return once and for all: "ne le pouvant moins aymer qu'elle avoit accoustumé, sçachant qu'amour estoit cause de ceste faulte, se delibera, satisfaisant à l'amour, de l'aymer de tout son cueur, et, obeissant à l'honneur, n'en faire jamays à luy ne à autre semblant" (p. 75).[60]   This necessarily solipsistic love is a matter of *choice*:

---

[57] "To repay himself in one hour what he thought he had merited."

[58] "Does such a long service merit the reward of such cruelty?"

[59] "The fruit of my labor will not be taken away by your scruples."

[60] "Not being able to love him less than she had before, knowing that love was the cause of this fault, she decided, satisfying her love, to love him from all her heart, and, obeying her honor, to never give a sign of it to him or to

Marguerite de Navarre uses the same word to describe Floride's decision as she uses to describe Amadour's decision to love Floride (Amadour "se delibera de l'aymer," p. 56). In some persons love can be combined with *deliberation,* which means that the economy of investment and return may also be a matter of choice, that is, not a fact of the natural order against which there is no defense. Similarly, in the rape scene, Amadour, having announced logically that he was willing to die for such a great prize, "n'estoit pas si prest à morir qu'il disoit" (p. 79), and prefers to lie to Floride's mother about what had happened. The notions that there are alternatives to a relationship based on service and payment, and that these alternatives can be chosen, are an argument in Floride's favor, in her advocacy of virtuous love. Floride's alternative also connects the representation of her love to an aspect of "feminine writing," one that refuses the linear economic language of "male" desire.[61]

The refusal of an economy of love, while clearly set in opposition to Amadour's "male" desire in Marguerite de Navarre's novella, is nonetheless also characteristic of the discourse of friendship that, as we have seen, is so markedly dominated by male examples. Cicero emphasizes the absence of hope of gain in relationships of true friendship:

> Ut enim benefici liberalesque sumus, non ut exigamus gratiam (neque enim beneficium foeneramur, sed natura propensi ad liberalitatem sumus) sic amicitiam non spe mercedis adducti,

------

anyone else."

[61] "Ainsi ce qu'elles désirent n'est précisément rien, et en même temps tout. Toujours plus et autre chose que cet *un* - de sexe, par exemple - que vous leur donnez, leur prêtez. Ce qui est souvent interprété, et redouté, comme une sorte de faim insatiable, une voracité qui va vous engloutir tout entier. Alors qu'il s'agit surtout d'une autre économie, qui déroute la linéarité d'un projet, mine l'objet-but d'un désir, fait exploser la polarisation sur une seule jouissance, déconcerte la fidélité à un seul discours. . .," Luce Irigaray, *Ce sexe qui n'en est pas un* (Paris: Minuit, 1977), p. 29.

sed quod omnis eius fructus in ipso sit amore, expetendam
putamus.[62]

The explicit exclusion of "profit" from relationships of perfect friendship
is also a commonplace in Aristotle's *Nicomachean Ethics*, and is
underlined in the commentary provided by Nicole Oresme, in the first
translation into French of the work: "Quant l'en voit que il ne sont amis
fors pour proffit, l'en puet de legier croire que il ne sont pas vrais amis,
et que il aiment plus le gaaing que la personne, et ne sont pas
vertueus."[63] We find, then, in friendship theory the opposition between
an economic model of investment and return, and a love of the "person"
detached from usefulness to the lover, or an enjoyment of the love itself,
as a virtuous activity. This discourse of generosity can only be applied
metaphorically to the situation in which Floride and Amadour find
themselves, but then so can Amadour's language of service and payment.
The resistance to an economic model underlying the relationship of love
is prefigured in the friendship with another for his own sake. Of course
Amadour is seemingly incapable of fulfilling the role of a true friend,
and it is Floride who best incarnates the generous ideal.[64]

Floride's insistence on choice, or some sort of deliberation, is in
agreement with the representation of *amor virtutis* as a love capable of
rational decision, as opposed to the blindness of *eros* or Cupid. We find

---

[62] "For as we are kind and generous, not so that we may demand repayment
- for we do not give favors with interest, but are by nature given to generosity -
so we believe that friendship is desirable, not because we are influenced by
hope of gain, but because its entire profit is in the love itself," *De amicitia*, p.
488 [9.31].

[63] "When one sees that they are friends only for profit, one can easily
believe that they are not true friends, and that they love more the gain than the
person, and are not virtuous," p. 421, on 8.6 [1157a 25].

[64] Even after the attempted rape Floride is willing to provide *beneficia* to her
friend, even though his actions have not merited any such consideration. She
warns him of a jealous husband of Lorette, a woman to whom Amadour is
speaking "propos d'amityé" on Floride's advice (p. 81).

in friendship theory a similar opposition, between uncontrolled passion and the deliberate choice of a friend. In Oresme's translation of the *Nicomachean Ethics*, in the section analyzing friendship as state or as activity (1157b 5-1158a 1), friendship ("amistié") is called a "habit," recalling scholastic terminology, as opposed to love, or "amacion" ("Amacion, c'est plaisance, desir, affeccion et mouvement de l'appetit en aucune chose," p. 423 n 6): "Et amacion ressemble a passion. Et amistié semble estre habit, car amacion puet estre es choses qui sont senz ame. Mais les amis ne reaiment pas l'un l'autre ou entreaiment senz eleccion; et eleccion vient de habit" (p. 423).[65] Oresme explains in his commentary that "Eleccion vient par deliberacion et de habit qui encline a eslire, et eleccion de reamer son amy vient d'amistié; donques est amistié un habit" (p. 423 n 8).[66] The *habitus* of friendship, the time spent together, the conversations, etc., at the same time allow a choice and incline toward a choice of friend, of loving him who has shown friendship towards you. Familiarity and rational decision are combined, just as, at the beginning of their relationship, Amadour makes sure to become like a son in the family of Floride.

In all these ways we have seen that the ideal of classical friendship provides a model for the tenth novella, a model in which the Christian associations are not excluded, but in which the essentially *human* element of their love is accounted for. Seen in the tradition of exemplary friendships it is obviously a failure; yet the reasons for this failure cannot be attributed to the woman, who lives up to the ideal of *philia*. It is Amadour's choice of an economy and strategy of desire incompatible with true friendship that destroys their contentment with each other. Marguerite de Navarre has reworked in women's favor a tradition that seemed to say that only men are capable of the generous virtue which characterizes perfect friendship.

---

[65] "Love resembles a passion. And friendship seems to be a disposition, for love can be in things that have no soul. But friends do not love each other without having chosen to do so, and choice comes from a disposition."

[66] "Choice comes through deliberation and from disposition which inclines to choose, and the choice of loving back one's friend comes from friendship; therefore friendship is a disposition."

The suicide of Amadour in battle and the death of Floride, joyfully departing from this world to see her "true" husband, are, however, hints of the anachronistic nature of perfect friendship. For the novella itself is not the final word on the subject. When Parlamente finishes, and opens the subsequent discussion, she is true to her name and offers more space for negotiation between men and women:

> Je sçay bien, mes dames, que ceste longue nouvelle pourra estre à aucuns fascheuse; mais, si j'eusse voulu satisfaire à celluy [her male *amy*] qui la m'a comptée, elle eut esté trop plus que longue, vous suppliant, en prenant exemple de la vertu de Floride, diminuer un peu de sa cruaulté, et ne croire poinct tant de bien aux hommes, qu'il ne faille, par la congnoissance du contraire, à eulx donner cruelle mort et à vous une triste vie. (p. 83)[67]

Parlamente has had to adapt the long story to the more easily bored audience, just as women should adapt their expectations to the flawed men they may want to be friends with. In other words, "perfect" friendship poses demands on the (male) friend that cannot be realized, and a more flexible approach will not only benefit the man but may make a woman's life happier, as well. The possibility of the *medius cursus* implies a (healthy) distrust of the friend, which, in turn, transforms the relationship into a somewhat more utilitarian one: do not expect the man to be without interest in his affection for you, and, conversely, it is in your interest to presume interest in the other. In this sense Floride and Amadour's friendship is not really fitting, and neither is, for that matter, that perfect relationship of good men in virtue advocated by the classics.

---

[67] "I know well, my ladies, that this long novella might be troublesome to some; but, if I had wanted to do justice to the one who told it to me, it would have been too long, and so I beg you, when you take Floride as an example, to diminish somewhat her cruelty, and to not believe that men are so good that, by learning the contrary, you should give them a cruel death and to yourselves a sad life."

# CHAPTER V

# MOROSE NOSTALGIA, INTEREST, AND THE END OF FRIENDSHIPS

Whereas in the previous chapter we have seen how the elaboration of friendship can involve an abundance of explanatory discourse, of motivation and justification, there are also remarkable instances of the *lack* of explanation serving as the measure of a relationship's perfection. The importance given at times to lack of justification is linked, I think, to a spasmodic but profound distrust of explanatory discourse as something corrupting, sullying, intruding. This perception of corruption of the immediate, non-discursive relationship arises from an underlying nostalgia, and an underlying suspicion of economic exchange. It is this morose nostalgia and this suspicion that will be the focus of the first sections of the present chapter.

## 1. Friendship, Money, and Moroseness

> L'amitié est tellement corrompuë, que seulement on la
> mesure à l'aune du proffict & utilité. - André Thevet,
> *Les Vrais pourtraits et vies des hommes illustres*
> (1584), 7.126.

> Tout ce qui semble estre profitable, comme les
> honneurs, les richesses, les voluptez, & tout ce qui est
> de ceste qualité, ne doyvent aucunement estre preposez
> à l'Amitié. - Pierre de la Primaudaye, *Academie
> francoise* (1581), 1.4.13, f. 41v.[1]

One of the recurrent themes in the theory and representation of friendship is the association between the end of "pure" friendships and the dominance of money and ambition among human beings. In his *De amicitia* Cicero formulates it succinctly: "pestem enim maiorem esse nullam in amicitiis quam in plerisque pecuniae cupiditatem, in optimis quibusque honoris certamen, & gloriae."[2] The end of friendship is a symptom of the general corruption of social relations by the influence of money: "sed corrupti mores, depravatique sunt admiratione divitiarum," says Cicero in his *De officiis*.[3]

Cicero's complaint finds its echo in Boccaccio's *Decameron*. In the conclusion to the tale of Gisippo and Tito (10.8), one finds a praise

---

[1] "Friendship is so corrupted that one only measures it by profit and utility." "All that seems to be profitable, such as honors, wealth, pleasures, and everything of this kind, should in no way be preferred to friendship."

[2] "Among most men, the greatest bane for friendships is the lust for money, among the most worthy men it is the competition for honors and glory." Cicero, *De officiis libri III. Cato Maior, vel de Senectute: Laelius, vel de amicitia . . . cum annotationibus Pauli Manutii* (Venice: Aldus, 1564), f. 119v (10.34). I have modified slightly the Loeb Classical Library translation by William A. Falconer.

[3] "But morals are corrupted and depraved by our worship of wealth" (f. 57r [2.20.71]).

of friendship, the *santissima cosa*, and an affirmation of its decline today:

> Li cui [dell'amistà] sacratissimi effetti oggi radissime volte si veggiono in due, colpa e vergogna della misera cupidigia de' mortali, la qual, solo alla propria utilitá riguardando, ha costei fuor degli estremi termini della terra in esilio perpetuo rilegata.[4]

The example of Gisippo and Tito is taken from the time of Octavian (before he was Augustus, as the narrator Filomena points out), during the triumvirate. This is, therefore, an example from a still virtuous past, perhaps impossible to reproduce today, in the climate of self-interest and greed. Many years later, in the *Ragguagli di Parnaso* (1612) by the Italian political commentator and satirist Traiano Boccalini, we find the starkest if somewhat ironic version of Cicero's and Filomena's condemnation of the worship of money. In a "dispatch" entitled "Generale Riforma dell'Universo da i sette Savii della Grecia, e da altri Letterati publicata di ordine di Apollo" (1.77), Apollo decides to convene the seven sages of Greece, two Roman philosophers (Cato and Seneca), and a modern Italian "sage" (Galileo's mentor Iacopo Mazzoni) in order to adopt a general reform of the world. He decides to do this after being asked by the emperor Justinian to approve a new law against suicide: horrified, he wonders how the world could be in such bad shape that men prefer committing suicide to living in it?[5] During the meeting

---

[4] "The most sacred effects of friendship are today most rarely seen in two people; [this is] the fault and the shame of mortals' miserable greed which, concerned only with usefulness to itself, has banished friendship beyond the outer confines of the earth, in perpetual exile," ed. Charles S. Singleton (Bari: Laterza, 1966), vol. 2, p. 290. Pietro Bembo will have a similar complaint, saying that in the present time one cannot trust friends, as everyone in the end will attempt to deceive the other (in Castiglione's *Libro del cortegiano*, 2.29). Federico, though, immediately defends modern friendships (2.30).

[5] Boccalini published several selections of his "dispatches"; I have used *De' Ragguagli di Parnaso* (Venice: Pietro Farri, 1612). There were many editions of this work throughout the seventeenth century, and translations into French, English, Dutch, Spanish, and German.

of the seven sages various solutions are proposed: the opening of men's chests so that their heart, i.e. their true sentiments, would be visible through a small window, a "finestrellino," the banning of sea voyages, etc. A common thread in the description of the world's ills is the predominance of "avaritia" and "ambitione" (pp. 333, 341, 349), the thirst for gold and silver (p. 335-336), and the resulting inequality among men (the "Mio e Tuo," p. 333). Boccalini's thoroughly pessimistic vision draws on a long tradition of golden age mythology, and is symptomatic of a profound, nostalgic association between purity of relationships and the absence of instrumental thought. For men to be virtuous with each other, there should be no third term in their relationship: no hope of financial gain, no gold or silver, no hope for preferment. The "finestrellino" to men's hearts is a physical depiction of this virtuous immediacy (the danger being, however, that one will kill the human being during surgery, p. 332).

The stripped-down, "pure" relationship that friendship is at times imagined to be in the Renaissance excludes *all* interest or motivation. When relationships are submitted to a final cause (especially of a material or generally utilitarian nature), this finality is immediately a sign of their ending, of their destruction. As soon as a *telos* is imagined, the relationship becomes less than perfectly human, and, paradoxically, such instrumental relationships then multiply, cancerously, in a general crisis before their agony. This weary view of the world considers the present to be close to an ending, just as relationships themselves have become finalized, furnished with an end. When Boccalini's Justinian proposes to add a law against suicide to the corpus of Roman law, it is clear that the world could not get any worse, and that the humans committing suicide stand for the world in general. One of the sages, Cato, proposes that another flood simply do away with all but a chosen few of the human race (p. 355). When Iacopo Mazzoni, the more recent Italian sage, invites the "Secolo" (a prosopopeia of the "present time") to be examined by the wise company, they find his body encrusted with layers of infected flesh, and, when those layers are removed, nothing but his bones is left (p. 363).[6] At the same time this morose vision is a

---

[6] The cutting-out of the infected flesh (the human race) from the body of the world is a parody of Ovid, *Metamorphoses* (1.190-191), when Jupiter is enraged by the vices of mortals: "cuncta prius temptata, sed inmedicabile corpus ense

nostalgic one; it projects into the past a gratuitousness and purity that have become lost amid the present corruption. This corruption destroys, finishes, human relationships by assigning to them an *end*. If relationships are based on a contract, an exchange of services or goods, they will end when the terms of the contract are fulfilled, or when the services provided are no longer useful.[7] This commonplace is a feature of Renaissance discussions of different types of love and friendship; for example, in a novel probably written by Nicolas Denisot, *L'Amant resuscité de la mort d'amour* (1558), we read: "si l'utilité estoit cause de la liayson d'amour: il seroit necessaire & consequent, que ceste utilité cessant, . . . cessast aussi l'amitié."[8] When the favor, the *beneficium*, one does for a friend is accompanied by the hope for a return favor, interest, or some other motivation, the favor *dies*: "or le bienfaict meurt & finist, s'il est recompensé," we read in a sixteenth-century translation of Lactantius's *Divinae institutiones*.[9]

The death of the favor, the death of friendship, the agony of society are all connected in this *morose* vision, that is, in the vision of those who are old and sense themselves close to death (and who are, ironically, themselves no longer capable of friendship): "At sunt morosi,

---

recidendum, ne pars sincera trahatur" (All things have been tried before, but that which is incurable must be cut away with the knife, lest the untainted part draw infection).

[7] See Aristotle, *Nicomachean Ethics*, 1156a 10 - 1156b 5, on the short duration of friendships based on usefulness or pleasure.

[8] "If usefulness were the cause of the bond of love, it would necessarily follow that once this usefulness ceased, so would friendship." Quoted from the Lyons edition of 1558, first edition 1555 (facsimile repr. Yorkshire, New York, The Hague: S. R. Publishers, Johnson, Mouton, 1971), p. 87.

[9] "Indeed the favor dies and finishes, if it is returned." *Lactance firmian des Divines Institutions, contre les Gentilz & Idolatres*, trans. René Fame (Paris: Galliot du Pré, 1543), 6.12, f. 137r. Sentences from Lactantius appear in Renaissance *florilegia* in the section devoted to *amicitia* (such as in the frequently edited and revised *Polyanthea* [1503] by Domenico Nanni Mirabelli).

& anxii, & iracundi, & difficiles senes," says Cicero.[10] Moroseness is, from this perspective, not connected to any real historical decadence, but to biological decadence; a discourse on the awfulness of present times is perhaps also connected insidiously with a discourse on one's body, on the decay of one's body. Even though Cicero himself wrote his treaties on friendship and old age under the menacing shadow of what he considered to be tyranny, the philosopher as a good philosopher refuses to validate the moroseness of old men. Their nostalgia is a personal, not a historical, perspective, and it is determined in part by the lack of respect they receive, in part by the frailty of their body (ibid.).[11] The reception of Cicero in the Renaissance is filtered through centuries of Christian thought, in which sadness, despair, and melancholy are symptoms of sloth, and thus antithetical to the life of the Christian faithful.[12] However, even if Renaissance writers could not ignore the condemnation of *acedia* or *accidia* (heaviness of the heart) by the Church, it is perhaps in the spirit of Cicero that Castiglione refuses the moroseness of old men, in his introduction to the second book of the *Libro del cortegiano* (1528):

> Non senza maraviglia ho più volte considerato onde nasca un errore, il quale, perciò che universalmente ne' vecchi si vede, creder si po che ad essi sia proprio e naturale; e questo è che quasi tutti laudano i tempi passati e biasmano i presenti, vituperando le azioni e i modi nostri e tutto quello che essi nella lor gioventù non facevano; affermando ancor ogni bon costume

---

[10] "But old men are morose, anxious, irritable, and difficult," (*De senectute*, f. 105v [18.65]). Aristotle finds, as does Cicero, that old men and morose men appear little inclined to friendship (*Nicomachean Ethics* 1157b14-15).

[11] Compare Lucretius, *De natura rerum*, 2.1149-1157.

[12] See, for example, [Thomas à Kempis], *De imitatione Christi*, 3.57.2: "Ad minus sustine patienter, si non potes gaudienter" (Paris: Imprimerie royale, 1640, p. 427); Erasmus, *Enchiridion militis christiani*, 116 (16th canon). The avoidance of despair is fundamental in the ongoing battle against temptation and adversity.

e bona maniera di vivere, ogni virtù, in somma ogni cosa, andar sempre di mal in peggio.[13]

What an irrational way of thinking for old men who otherwise can show such wise judgment, Castiglione responds, since that would mean that the world would have long since become the worst of all possible worlds.[14]  This is obviously not the case.  Castiglione's argument against historical despair is repeated by Pierre de Ronsard, in the exordium to his first major political poem treating the religious strife in France, the *Discours des misères de ce temps* (1562), addressed to Catherine de Médicis.[15]  Citing Tacitus and Seneca, the jurist and historiographer Louis Le Roy similarly discounts this pessimistic vision of history, and connects it to the moroseness of old people:

La plainte est vieille que les moeurs empirent de jour en jour. Si ainsi estoit, les hommes seroient pieça parvenus au comble de toute meschanceté, et n'y auroit plus d'integrité en eux, ce qui n'est vray. ( . . . ) Il est croyable telle plainte estre procedee premierement des vieillars: lesquels passee la fleur de

---

[13] "Not without astonishment have I asked myself several times where an error originates, which, since it is universally seen among old people, perhaps it is proper and natural to them; and this error is that almost all praise the past and blame the present, condemning our actions and ways and all that they in their own youth did not do, and affirming in addition that all good habits and good ways of living, all virtue, in sum everything is going from bad to worse," *Il libro del cortegiano*, 2.1, eds. E. Bonora, P. Zoccola (Milano: Mursia, 1972), p. 103.

[14] "E veramente par cosa cosa molta aliena dalla ragione e degna di maraviglia, che la età matura, la qual con la lunga esperienza suol far nel resto il giudicio degli omini più perfetto, in questo lo corrompa tanto, che non si avveggano che, se 'l mondo sempre andasse peggiorando e che i padri fossero generalmente migliori che i figlioli, molto prima che ora saremmo giunti a quest'ultimo grado di male, che peggiorar non po" (ibid.).

[15] "Si, depuis que le monde a pris commencement, / Le vice d'age en age eust pris accroissement, / Il y a jà long temps que l'extreme malice / Eust surmonté le monde, & tout ne fut que vice," in ed. Paul Laumonier, *Oeuvres complètes*, vol. 11 (Paris: Didier, 1946), p. 19, vv. 1-4.

l'aage plaine de lyesse, quand ils entrent en extreme viellesse
où il n'y a que tristesse, ils regrettent les plaisirs de jeunesse se
voyans affoiblis des sens, et debilitez de tous membres.
Quelquefois aussi estans mesprisez de ceux qui les honoroient
paravant, et deceuz par la faulse opinion qu'ils ont des choses,
pensent n'y avoir plus de foy, ne d'amitié, ou d'honnesteté
entre les hommes: racontans aux plus jeunes merveilles de leur
premier aage.[16]

The Ciceronian avoidance of historical pessimism is reproduced by Le
Roy as an antidote to his own occasional lapses in optimism, as he
cannot keep himself from deploring the sectarian violence and chaos in
French society. His summation "Tout est pesle mesle, confondu, rien
ne va comm'il appartient" characterizes the cancerous, anarchic
proliferation of corrupt human activity.[17]  The rejection of old age's
moroseness seems a conventional, rhetorical gesture, ensuring a
distinction between the life of the body and the life of the world, and
thus ensuring the validity of pessimistic observations when they are
forced upon the author by what he perceives to be real decline and
decay.

---

[16] "The complaint is old that mores are getting worse day by day.  If this
were the case, men would already have reached the height of evil, and there
would no longer be any honesty among them, which is not the case. ( . . . )
It seems as though this complaint may have come first from old men who, the
flower of their joyful age having passed, when they enter into extreme old age
where there is nothing but sadness, they regret the pleasures of youth, seeing
their senses and their limbs weakened.  Sometimes also, looked down upon by
those who used to honor them, and deceived by the false opinion that they have
of things, they think that there is no longer loyalty or friendship or honesty
among men: reciting to the younger the marvels of their youth," *De la
vicissitude ou variété des choses en l'univers* (Paris; P. l'Huillier, 1575; repr.
Paris: Fayard, 1988), Book 11, pp. 421-422.

[17] "Everything is upside down, confused, nothing is going as it should," *De
la vicissitude*, Book 10, p. 381.  See also Ronsard who, having refused to see
a general historical decline, writes in the same *Discours*: "tout à l'abandon va
sans ordre & sans loy" (p. 28, v. 166), and "Tout va de pis en pis" (p. 29, v.
185).  Ronsard in particular could be echoing Virgil: "Sic omnia fatis in peius
ruere ac retro sublapsa referri" (*Georgics* 1.199-200).

The perception of decline and decay, even when it is detached from the moroseness of old men, takes certain typical forms which are reflected in many Renaissance discussions of friendship. For friendship often belongs to an anterior mode of being, before finality and interest cast their shadow on the world. Literature has a peculiar place in the nostalgic vision because it is the imaginary space in which "pure" relationships can be realized, and yet the very means by which they are realized seem to work against their purity. In a general sense the corruption of contemporary society is mirrored in the decline of the writer, who must write in a time when "rien ne se dit, qui desia ne soit dit," nothing is said which has not been said before. This phrase from Terence is quoted by the Neoplatonic hermetic philosopher Blaise de Vigenère, a contemporary of Montaigne, in his translation of Plato's, Cicero's, and Lucian's dialogues on friendship.[18]    For Vigenère's predecessor Jean Collin, however, who translated Cicero's De amicitia in 1537, the state of contemporary society was more of a positive inspiration. Collin undertook this translation "pour ce que plusieurs sont ou temps present studieux & amateurs de toute bonne doctrine & vertu plus que jamais."[19]  For Vigenère, in 1579, the world is not the same.

---

[18] *Trois dialogues de l'amitié: Le Lysis de Platon, et le Laelius de Ciceron; contenans plusieurs beaux preceptes, & discours philosophiques sur ce subject: Et le Toxaris de Lucian; ou sont amenez quelques rares exemples de ce que les Amis ont fait autrefois l'un pour l'autre* (Paris: Nicolas Chesneau, 1579). Terence's maxim is quoted on p. 9 of the prefatory epistle. Vigenère is echoing also the subtitle, and title of Book 12 of Le Roy's *De la vicissitude*: "S'il est vray ne se dire rien qui n'ait esté dict paravant."

[19] "Because several in these times are more than ever studious and lovers of all good learning and virtue." *Le livre de amytie de Ciceron* (Paris: Arnoul & Charles les Angeliers, Vincent Sertenas, 1537), [p. 23].  Jean Collin's translation was reprinted several times in the sixteenth century, together with French translations of Cicero's *De officiis* and other moral treatises.  See Valerie Worth, *Practising Translation in Renaissance France: The Example of Etienne Dolet* (Oxford: Clarendon, 1988), pp. 14-15, and pp. 23-25 on the characteristics of Collin's text.  A more cautious optimism than Collin's can also be found in remarks on friendship in Pietro Bembo's *Gli asolani* (1505), Book 2, where Gismondo describes the advent of friendship in earlier times, its growth, and its survival today; the world still desires friendships: "ancora se ne

The serene times of François Ier have given way to a time of "Barbarie," and the world has become "un si malin, inique, perverty, seditieux, mutin, ingrat & desbauché siecle . . . indigne d'un si bon, si benin, gracieux, debonnaire, & pacifique Monarque [Henri III]" (p. 5 of the preface).[20]    Vigenère's abundant adjectives accumulate just as contemporary books multiply in direct proportion to their increasing lack of substance. The new books only imitate old ones, and this imitation somehow allows them to balloon into a chaotic, promiscuous, meaningless mass:

> Et n'est plus la saison de faire aucune difficulté ne conscience, de diversifier les bons livres anciens en une infinité de nouveaux.   Car tout ainsi que de divers accouplemens de quelques deux douzaines de lettres, viennent à se former tant de milliers de syllabes: Et de la transposition des syllabes, plus grand nombre de dictions encore: De la diverse collocation des dictions, innumerables clauses complettes: Et de ces clauses finablement a se teistre infinis traictez, livres, tomes, volumes: En semblable; De ces volumes, tomes, livres, traictez, empruntant non les mesmes clausules, dictions, syllabes, & caracteres; mais des pages toutes entieres, des fueillets & cayers aussi; se compilent en peu de temps de beaux gros magazins de livres, à l'exemple d'une Baleine qui devore infinies esquadres

---

[of friendships] tien vago il mondo: come che poi di tempo in tempo tralignando a questo nostro maligno secolo il vero odore antico e la prima pura dolcezza non sia passata" (ed. Milano: Società de' Classici italiani, 1808, pp. 151-152).

[20] "Such an evil, unjust, perverted, seditious, rebellious, ungrateful and debauched world, unworthy of a monarch so good, graceful, of such a noble nature, and so peace-loving."   See also his contemporary Pierre de la Primaudaye: "Or pource qu'aujourd'huy la malice des hommes est si grande, qu'il n'y a rien si sainct & sacré, qui ne soit violé, perverty & confondu, ce n'est merveille, si on abuse impudemment de ce nom d'Amy, tant reveré entre les Anciens. . ." (*Academie francoise*, Paris, Guillaume Chaudiere, 1581, 1.4.13, f. 42r).

de moindres poissons, pour en former ceste lourde excessive masse (pp. 9-10 of the preface).[21]

Montaigne's complains similarly in his essay on "Vanité": "L'escrivaillerie semble estre quelque simptome d'un siecle desbordé."[22] In Vigenère's diatribe we find this asiatic hypertrophy of writing linked to the need to imitate, and, by implication, to friendship which in its singularity and infrequency is precisely the opposite of promiscuous writing.  For Vigenère's preface introduces, of course, three famous dialogues on friends.  Certain metaphors used by Vigenère himself ("accouplemens," "former," "devorer") suggest fecundity, growth, ingestion.  In all, though, the growth of books appears perverse and pathological, since books constitute themselves in a purely *formal* way, by "collocation," piecing-together, and not by invention.  The hypertrophy of empty, imitative, anonymous writing mimicks the corruption of a world characterized by what Cicero called "admiration of wealth."

Another translation of the *De amicitia* appeared at the beginning of the following century, by the eloquent cardinal Jacques Davy Du Perron.  He makes explicit what was suggested in the profuse preface of his predecessor Blaise de Vigenère.  The relationship of friendship is smothered in a period dominated by interest:

---

[21] "And it is no longer necessary to have any scruples about diversifying the good old books into an infinite number of new ones.  For just as from diverse couplings of several couple of dozens of letters, so many thousands of syllables are formed, and from the transposition of syllables, a greater number of expressions, from the diverse composition of expressions, innumerable complete clauses, and from these clauses finally an infinite number of treatises, books, tomes, volumes are woven.  Similarly, from these volumes, tomes, books, treatises, borrowing not only the same clauses, expressions, syllables, and characters, but entire pages, leaves, and notebooks also, are compiled in little time nice large magazines of books, following the example of a whale that devours infinite squadrons of smaller fish, in order to form this heavy excessive mass."

[22] "Scribbling seems to be some sign of a world out of control." *Essais*, 3.9, eds. Pierre Villey, Verdun-L. Saulnier (Paris: Presses univ. de France, 1965), p. 946.

> Car si jamais il fut besoin de mettre la main à cét oeuvre, & si
> jamais la corruption du siecle & des moeurs l'ont requis, c'est
> maintenant que le defaut d'amitié se trouve non seulement si
> commun parmy nous, mais qu'il en arrive des interests tels que
> je ne sçay s'il y en peut avoir de plus grands.[23]

Du Perron accuses the "despravation de nostre siecle, auquel les amitiez ne sont pas plustost nées qu'estouffées; auquel un ombre d'interest, un Idole de vain honneur fait diviser celles mesmes qui sont fondées sur le sang & sur la nature" (p. 7).[24] As we saw in Boccalini's dark satire, it is avarice and ambition, interest and vain honor, in an anarchic society that signal the end of friendship, of the social sympathy that naturally binds men. As in Vigenère's preface, what is substantial and natural is smothered by the cancerous growth of personal interest and quarrels encouraged by a lack of social order. The death of human virtuous exchange, of "duties," in the sense of the Ciceronian *officium*, and of "favors," in the sense of the Senecan *beneficium*, will be the eventual result of the generalized calculus to which human relationships are submitted. One senses that it appears to be the gratuitous, that which is not submitted to interest, which guarantees, in the minds of these authors, the humanity of relationships, and which risks disappearing. This dark vision of society and relationships, this sense of ending and of finality, are linked undoubtedly to the divisions and disorder caused by the religious wars in France and the religious crisis in general. Friendship, that agreement or consensus of all things divine and human that links two human beings ("omnium divinarum humanarumque rerum . . . summa consensio," *De amicitia*, f. 115v [6.20]) has its social

---

[23] "For if ever it was necessary to accomplish this task, and if ever the corruption of the world and our mores have required it, it is now that the lack of friendship is to be found not only so wide-spread among us, but is also now that this corruption has engendered such great interests that no greater ones can exist." *Laelius ou de l'Amitié* (Paris: Antoine Estiene, 1618), p. 5 of the dedicatory epistle.

[24] "Perversion of our time, in which friendships are smothered as soon as they are born; in which the shadow of interest, the idol of vain honor divide even those friendships that are based on blood and nature."

analogue, and when the latter is so visibly destroyed, would personal relationships not follow?[25]

## 2. Friendship and "Usury"

A more conceptual link between the theory of friendship and the "admiration of wealth" deplored especially by a whole line of sad writers is the problem of interest in its strictly economic sense.   The link between friendship and interest is already present among the Latin moral philosophers.   Cicero establishes the distinction between giving a *beneficium* (a favor) and *faenerari* (lending at interest, or in the hope of a return).  Although a friendship may turn out to be advantageous, when one begins a friendship, the latter cannot be thought of as an investment:

> Ut enim benefici, liberalesque sumus, non ut exigamus gratiam, (neque enim beneficium feneramur) sed natura propensi ad liberalitatem sumus: sic amicitiam, non spe mercedis adducti, sed quod eius omnis fructus in ipso amore inest, expetendam putamus. (f. 118v [9.31])[26]

---

[25] The most obvious literary example of the disintegration that the religious wars represented is the work of Agrippa d'Aubigné.   On this aspect of his poetry, see Jean-Raymond Fanlo, *Tracés, ruptures: la composition instable des 'Tragiques'* (Paris: Champion, 1990), especially pp. 43-105.   See, on the "crisis" of the Renaissance in France, *L'Automne de la Renaissance 1580-1630*, eds. Jean Lafond, André Stegmann (Paris: Vrin, 1981), and *Humanism in Crisis: The Decline of the French Renaissance*, ed. Philippe Desan (Ann Arbor: Univ. of Michigan Press, 1991).   See also Géralde Nakam, *Les 'Essais' de Montaigne, miroir et procès de leur temps: Témoignage historique et création littéraire* (Paris: Nizet, 1984).

[26] "For as we are generous and liberal, not so that we may require repayment - for we do not put our favors out at interest, but are by nature given to liberality - so we believe that friendship is to be desired not because we are influenced by the hope of gain, but because all its profit is in the love itself."

The phrase in Cicero *neque enim beneficium feneramur* is echoed in Seneca: "demus beneficia non foeneremus" (*De beneficiis*, p. 8 [1.1.9]).[27] In the case of Cicero's formulation the deponent *faenerari* more clearly than the active verb in Seneca means "to lend with interest" rather than "to lend (i.e., to give in hope of repayment)," and that is the way Cicero's French translators understood him. Jean Collin says, "car nous ne baillons le bien faict a usure" (p. 49), and both Blaise de Vigenère (p. 70) and the cardinal Du Perron (p. 39) retain "usure" in their translations. Similarly, in the translation by Simon Goulart of Seneca's *De beneficiis*, we read: "Faisons plaisir de grace, & ne le prestons pas à interest."[28] In other words, the favor done for a friend is perhaps more clearly one in which *interest* or *usury* does not play a role.

In Cicero's description of true liberality, another distinction is made, that between *spes mercedis* (hope of gain) and *fructus [qui] in ipso amore inest* (compensation that is in the love itself).[29] This concerns again the spirit in which a *beneficium* is made, and on which friendship

---

[27] "Let us give favors, not lend with interest." I have used *Lucii Annaei Senecae sanctissimi philosophi lucubrationes omnes. . .* (Basel: Johannes Frobenius, 1515).

[28] *Les Oeuvres morales et meslees de Senecque* (Paris: Jean Houzé, 1595), f. 3v.

[29] The French translations are fairly close to each other. Jean Collin: "esperance de quelque salaire," and "le fruict delle est & consiste en amour" (p. 49). Blaise de Vigenère: "esperance de quelque loyer & guerdon," and "le fruict qu'on en peut percevoir consiste en l'Amour" (p. 70). Du Perron: "esperance de la recompense," and "son fruict est constitué en l'acte mesme d'aymer" (p. 39). The persistence of "esperance" and "fruict" indicates, I think, the interference of religious vocabulary (*actus spei*, the motivation of love by the hope for salvation, and *fruitio*, the enjoyment of God). See La Primaudaye: "Aimer (dit Ciceron) n'est autre chose que vouloir faire beaucoup de bien & plaisir à quelcun, sans en esperer aucune recompense. Autrement l'Amitié seroit une pure marchandise, au lieu qu'elle doit estre comme la charité gratuite" (*Academie francoise*, 1.4.13, f. 42r). Echoing Cicero again, he speaks later of perfect friendship's reward consisting in "l'amour seule de celuy que l'on aime" (1.4.13, f. 43v).

is based; the love itself of the other should provide the motivation for the favor - not the favor, nor the hoped-for return. Seneca elaborates this autotelic nature of the favor:

> Quid est ergo beneficium? Benevola actio, tribuens gaudium, capiensque tribuendo, in id, quod facit, prona et sponte sua parata. Itaque non quid fiat aut quid detur, refert, sed qua mente. Quia beneficium non in eo, quod fit, aut datur, consistit, sed in ipso dantis, aut facientis animo. (p. 10 [1.6.1])[30]

Cicero's and Seneca's analyses of the *beneficium* combine with the Aristotelian distinction between friendship in virtue and friendship born out of usefulness or pleasure. In his essay, "De l'affection des pères aux enfans" (2.8), Montaigne provides an analysis of father-son relationships based on the notion of the "bienfaict" that reproduces an economy of giving gleaned from these classical sources:

> Qui bien faict, exerce une action belle et honneste; qui reçoit, l'exerce utile seulement; or l'utile est de beaucoup moins aimable que l'honneste. L'honneste est stable et permanent, fournissant à celuy qui l'a faict, une gratification constante. L'utile se perd et eschappe facilement; et n'en est la memoire ny si fresche ny si douce. Les choses nous sont plus cheres, qui nous ont plus cousté; et il est plus difficile de donner que de prendre. (p. 387)[31]

---

[30] "What then is a benefit? It is the well-wishing act [of someone who] bestows joy and derives joy from the bestowal of it, and is inclined to do what he does from the prompting of his own will. And so what counts is, not what is done or what is given, but the spirit of the action, because a benefit consists, not in what is done or given, but in the intention of the giver or doer." See also Seneca's 9th letter to Lucilius: "Ista quam tu describis [amicitia . . . causa utilitatis], negociatio est, non amicitia, quae ad commodum accedit, quae quid consecutura sit spectat" (p. 199 [9.10]).

[31] "Whoever does a favor, performs a beautiful and morally good action; whoever receives the favor, performs only a useful action; the useful is much less to be loved than the morally good. The morally good is stable and permanent, furnishing constant gratification to him who did the favor. The

As Montaigne points out (p. 386), this is more or less a paraphrase of Aristotle (*Nicomachean Ethics*, 1168a 10-28); the Aristotelian argument seems readily available. These commonplaces are also repeated in Christian reflections on friendship.[32] The economic language already present in Cicero's rejection of the *faeneratio* continues in his rejection of the *spes mercedis*. Renaissance readers of Cicero were immediately reminded of the condemnation of usury, and the language of "hope of profit" only reinforces that association. For usury is often defined as an illegitimate *spes lucri*, a hope for money, for example among the scholastics: "usura est spes qua ex vi mutui aliquid speratur principaliter ultra sortem."[33]

---

useful is lost and escapes easily; and the memory of it is neither as fresh nor as sweet. The things that have cost us more, are dearer to us, and it is more difficult to give than to take."

[32] See Pierre de Blois, *De amicitia christiana*, cap. 4: "Non enim amor ille nomine vel honore amicitiae dignus est, qui alicuius mundanae utilitatis abtentu contrahitur. Amicitia siquidem ipsa sui causa est, ipsa sibi merces, et longe infra fines amicitiae amor ille subsistit, quam ex spectatio ambitiosa, vel spes quaestuaria antecedit" (in ed. M.-M. Davy, *Un traité de l'amour du XIIe siècle*, Paris, E. de Boccard, 1932, p. 122). See also Ethelred of Rievaulx, *De spirituali amicitia*, 2: "Cum igitur in bonis semper praecedat amicitia, sequatur utilitas; profecto non tam utilitas parta per amicum, quam amici amor ipse delectat" (*Patrologiae cursus completus*, 195: 678A); this sentence is found as well in the digest made of Aelred's work, called *Liber de amicitia*, and falsely attributed to Augustine (*Patrologiae cursus completus*, 40: 837, cap. 10). Aelred also speaks of the absence of "spes futurae utilitatis" in the friendship between Jonathan and David (ibid., 677D).

[33] "Usury is the hope through which, by force of a loan of money [as opposed to the *commodum*, the loan of goods], something is hoped for principally beyond the amount lent." Jacques Almain, *De penitentia* dist 15 qu 2 "De usuris," in *Aurea clarissimi et acutissimi Doctoris theologi Magistri Iacobi Almain Senonensis opuscula* (Paris: Claude Chevallon, 1518), f. 41v. On the attitude of the Faculty of Theology in Paris towards usury in the early sixteenth century, see James K. Farge, *Orthodoxy and Reform in Early Reformation France: The Faculty of Theology of Paris: 1500-1543* (Leiden: E. J. Brill, 1985), p. 121.

The language of moral philosophy is woven inextricably into economic terms which, in turn, are inseparable from both evangelical-humanist and scholastic doctrines on the problem of interest. The New Testament commonplaces are found in the exhortations to love one's enemies in Luke 6, and there is much commentary on Luke 6:35, "Date mutuum nihil inde sperantes."[34] In his *Paraphrases* Erasmus advises Christians not to hope even for the return of the loan.[35] The scholastics, while vigorous in their condemnation of usury, allow for various instances in which something in addition to the principal may be paid back to the lender.[36] The sixteenth century witnesses a gradual relaxation of the condemnation of usury, the most notable example of

---

[34] "Give a loan without hoping for anything from it." The Vulgate translation is, in fact, a distortion of the Greek, δανείζετε μηδὲν ἀπελπίζοντες (lend, not despairing in any way). The meaning of ἀπελπίζειν as "hope to receive back" is a hapax, and thus highly doubtful. Both Erasmus and Henri Estienne end up accepting the Latin version, however. See Erasmus's note to *nihil inde sperantes* in his *Novum Testamentum complectens . . . cum annotationibus* (*Opera omnia*, Loudun, P. Vander Aa, 1705, vol. 6, 256D), and Estienne's *Thesaurus linguae graecae* (rev. ed. Paris, Firmin Didot, 1831, vol. 1, part 2, 1265D).

[35] "Si mutuum dederitis his, à quibus speratis vos recepturos sortem, quid dignum facitis Evangelico vigore? ( . . . ) Non est purum officium, quod spe redituri officii confertur. Si tuam opem desiderat proximus, & petit mutuum, dato, etiamsi nulla spes sit reddendae pecuniae" (on Luke 6:34 in *Opera omnia*, vol. 7, 348A-B). On humanist attitudes towards commerce and wealth, see Winfried Trusen, "Handel und Reichtum: Humanistische Auffassungen auf dem Hintergrund vorangehender Lehren in Recht und Ethik," in ed. Heinrich Lutz, *Humanismus und Ökonomie* (Weinheim: Acta humaniora, 1983), pp. 87-103.

[36] See Johannes Altensteig, *Lexicon theologicum*, under "Usura" (pp. 597 ff.), who allows for *interesse* which is not excessive, and which is conceived of as payment for actual damages occurred to the lender because of the loan (*damnum emergens*) and for projected profit the lender would have made if he had not lent his money (*lucrum cessans*). See also the discussion in John T. Noonan, *The Scholastic Analysis of Usury* (Cambridge: Harvard Univ. Press, 1957), especially the summary, pp. 80-81.

which is the realistic approach of Charles Du Moulin.[37]   In general, however, there is still an opprobrium attached to the very notion of money that must be repaid in addition to the money lent.

In part, this opprobrium stems from the idea that interest comes out of *nothing*.  When Panurge, in order to justify his squandering of immense revenues of the domain of Salmigondin, praises debts, in Rabelais's *Tiers livre* (1546), he connects credit to the creating of something out of nothing.[38]   Perhaps Panurge's defense derives from Plutarch's essay, *De vitando aere alieno*, where he plays on the meanings of τόκος (an offspring, a child, or interest).  It is, however, just as likely that underlying this notion of credit and debt we find the scholastic conception of interest as *id quod non est*, as Aquinas formulates it, in responding to the question "Utrum accipere usuram pro pecunia mutuata sit peccatum," whether accepting usury for lent money is a sin: "Dicendum quod accipere usuram pro pecunia mutuata est secundum se iniustum, quia venditur id quod non est" (*Summa theologiae* II-2 qu 78 art 1 resp).[39]   Lending in the hope of receiving (excessive) interest, according to Aquinas, establishes inequality, since it does not generate revenue through an equal exchange of goods (ibid.). The implication is that interest as such is artificial, not inherent in the exchange, and that it involves something like a perverse fiction.  The other implication is that interest somehow exceeds things as they are in themselves, and as they are in relation to other things.  Interest is in relation to *nothing*, and partakes of the general condemnation of human creation *ex nihilo* that one finds in the medieval theological tradition.

---

[37] In his *Tractatus commerciorum et usurarum*, translated into French in 1547.  I have consulted his *Sommaire du livre analytique des Contrats, Usures, Rentes constituées, Interests, & Monnoyes* (Paris: Jean Houzé, 1586), where the discussion of Luke 6:35 is on f. 41v and ff.  Du Moulin allows lending with moderate interest to those who do not need the money, but wish to have it in order to "negocier ou acquerir & amplifier leur bien" (f. 34v).

[38] *Le tiers livre*, ed. M. A. Screech (Geneva: Droz, 1974), Chapter 3, p. 39.

[39] "It should be said that accepting usury for lent money is inherently unjust, because it is selling that which is not."

Interest also detracts from concentration on the person to whom one gives the loan, for one gives the loan not in order to do good to the person, but out of hope for money, *spe lucri*. In this sense a third term is introduced into the relationship, something exceeding the love of the other for his own sake, and ultimately displacing it. In the end this third term is only a love for oneself, for one's own gain, and involves a glorification of the self that is rejected, similarly to creation *ex nihilo*, in the theological tradition.[40] Interest, that which is the sale of what is not (*id quod non est*), is a perverse concentration on the self in all these ways.

The parallel to friendship seems clear: when relationships of friendship are submitted to ends outside of the love of the other for his own sake, then the perception is that the friendship is not perfect, but partakes of the general corruption of social relations. Submission to an end is, as I have suggested above, literally the death of friendship. Interest is precisely such an end, for it arises out of what is not, a sort of cancerous bloating that is conveyed by the parasitical profusion of writing evoked in Blaise de Vigenère's preface to his translations of the three friendship treatises. Perfect friendship resists that empty augmentation, the "lourde excessive masse." On the other hand, interest is also *motivation*, in the sense that it explains why, for example, one would help this person rather than that person, why one would be friends with some but not with others. In classical moral philosophy this question does not really arise, since friends are such because of their resemblance in enacting virtue. In the Renaissance, however, virtue seems to function less happily as a final cause, partly because it is a conceptually more natural move for some writers to separate the person

---

[40] The problem is especially acute when the creature loves God, for a love of God that is motivated purely by the hope for salvation is not good. The solution is that the love of God for himself must precede the hope for salvation. See Jacques Almain: "Actus spei est desiderium quo desideramus deum nobis vel passio causata ex illo desiderio: vel tale desiderium quo desiderio causatur ex amore dei: vel ex amore mei. Si primum: ergo actus charitatis est praevius ad actum spei. Si secundum: ergo iste actus videtur esse malus: quia amo deum propter me" (*Moralia acutissimi et clarissimi Doctoris theologi magistri Jacobi Almain: cum eiusdem Jacobi: et David Cranston Scoti additionibus*, Paris, Claude Chevallon, 1520, f. 51r). On this problem see also Aquinas, *Summa contra gentiles*, 3.153.2, where grace causes hope.

from his virtue, and thus to assimilate virtue to a property one may possess like wealth or beauty.[41]   Any teleology of relationships may then be felt to introduce a third term, that which is not, into that which just *is*.

## 3. Montaigne's Friendship: Sublime Inaccessibility

"La nostalgie est immotivée." - Vladimir Jankélévitch[42]

Montaigne reproduces many of the commonplaces that make up the often nostalgic rhetoric of friendship.[43]   True friendships are extremely rare, if there are any at all, for, as Diogenes Laertius quotes

---

[41] See on this problem the discussion of Antoine Hotman in Chapter II.

[42] "Nostalgia is unmotivated" (from *L'irréversible et la nostalgie*, Paris, Flammarion, 1974, p. 352).

[43] See the fine discussion in Barry L. Weller, "The Rhetoric of Friendship in Montaigne's *Essais*," *New Literary History* 9 (1977-1978): 503-523. See also Philippe Desan, *Les Commerces de Montaigne: le discours économique des 'Essais'* (Paris: Nizet, 1992), pp. 146-162, who correctly sees friendship as an attempt to reserve a space of human relations outside of economic exchange, and Ullrich Langer, *Divine and Poetic Freedom in the Renaissance: Nominalist Theology and Literature in France and Italy* (Princeton: Princeton Univ. Press, 1990), pp. 182-190, where the paradoxes of a sovereign self in friendship are explored.   Also Richard L. Regosin, *The Matter of My Book: Montaigne's 'Essais' as the Book of the Self* (Berkeley: Univ. of California Press, 1977), pp. 9-20, and Floyd Gray, "Montaigne's Friends," *French Studies* 15 (1961): 203-217.   A good discussion of Montaigne's refusal of the discourse of virtue in the friendship essay can be found in Elisabeth Caron, *Les 'Essais' de Montaigne ou les échos satiriques de l'humanisme* (Montreal: Editions CERES, 1993), pp. 149-159.   Finally, on the differences that separate Montaigne's feeling of friendship from certain medieval conceptions of friendship, see the insightful comments by Brian Patrick McGuire, *Friendship & Community: The Monastic Experience 350-1250* (Kalamazoo, MI: Cistercian Publications, 1988), pp. 423-425.

Aristotle as saying (*Lives*, 5.21), and whose saying Montaigne reiterates in his own version, filtered through the Latin translation of Diogenes, "O mes amis, il n'y a nul amy" (meaning "Oh, my friends, there is no *real* friend") (*Essais*, 1.28, p. 190). In his essay "De trois commerces," the three sorts of relationships being with other men, women, and books, Montaigne prefers the latter, for sexual relationships decline with age, and friendship with men "est ennuyeux par sa rareté" (3.3, p. 827).[44] The infrequency of true friendship is tied to a sense of the passage of time, in personal and historical terms. For Montaigne's true friend is dead, and their relationship belongs to the domain of the past.[45] Even while Etienne de la Boétie was still alive, their friendship was marked by the nearness of the end, by a sense of lateness, "ayant si peu à durer, et ayant si tard commencé" (p. 188).[46] But this same sense of anachronism provides a sort of perfection, for, having begun so late, their friendship could avoid imitating other, looser friendships, and be more of its *own*: "elle n'avoit point à perdre temps, et à se regler au patron des amitiez molles et regulieres" (pp. 188-189).[47] On the other hand, when Montaigne *writes* about his relationship, he reflects on his own friendship through the reading of the Ancients (Cicero, Aristotle, Lucian, Plutarch). His friendship with La Boétie has as its "patrons" (models) not contemporary examples, but classical moral philosophers and their examples. These philosophers do not fully account for his own friendship (in much the same way as Plato and Aristotle did not account

---

[44] Like Aquinas, however, Montaigne praises conjugal relationships that are based on friendship rather than love, and even uses the famous adages *homo homini deus* and *homo homini lupus* (3.5, p. 852).

[45] See Weller, "The Rhetoric of Friendship," pp. 504-505: "When one writes of his friends, they are already as though dead, and language is the cenotaph by which they are remembered." Weller traces this sense of distance and absence to Petrarch, who "made friendship seem like a far country, a province of antiquity, from which he and his contemporaries would remain forever in exile" (p. 504).

[46] "Having so little time to last, having started so late."

[47] "It did not have any time to lose, and fashion itself on the model of soft and regular friendships."

for the existence of the New World): "les discours mesmes que l'antiquité nous a laissés sur ce subject, me semblent láches au pris du sentiment que j'en ay" (p. 192).[48] This anachronistic friendship has been able to capture a purity, an originality which its belatedness seemed to deny to it; it has resisted general decay and imitative hypertrophy so effectively evoked by Blaise de Vigenère and, in other essays, by Montaigne himself.

How can I express the "sentiment que j'en ay," that feeling that the friendship is true and that it is singular, my own? The very formulation establishes a perspective on the relationship that is always ultimately subjective. For the identification of the relationship becomes the identification of a *feeling* or personal notion, and not, for example, the identification of a series of actions by which the friends have demonstrated their friendship, in the manner of the friends in Lucian's *Toxaris*, or in the examples cited by Cicero. Even if society and history should provide points of comparison to his friendship, Montaigne as it were reserves the right to assent to or reject those comparisons.[49] Perfection is not thought of in terms of the virtuous choices enacted by the friends, and thus cannot be measured from the outside, but is irreducibly private.[50] Which does not, however, mean that Montaigne

---

[48] "Even the writings that antiquity has left us on that subject seem weak in comparison to my feeling."

[49] The passing of ethical relationships through the "assent" of subjectivity in the ethics of Renaissance humanism is discussed by Nancy S. Struever, *Theory As Practice: Ethical Inquiry in the Renaissance* (Chicago: University of Chicago Press, 1992). She uses Paul Ricoeur's distinction between *doxa* (opinion), *foi* (Christian faith), and *assentiment* (Cartesian assent), and makes Montaigne into a forerunner of such assent. For Montaigne, "[b]elief as *assentiment* is radically internalized, closely held; no one assents for you" (p. 183). I find the "communal certification" of belief that saves the subject from solipsism slightly more problematic than Struever allows.

[50] As Hugo Friedrich saw well, in *Montaigne* (trans. Berkeley: Univ. of California Press, 1991), pp. 244-245. See, following Friedrich, Timothy J. Reiss, "Montaigne and the Subject of Polity," in *Literary Theory / Renaissance Texts*, eds. Patricia Parker, David Quint (Baltimore: Johns Hopkins University Press, 1986), pp. 115-149. On this point I disagree with Eric MacPhail,

deprives this relationship of all social significance. Montaigne refers once again to Aristotle in assigning social benefit to friendship, as the culmination of the social bind to which nature impels us ("Or le dernier point de sa perfection [de la société] est cetuy-ci [l'amitié]," 1.28, p. 184).[51] But the articulation of the inner "sentiment" of friendship with the life of social activity is unclear.

Montaigne does, nevertheless, attempt to express this friendship; much of the essay is devoted to rejecting traditional forms of friendships as models, in order to arrive at a faithful representation of his own friendship.[52] He reviews different sorts of friendship ties consecrated by moral philosophy - "naturelle, sociale, hospitaliere, venerienne," the ties of nature, of society, the tie of hospitality (which in fact is not discussed in this essay), and erotic desire - and finds that these friendships "meslent autre cause et but et fruit en l'amitié, qu'elle mesme" (p. 184).[53] Montaigne's own friendship with La Boétie was a relationship "sans mélange": *propter se*, as classical moral philosophy and its Christian versions would say. Friendship must, we have seen, radically resist *interest*; friendship must avoid the supposition of any efficient or final cause and avoid the appearance of an effect ("cause et but et fruit") foreign to the relationship itself. But what is the relationship "in itself," especially when one wants to represent it to others? When it is no longer a matter of relating examples of virtuous behavior towards each other and in the civic realm, but when representation involves the transmission of a "sentiment," the solution is not obvious. Representing a relationship is making it understood, which, in turn, often implies some sort of a teleology, motivation, interest.

---

"Friendship as a Political Ideal in Montaigne's *Essais*," *Montaigne Studies* 1 (1989): 177-187.

[51] "The ultimate point of the perfection of society is friendship."

[52] Again, the similarity to his utopian description of the New World is evident. See 1,31 ("Des cannibales"), the initial consideration of possible Ancient awareness of America, and the celebrated passage referring to Plato's *Laws*, where the New World is described in the traditionally utopian, negative way (pp. 206-207).

[53] "Mix in a cause and goal and product different from friendship itself."

This is particularly true of a period when a-teleological writing, one that does not involve moral, esthetic, religious persuasive ends, is quite rare. In other words, the question "what feeling or notion do I have" is practically inseparable from the question "why, or for what purpose, do I have this feeling."

In fact, one could perhaps only point to Montaigne as someone who on occasion seems to propose such un-motivated, a-teleological writing. In "De trois commerces," having preferred books to people, the essayist suggests that his activities have no extension or imperative for anyone else, no purpose outside of themselves:

> Je vis du jour à la journée; et, parlant en reverence, ne vis que pour moy: mes desseins se terminent là. J'estudiay, jeune, pour l'ostentation; depuis, un peu, pour m'assagir; à cette heure, pour m'esbatre; jamais pour le quest. (3.3, p. 829)[54]

The lack of "quest" of Montaigne's studies can be understood primarily as a lack of monetary interest, but it can be understood more broadly, as well, as a lack of goals. Reading is not directed towards an end outside of itself, it is precisely not "desire" of something else. It is done "pour m'esbatre," in order to amuse myself. Having only oneself as a goal comes close to having no goal whatsoever, at least when Montaigne is read by anyone other than himself. Thus, when in his final essay, "De l'expérience" (3.13), Montaigne writes about his petty likes and dislikes, his kidney stone, his preference for melons over salads, etc., his writing appears to be entirely removed from esthetic, moral, religious aims outside of himself, even if many of his statements are in agreement with contemporary "régimes de vivre."[55] Supposing only a private end to this writing seems indistinguishable from supposing no end at all. In

---

[54] "I live from day to day; and, speaking carefully, I live only for myself: my intentions finish there. When I was young I studied for show; then, a bit, in order to become wiser; now, in order to have fun; never for any gain."

[55] See on this point Jean Céard, "La culture du corps: Montaigne et la diététique de son temps," in eds. Marcel Tetel, G. Mallary Masters, *Le parcours des Essais: Montaigne 1588-1988* (Paris: Aux amateurs de livres, 1989), pp. 83-96.

this sense, "autotelic" (self-directed) writing and "a-teleological" (non-directed) writing cannot be easily distinguished.

Montaigne more or less says so himself, in his little preface "au lecteur" to the readers of his *Essais* in 1580: "je ne m'y suis proposé *aucune fin*, que domestique et privée."[56] This radically modest, private writing will not, or should not, be *read*: "ce n'est pas raison que tu [the reader] employes ton loisir en un subject si frivole et vain" (ibid.).[57] There is no *raison*, no reason, purpose, why a reader would read Montaigne (i.e., his writing is a-teleological), which is the same thing as saying that the essayist's "goal" is utterly private, i.e., autotelic. When Montaigne attempts to define the "sentiment" which indicated a perfect friendship, in a sense much of the project underlying the *Essais* is involved in that definition. Above all, a love motivated only by itself, and only by the other for his own sake, implies a writing that consistently must refuse subordination to an end other than itself.

The essay is, however, "On Friendship," and the friendship between Montaigne and La Boétie demands to be represented, communicated, understood: "Si on me presse de dire pourquoy je l'aymois, je sens que cela ne se peut exprimer, qu'en respondant: Par ce que c'estoit luy; par ce que c'estoit moy" (p. 188).[58] The question asked of Montaigne is not "what did you feel?" but "*why* did you love him?" As soon as others are envisaged, Montaigne imagines them to be asking for the reason, purpose, or end of the friendship; in other words, everyone other than Montaigne and La Boétie is submitted to interest and purpose. Their friendship is by the very nature of the question put to it anachronistic, singular in respect to "interested" contemporaries, and singular in respect to the more practice-oriented Ancients.

---

[56] "I have proposed to myself no goal except a domestic and private one," p. 3, my italics. In 1580, it is "nulle fin" rather than "aucune fin." On the possible rhetorical and legal contextual senses of "avertissement" and "fin" here, see Michel Simonin, "*Rhetorica ad lectorem*: lecture de l'avertissement des *Essais*," *Montaigne Studies* 1 (1989): 61-72, and especially 64-65.

[57] "This is no reason for you to use your leisure on such a frivolous and vain subect."

[58] "If one pressures me to say why I loved him, I feel that that cannot be expressed, except in saying: because it was he, because it was I."

The brilliant and "sublime" response of Montaigne, "Par ce que c'estoit luy; par ce que c'estoit moy," literalizes the classical *propter seipsum*, καθ᾽ αὐτόν, of perfect friendship, and introduces, in the symmetry of its formulation, an echo of charity's *sicut teipsum*, as you [love] yourself. The response also refuses the final cause, purpose, that the question implied.[59] For Montaigne's formulation, in the last version of the text, consists in a semantic repetition: in respect to the question posed no new information is introduced (I loved him because I loved *him*, and *I* loved him), and the response repeats itself in its two parts while exchanging pronouns. This repetition, while it is a figure of the *consensio* of Cicero's friendship (*De amicitia*, 6.20), also avoids any semantic *augmentation* and thus avoids interest and finality. There is nothing else, no purpose, no usefulness, there is *only* he and I. The language of Montaigne's response is a perfect incarnation of the singularity, and the a-teleological nature, of his friendship with La Boétie.

Montaigne's formulation is semantically "poor," and yet it transmits the gratuitousness and force of "le sentiment que j'en ay" to the reader by its very semantic poverty, and by the play on reference, first to *him*, then to *me*. The language opens up to the real person "for his own sake," that is, without ascribing attributes to him, without

---

[59] This aspect of Montaigne's views on friendship was somewhat imperfectly understood by his assiduous reader (and imitator) Pierre Charron. Systematizing the essay and vaguely inspired by Cicero and Aristotle, Charron writes on the one hand that "Qui ayme pour la vertu ne se lasse point d'aymer" and indicates this kind of friendship as the noblest and strongest; on the other hand, he reproduces Montaigne's understanding of obligation as a sort of limit to free choice, and praises friendship's complete voluntariness: "ou elle [l'amitié] est libre et volontaire comme entre compagnons et amis, qui ne se touchent et tiennent de rien que de la seule amitié: et cette est proprement et vrayement amitié" (*De la sagesse*, 3.7, 2nd ed. 1604 [1st ed. 1601], repr. Paris, Fayard, 1986, pp. 638-639). Montaigne says little or nothing about the first condition (of virtue) which may very well constitute for him a sort of moral limitation on the personal "sentiment." On Montaigne's difference here vis-à-vis Aristotle's concept of friendship, see some insightful remarks in Lambros Couloubaritsis, "L'amitié selon Montaigne et les philosophes grecs," in ed. Kyriaki Christodoulou, *Montaigne et la Grèce* (Paris: Aux amateurs de livres, 1990), pp. 164-178, and especially p. 175-176.

describing him. For, the implication seems to be, if attributes were involved, the "person" himself would escape. It is by referring, not by signifying, that we capture the real; yet, in turn, the very act of referring makes the real into something not recuperable by signification.[60]

The disjoining of the real *propter se*, as such and for itself, and meaning as semantic, teleological description carries with it the risk of unintelligibility to anyone except the speaker or writer. Montaigne refers not to a person standing in front of us readers, but to a dead person. The openness to the real "as such" is fundamentally without information about the real, although it conveys the "sentiment" which the real has provoked in the writer. It is extremely difficult to distinguish between, on the one hand, the refusal to impose teleology onto what is conceived of as prior to teleology, as "other," and, on the other hand, the idolization of the self, which is the source and speaker of the "other" to which it has bound itself in perfect friendship.[61] In other words, total respect for the other may mean total absorption of the other into oneself. Montaigne has reduced, or elevated, the combination of two wills without "couture" to its *degré zéro*. But in so doing, he has compromised irredeemably the classical connection between the virtuous consensus of wills and exemplary social activity, and he has made the entire abandonment to the other person identical, from the outside, to a complete self-absorption.

The alexandrine "Par ce que c'estoit luy; par ce que c'estoit moi" places the paratactic relationship that is perfect friendship at the heart, at the caesura, of the sentence. The two equal members of the line are arrayed one to the other so that their unmediated juxtaposition may dominate their hypotactic beginnings, in a way reminiscent of the examples of "ravishing" poetic language given in the pseudo-Longinian

---

[60] See Regosin, *The Matter of My Book*, p. 28: "A fundamental characteristic of the perfect union of friendship is that it is most profoundly a prelinguistic or extralinguistic phenomenon." This is true not of *all* "perfect" friendship, but of Montaigne's. Although Regosin conflates the semantic and the linguistic, his intuition seems right. See also Weller, "The Rhetoric of Friendship," pp. 514-515.

[61] We are reminded of Kierkegaard's condemnation of *philia* as the incarnation of self-love. See Chapter II.

*Peri hupsous*, which Boileau will translate in 1674 as the *Traité du sublime*.[62]

The caesura of Montaigne's phrase marks several overlapping moments: the point of contact between himself, in himself, and myself, in myself; but also a rejection of the subordination or hypotaxis that the anaphoric beginnings of the members of the alexandrine put forth; furthermore the rejection of any *expressed* conjunction, just a pure apposition, a pure positioning in space. The repetition is also, as it were, a paradoxical rejection of time: the reading of the sentence is always, necessarily, an unfolding of meaning, an accumulation of meaning, and thus open to the impure that time may bring, but in the case of this *allongeail* the repetition creates the illusion of starting the same thing *again*, such that the fact that one half of the alexandrine comes after the other half seems occulted. When Boileau translates Longinus' evocation of Sappho's "sublimity," he also uses an alexandrine: "Elle gèle; elle brûle; elle est folle; elle est sage" contains a similar effect of simultaneity.[63]   Whereas Boileau's version of Longinus' line communicates not only the effect of what is felt, but also *what* is felt, in Montaigne's case the lexical and semantic poverty of his sentence is striking. Content is reduced to the bare minimum; the fact of parataxis, the fact of deixis, the fact of reference: that is about it.[64]

---

[62] See the illuminating study by Philip Lewis, "L'anti-sublime, ou la rhétorique du progrès," in *Rhétoriques fin de siècle*, pp. 117-145.   Lewis usefully contrasts the extra-rhetorical immediacy of the concept of the sublime in Boileau with a progressive, rhetorical notion found in Perrault's description of the sublime style.

[63] Nicolas Boileau, *Traité du sublime*, in *Oeuvres complètes*, eds. Antoine Adam, Françoise Escal (Paris: Gallimard, 1966), chap. 8, p. 357. See Lewis, "L'anti-sublime," p. 123.

[64] Montaigne's momentary refusal of discursivity is also the reduction of rhetoric to an evocation of the absolutely singular, and as such perfectly general. Nothing in the sentence distinguishes the *luy* or the *moy* from any other person enunciating the sentence.   This is what Louis Marin has pointed out lucidly in his analysis of Pascal's *Art de persuader*: "en fin de ce compte infini, ce singulier dans sa dernière différence, "celui-ci" dans "cet instant" et dans "ce lieu-ci," est parfaitement indifférent, indiscernable de tous les autres" (in "Une

Montaigne's sublime reduction of friendship discourse operates, as we have seen, on the background of what is felt by contemporaries to be the bloated efflorescence of interested relationships, similarly to what Longinus deplores in the last extant chapter of the treatise.[65]

Montaigne goes on to describe the "force inexplicable et fatale" (p. 188) of his union with La Boétie, and the way in which this force caused them to lose all sense of self, and all sense of what belonged to one or the other: "Je dis perdre [notre volonté], à la verité, ne nous reservant rien qui nous fut propre, ny qui fut ou sien ou mien" (p. 189).[66] The abolition of difference between the two friends leads to an abolition of that which characterizes the corruption and interest of the world around them, the *sien* and *mien*, the *mio* and *tuo* of Boccalini's and so many other writers' despairing satire. At the same time the Attic and apodictic formulations contrast with the prolixity of, say, a Blaise de Vigenère evoking the hypertrophic decay of writing, and the excess of commentaries and glosses criticized by the Montaigne of the third book.

Montaigne's language also comes close to what can be called "mystic" speech, a paradoxical renunciation of subjective modifying or representing in an attempt to convey the power of what simply *is*, what

---

rhétorique 'fin de siècle': Pascal: *De l'art de persuader* (1657-1658?)," in *Rhétoriques fin de siècle*, p. 95). Montaigne, however, in the pride of modesty that Pascal so detested, refuses in this instance to make the next move, and to see that absolute indifference as the ever-present ground of all rhetoric. It still is possible for Montaigne, at some moments at least, to be distinctly private and domestic.

[65] In Boileau's translation, Longinus deplores "ce temps où la corruption regne sur les moeurs et sur les esprits de tous les hommes" (*Traité du sublime*, p. 401): "Comment, dis-je, se pourroit-il faire que dans cette contagion generale il se trouvast un homme sain de jugement, et libre de passion; qui n'estant point aveuglé ni seduit par l'amour du gain, pût discerner ce qui est veritablement grand et digne de la posterité?" (pp. 401-402). The sublime acquires a force that is all the more marked as it contrasts with present "decay."

[66] "I say lose our will, in truth, reserving nothing of our own, nothing that was his or mine."

is absolutely beyond one's rational efforts.[67]   In spite of occasional references, and an important concession to mystical theology in the "Apologie de Raimond Sebond" (2.12),[68] Montaigne's project seems, however, profoundly alien to the claims and effects of ecstatic theology. The essayist is in general deeply committed to discursive communication and deeply suspicious of ecstasies of any kind.  Just before the end of the last essay, Montaigne evokes Socrates one last time, a Socrates whom he has praised almost without exception in the essays: "Ces humeurs transcendentes m'effrayent, comme les lieux hautains et inaccessibles; et rien ne m'est à digerer fascheux en la vie de Socrates que ses ecstases et ses demoneries" (3.13, p. 1115).[69]  Montaigne's own "ecstatic" evocation of La Boétie seems less tied to a conscious mystical inspiration but instead, as I have suggested, to a complex ethical attitude.

For the inexplicability of true friendship partakes of a nostalgic attitude which equates motivation and explanation with economic interest.  It also sets up the person to be loved in his otherness as ultimately distinct from the choices the person makes, the attributes he possesses.  I have argued at the beginning of this book that this emphasis in some early modern writers is something different from friendship

---

[67] See Michel de Certeau, "L'énonciation mystique," *Recherches de science religieuse* 64, 2 (1976): 183-215; Gérard Defaux, "Montaigne et la rhétorique de l'indicible: l'exemple 'De la tristesse' (I,2)," *Bibliothèque d'Humanisme et Renaissance* 55 (1993): 5-24.  See, for a contemporary example, the life of Saint Teresa of Avila (first available in its complete form in 1565), especially the beginning of Chapter 10.

[68] See Jan Miernowski, "The Law of Non-Contradiction and French Renaissance Literature: Skepticism and Negative Theology," *South Central Review* 10, no. 2 (1993): 49-66.

[69] "These transcendent moods scare me, as do elevated and inaccessible places, and nothing is more difficult for me to digest in the life of Socrates than his ecstasies and daimonic episodes."

"theory" as it is inherited from classical moral philosophy and from the intermittent parallels with Christian charity.[70]

Montaigne's "sublime" response finds a textual echo in the preface to the 1595 edition of his essays composed by his "fille d'alliance" Marie de Gournay. She laments the absent friend in much the same way that Montaigne had lamented the absence of La Boétie.[71] Her preface develops commonplace rhetoric on friendship (especially the friend as another self), and she imagines, as Montaigne did, the question of friendship's *motivation*:

> Ils demandent où est la raison: la raison mesme c'est aymer en ces amitiez. On ne plaint pas ce mal-heur qui veut; car voicy le seul mot du contract au marché de l'amitié perfaicte: Toy et moy nous rendons l'un à l'autre, par ce que nous ne sçaurions si bien rencontrer ailleurs.[72]

Gournay has reformulated Cicero's *omnis eius fructus in ipso amore inest*, the entire profit (or return) is in the love itself (*De amicitia*, 9.31), as "la raison mesme c'est aymer." In Cicero the choice of wording seems to emphasize the economic or legal connotations: *fructus* in Roman law has a primarily agricultural sense, as "fruits of a piece of land (*fundus*)" (see *Institutes* 2.1.35-37), but can also mean more generally the return on property (*Inst* 4.17.2-4). *Fructus* is normally opposed to *res ipsa*, the thing or property itself (*Inst* 4.17.2); Cicero's sequence *fructus - in ipso amore* announces the formulation in Justinian's

---

[70] See Chapter II and the discussion of the enactment of virtue as an integral part of what the person as such is felt to be, in classical ethics.

[71] See François Rigolot, "L'amitié intertextuelle: Etienne de la Boétie et Marie de Gournay," in *L'esprit et la lettre: Mélanges offerts à Jules Brody*, ed. Louis van Delft (Tübingen: Gunter Narr, 1991), pp. 57-68.

[72] "They ask where the reason [for our friendship] is: the reason itself is to love in these friendships. Not anyone can complain about this misfortune; for here is the only word of perfect friendship's contract: You and I give ourselves to each other because we could not 'find as well' elsewhere." From "Marie de Gournay: Préface à l'édition des *Essais* de Montaigne," ed. François Rigolot, in *Montaigne Studies* 1 (1989), pp. 51-52.

laws. *Fructus* has become in Gournay's formulation a somewhat larger term, echoing Montaigne's "pourquoy je l'aymois." The term "raison" focuses more on the *motivation*, the final cause of the relationship. Gournay's "raison," though, also has economic and legal meanings, more so than Montaigne's phrase. "Raison," from the Latin *ratio*, can mean a financial "accounting," an "account," and then metaphorically an "explanation." The economic and legal subtexts are rendered entirely explicit in what follows: "le seul mot du contract au marché de l'amitié perfaicte." Gournay seems to have reconnected "perfect" friendship to the notion of economic exchange and augmentation. The difference, though, is the extreme brevity of such a contract, and its elliptical nature: *what* is exchanged is not really clear, it is just clear that the two friends would not have been able to "si bien rencontrer," to find as well, to meet as well, to do as well, elsewhere. What is this "si bien"? That question is never answered, and it escapes, in this rhetoric of friendship, the impingement of "reasons." Marie de Gournay's version of perfect friendship hovers, then, perilously close to the economic exchange the nostalgic rhetoric of friendship abhors, but is able to short-circuit it after all.

## 4. The Princess's Inexplicable Choice

Montaigne's sublime response will find another remarkable echo in the masterpiece of the seventeenth-century novel, the *Princesse de Clèves*. Although the rhetoric of the inexplicable, and the apodictic, has decidedly different connotations and perhaps filiations in the century following Montaigne's time, the motivation of friendship tends in Madame de Lafayette's novel to return to similar semantic constellations.

Perhaps this is because the demonstrations of nostalgia and disgust at the present-day world we find in Montaigne's time, themselves often derived from classical sources, seem like a permanent part of culture, a sort of corner of the house of commonplaces whose arguments and embellishments may be used by any writer at any time. Friendship is one of those commonplaces, but it has taken a sort of "inner" turn after Montaigne, after the essayist's insistence on the *sentiment que j'en ay*. In Madeleine de Scudéry's *Clelie, Histoire romaine* (published from 1654 on), we find an extended discussion of *amitié*; one of the questions discussed is "si les bien-faits faisoient plustost naistre l'amitié, que l'amitié mesme, ou que le grand merite sans bien-faits."[73]  Whereas the framework of the discussion of the *beneficium* seems classical, even Senecan, the substance shows that friendship here is not conceived as a voluntary choice of a virtuous friend, but touches on areas within oneself over which one is not "master" (p. 363).  The character Zenocrate distinguishes between gratitude (caused by favors) and friendship:

> Car enfin l'amitié & la reconnoissance sont deux choses differentes, ainsi je suis persuadé que l'on doit avoir de la reconnoissance pour tous ceux de qui on reçoit des bien-faits, & de l'amitié seulement pour ceux qui touchent nostre coeur, ou par leur merite, ou par leur amitié ou par nostre inclination. (p. 362)[74]

In other words, a completely internalized sort of friendship is possible, one that arises out of "inclination," out of our heart: this inner sentiment is theoretically disconnected from virtue or merit, and is thus inaccessible to the calculus of moral ends.  Scudéry's definition is taken up later in her *Morale du monde*, where "Antenor" proclaims: "L'amitié parfaite . . . est naturelle, sa source doit estre dans le coeur, elle doit estre sans interest, unir parfaitement, & durer toujours."[75]

In Madame de Lafayette's *La Princesse de Clèves* (1678), we find a supreme example, an example beyond any *exemplum*, of perfect friendship.  The friendship is, however, not mutual, and the perfection

---

[73] "Whether favors caused friendship to be born, rather than friendship itself, or great merit without favors." [Madeleine de Scudéry,] *Clelie, Histoire romaine*, part 5, book 1 (Paris: Augustin Courbé; Amsterdam: Jean Blaev, 1660), p. 360.

[74] "For finally friendship and gratitude are two different things; so I am persuaded that one must be grateful to all those from whom one receives favors, and friendship only for those who touch our heart, whether by their merit, by their friendship, or by our inclination."

[75] "Perfect friendship is natural, its source must be in the heart, it must be without interest, unite perfectly, and last forever." Madeleine de Scudéry, *La Morale du monde, ou conversations* (Amsterdam: Pierre Mortier, 1686), p. 170. The "Histoire et conversation d'amitié" is found on pp. 156-218.

of the *sentiment* is in the end solipsistic, and anachronistic. The novel is a sort of reaching-back to an earlier historical state, and within that state, to an earlier personal moral state. The action takes place not in the reign of Louis XIV but during that of Henri II. The political event at the center of the novel is the death of the king at a jousting tournament, and everything changes after his death ("Enfin, la cour changea entierement de face."[76] The novel is less interested in "epochal" changes than in changes in the personal composition of the court, but there is a sense of a more general decline, after the death of the chivalric king, the disfavor of his flamboyant mistress, and the new dominance of a queen known for her cleverness and secrecy. The first words of the novel indicate the shadow of the king's impending death, and the autumnal splendor of his court: "La magnificence et la galanterie n'ont jamais paru en France avec tant d'éclat que dans les dernières années du règne de Henry second," (p. 1107).[77] Already in the seventeenth century a slightly mean-spirited critic, Valincour, noted that the way in which Madame de Lafayette formulates the magnificence of the court leads one to believe that the court of Louis XIV was inferior to that of Henri II.[78] This unequalled splendor is found in the *last* years of the reign, just as the unequalled friendship between Montaigne and La Boétie was to flourish so briefly ("ayant si peu à durer," *Essais*, p. 188). The sense of the inimitable and the final, the closing of an era and a life, is found in the last words of the novel, when the still young Madame de Clèves has decided to retire from the court: "sa vie, *qui fut assez courte*, laissa des exemples de vertu *inimitables*" (p. 1254, my italics).[79] The radical perfection of the princess's virtue is inseparable from its strangeness or its anachronism in relation to a court dominated by feverish activity and all-powerful interests. The last sentence contains

---

[76] "Finally, the court's appearance changed completely." Ed. Antoine Adam, *Romanciers du XVIIe siècle* (Paris: Gallimard, 1958), "Bibliothèque de la Pléiade," p. 1219.

[77] "Magnificence and galantry have never appeared in France with as much splendor as in the last years of the reign of Henry II."

[78] See Adam's note 1 to p. 1107 (p. 1471).

[79] "Her life, which was quite short, left inimitable examples of virtue."

a curious oxymoron, "inimitable examples"; the life of Madame de Clèves is an example taken from a different world, and is therefore no longer imitable by the present one. The "inimitable example" is not an example, for it is a model without being a model to be followed.[80]  In part, the "example" of the princess cannot be followed because the court is no longer capable of understanding her relationship with her husband; in part, the representation itself of her relationship seems to preclude its imitation.

The world of *La Princesse de Clèves* is imbued with a double nostalgia, then: the court of Henri II was inimitable, and, within this splendid court *already*, the virtue of the princess was inimitable. It is as if the nostalgic vision comprised a mechanism of infinite regression, as if the tendency toward the superlative in Madame de Lafayette's epideictic rhetoric made the present necessarily a spectacle of decline. The anachronistic virtue of Madame de Clèves, is all the more salient as it is seen against the background of the court in the novel itself. Even if France of 1678 can hardly be compared to the political climate of Montaigne's time, the description of the court we find in Madame de Lafayette's novel participates in the rhetoric of interest whose avatars we have seen among the translators of Cicero, and in the critique of "mixed" friendships that sets up perfect friendship in the famous essay of Montaigne. The dominance of interest, itself a commonplace in court and anti-court literature throughout the fifteenth and sixteenth centuries, is evoked brilliantly:

> L'ambition et la galanterie étoient l'âme de cette cour, et occupoient les hommes et les femmes. Il y avoit tant d'intérests et tant de cabales différentes, et les dames y avoient tant de part que l'Amour estoit toujours meslé aux affaires et les affaires à l'Amour.  Personne n'estoit tranquille, ni indifférent; on songeoit à s'élever, à plaire, à servir ou à nuire; on ne connaissoit ni l'ennui, ni l'oisiveté, et on estoit toujours occupé des plaisirs ou des intrigues. ( . . . ) Les intérests de grandeur et d'élévation se trouvoient souvent joints à ces autres intérests

---

[80] On the interpretation of the beginning and ending lines, and a definition of the example and its subversion by Madame de Lafayette, see John D. Lyons, *Exemplum: The Rhetoric of Example in Early Modern France and Italy* (Princeton: Princeton Univ. Press, 1989), pp. 3-20, 196-200, 217-236.

> moins importans, mais qui n'étoient pas moins sensibles. Ainsi
> il y avoit une sorte d'agitation sans désordre dans cette cour
> . . . (p. 1118).[81]

These sentences convey perfectly the febrile "agitation" of the court: the
chiasmus "Amour . . . meslé aux affaires et les affaires à l'amour"
renders indistinguishable interest and feeling. The series of infinitives
"à s'élever, à plaire, à servir ou à nuire" expresses at the same time
continuous activity, which is somehow deprived of value, and the
substitutable nature of these actions. To render someone a favor, or to
do someone a disfavor, are more or less the same, part of the to and fro
of the court. All actions are assimilated to each other under the pressure
of interest. So the splendor of the court has an empty, yet hypertrophic
side to it; it is against the relief of this always impure agitation that the
unique, inimitable relationship between the princess and her husband
places itself.

    This relationship is perhaps only imperfectly expressed in the
seventeenth-century language of love. As is the case in the preceding
century, the words "amitié" and "ami" are used in diverse senses, and
are an imperfect guide to male-female relationships, especially since the
introduction of the "amitié tendre" blurred the line between voluntary
friendship and a sentimental, affectionate inclination close to love.[82] At
most one could associate "amour d'estime" (love born out of admiration

---

[81] "Ambition and amourous affairs were the soul of this court, and occupied
men and women alike. There were so many interests and different cabals, and
women were so much involved that love was always mixed with political
dealings and political dealings with love. No one was calm or indifferent; one
planned to climb, to please, to serve or to damage; one knew neither boredom
nor idleness, one was always occupied with pleasures or intrigues. ( . . . ) the
interests of success and promotion were often linked to these other interests
which were less important but no less felt. So there was a sort of agitation
without disorder at this court. . . . "

[82] See Scudéry, *La Morale du monde*, p. 174: "Je vous renvoye . . . à une
Conversation de Clelie, ou l'amitié tendre est representée d'une maniere qu'on
ne connoissoit pas auparavant; car par la vertu qui l'accompagne elle est amitié
toute pure, mais par la tendresse qui la suit toujours elle ressemble fort à une
amour sans foiblesse."

or respect) and virtuous friendship in classical moral philosophy. This association seems justified when the princess scandalously confesses to her husband that she has good reasons to want to leave the court, implying that she loves another man: "Songez que pour faire ce que je fais, il faut avoir plus d'amitié et plus d'estime pour un mari que l'on n'en a jamais eu" (p. 1194).[83] "Amitié" seems here synonymous with "affection," "sympathy," and it is used in apposition with "estime," implying that it is without hope of material gain or physical pleasure. When Monsieur de Clèves falls seriously ill and his wife shows her deep affliction at his illness, the word "amitié" appears again: her lover Monsieur de Nemours despairs at this show of conjugal affection, for "il jugeoit aisément combien cette affliction renouvelloit l'amitié qu'elle avoit pour M. de Clèves, et combien cette amitié faisoit une diversion dangereuse à la passion qu'elle avoit dans le coeur" (p. 1234).[84] It is friendship indeed which opposes itself to dangerous passion, and which provokes the confession of the princess, in a gesture of honesty that recalls the union of individual wills and the lack of secrets characteristic of true friends.[85] At the same time Madame de Clèves's confession is

---

[83] "Remember that in order to do what I am doing, one needs more love and esteem for a husband than one has ever had."

[84] "He judged easily how much his affliction renewed the friendship that she had for M. de Clèves, and how much this friendship was a dangerous diversion from the passion she had in her heart." In a note to this passage Antoine Adam remarks with lucidity that one must understand "amitié" here in the sense of "friendship" current in the sixteenth and seventeenth centuries, which is not based on the presence of desire (p. 1492).

[85] In a different context, echoing Seneca, Montaigne remarks: "L'unique et principale amitié descoust toutes autres obligations. Le secret que j'ay juré ne deceller à nul autre, je le puis, sans parjure, communiquer à celuy qui n'est pas autre: c'est moy" (1.28, p. 191). The inability of men to treat women as true friends is demonstrated by the fact that they cannot be completely honest to women, according to Moderata Fonte (Modesta Pozzo di Zorzi): "non essendo veri amici essi [men], non sanno ne anco trattar gli altri da tali: che in vero l'huomo, che sia vero amico d'un altro, deve proceder seco con ogni libertà, e senza alcun'arte, ne rispetto, ne altra inchietta, ne altro fine non altramente trattandolo, che si faccia il fratello, il padre, o 'l figluolo, cioè con quella maniera, e licenza di viver, di praticar, e di comandarle anco con baldanza

a "favor," a *beneficium*, to her friend and husband: she attempts to deliver herself from a violent passion that threatens to destroy her relationship to her husband, by demonstrating once and for all her faithfulness to him.

Tragically, her friendship is one-sided. When Monsieur de Clèves her conjugal "friend," who is in fact violently in love with her, understands the reasons for her reluctance to follow the activities and obligations of the court, he is literally mortally wounded. The *beneficium* of Madame de Clèves, the gift of her honesty to her husband, has the most tragic consequences precisely because he can only suppose an *interest*, a *motivation*, underlying her action. When he has Monsieur de Nemours followed and it appears that he has spent a night with his wife at Coulommiers, her honesty appears to fit a dark pattern, an interest. This interest is, he implies, to cause his death:

> Vous versez bien des pleurs, madame, luy dist-il, pour une mort que vous causez et qui ne vous peut donner la douleur que vous faites paroistre. ( . . . ) Pourquoi m'éclairer sur la passion que vous aviez pour M. de Nemours, si vostre vertu n'avoit pas plus d'étendue pour y résister? Je vous aimois jusqu'à estre bien aise d'estre trompé. . . . (p. 1234)[86]

Rather than see Madame de Clèves's extraordinary confession as a "generous" albeit desperate act of friendship, her honesty is, in his eyes, at best a weakness, at worst only another trick. The gesture of friendship is also the gesture which ultimately forces an end to their relationship; had Madame de Clèves not spoken, her husband says, "j'eusse, peut-estre, ignoré toute ma vie que vous aimiez M. de

---

secondo il suo bisogno, dando all'incontro altratanta baldanza all'amico di far con lui il simigliante, non gli mancando in cosa niuna. . ." (*Il merito delle donne*, Venice, Domenico Imberti, 1600, p. 67).

[86] "You shed many tears, Madame, for a death you are causing and that cannot give you the pain you are showing. ( . . . ) Why did you let me know the passion you had for M. de Nemours, if your virtue did not have more strength to resist it? I loved you so much that I would have been happy to be deceived. . . ."

Nemours" (p. 1234).[87] Just before dying he seems to be half persuaded
by his wife's protestations of innocence, but it is all too late. Seen from
this perspective, Madame de Clèves's confession is almost gratuitous,
without hope of return, for she is the true friend of a husband who, even
if he is "capable de conserver l'amour dans le mariage" (p. 1247),[88] is
not capable of being a true and generous friend. In his furious and
mortal jealousy he suspects her of the worst betrayal and hypocrisy,
which means that the *liberalitas* of the wife finds no corresponding dis-
interestedness in the husband.

In respect to Monsieur de Nemours, too, the princess's scandalous
honesty will have dire consequences. Ironically, he will not be able to
keep himself from talking about his adventure to a "friend," the Vidame
de Chartres, whose untrustworthiness and scheming nature is well
documented in the novel. Nemours is incapable of selecting a true
friend, partly because he is not one, and partly because there simply are
none. In betraying his secret Nemours has made Madame de Clèves's
confession enter into the movement of interests at the court, and has
made it susceptible to the search for motivation that so haunts her
husband. In all these ways the confession at Coulommiers is the sign of
a singular, and sadly anachronistic friendship in the heart of the
Princesse de Clèves.

The final conversation of the lovers centers on the relationship
between Madame de Clèves and her now dead husband. We find a
situation reminiscent of Montaigne's ("si on me presse de dire pourquoy
je l'aymois. . ."); the question put again and again to the wife concerns
the *reason* for her faithfulness to her husband. Her response is
articulated through the notion of "devoir," her duty, which recalls, in
addition to and beyond all religious connotations, the *officium* of
classical, especially Ciceronian, moral philosophy: "Mon devoir,
répliqua-t-elle, me deffend de penser jamais à personne, et moins à vous
qu'à qui que ce soit au monde, *par des raisons qui vous sont inconnues*"

---

[87] "All my life I would have, perhaps, not known that you loved M. de
Nemours."

[88] Praise immediately tempered by what follows: "peut-estre aussi que sa
passion n'avoit subsisté que parce qu'il n'en avoit pas trouvé en moy" (ibid.).

(p. 1245, my italics).[89]   The bind which ties the princess to her
husband seems *a priori* beyond any comprehensible motivation, and it
is in effect a tie which, in the eyes of Nemours, appears precisely
without motivation (and thus absurd): "quel fantôme de devoir opposez-
vous à mon bonheur?   Quoy! madame, une pensée *vaine et sans
fondement* vous empeschera de rendre heureux un homme que vous ne
haïssez pas?" (ibid., my italics).[90]   Although the princess emphasizes
the extreme difficulty of her undertaking, she has no doubts whatsoever
about the absolute necessity of her sacrifice, and she refuses to allege
religious or social precepts which, in any case, would hardly justify her
choice.   Her tragic friendship has led to an imperious need for "repos"
(rest), one that makes the idea that Monsieur de Nemours may be
unfaithful to her intolerable, and one that conjures up the vision of her
deceased friend whenever she is tempted to cede to her passion.   In the
context of the novel, Madame de Clèves's "repos" is irreducibly
personal, the absence of all contact with others.   It arises out of her
intimate choice, and has as its end only herself; in this sense it is close
to the autotelic "sentiment" Montaigne attempts to convey in his essay.
The desperate Monsieur de Nemours criticizes this closed-off state of his
beloved: "Vous seule vous opposez à mon bonheur; vous seule vous
imposez une loy que la vertu et la raison ne vous sçauroient imposer" (p.
1249).[91]   The choice of words is significant: Madame de Clèves's
friendship is beyond virtue and reason, thus outside the realm even of
classical perfect friendship.   Her absolute need for "repos" also makes
it incomprehensible to others.   Montaigne's friendship, by its very
absoluteness, without "mélange" or heterogeneity, cannot really be
signified to others.   This ineffable aspect of friendship is conveyed by
Montaigne in a repetition which refuses the semantic augmentation

---

[89] "My duty, she replied, prohibits me from ever thinking about anyone, and
less about you than about anyone else in the world, for reasons that are
unknown to you."

[90] "What ghost of a duty do you oppose my happiness with?   What!
madame, an empty and groundless thought will keep you from making happy
a man you love?"

[91] "You alone oppose yourself to my happiness; you alone impose on
yourself a law which neither virtue nor reason could impose on you."

necessary for information to be transmitted.   Monsieur de Nemours unwittingly reproduces this repetition in his lament: "vous seule vous . . . vous seule vous. . . ."   This time it is from the outside, and the *lui - moi* dialectic at the heart of Montaigne's feeling of his friendship is replaced by Nemours's *vous seule*.   Perhaps one is not so different from the other.   The princess remains sovereign, and alone.

Montaigne's and Madame de Lafayette's discourse of "true" friendship connects here to the old lament of morose writers, expressed by Blaise de Vigenère and discussed elaborately by Louis Le Roy: "Rien ne se dit, qui déjà ne soit dit."   Friendship is perfect also because it cannot be *said* to others, it cannot therefore be imitated.   Friendship is said to oneself so that it may be excluded from this movement, agitation, interest, this cancerous growth of writing in a time of decay.   It is also *recalled* to oneself as having passed, and as being anachronistic in the context of today's world.   In spite of its connotations of youth and purity, friendship in some writers participates in an obsession with the end, both in personal and in cultural terms.

This obsession with ending also betrays a profound distrust of finality, in the sense of teleological motivation, and implies in this distrust of motivation, a suspicion of the coherent representation of human relations.   Perfect relationships, for the other's own sake, must be construed entirely outside of interest, and thus perhaps beyond understanding.   One is left with the impression that capturing what is the essentially and ideally human comes to mean the exclusion of reasoned moral discourse.   This exclusion can make what is "human" into a private, incommunicable transcendence.

I think that this is a peculiar development in some literary works of early modern Europe,   and it arises in part out of literary representation's historical dialogue with moral philosophy.   It results in, I believe, a certain more modern incompatibility between ethical thought and the esthetic fictional worlds of literature.   Literature no longer can claim to make us wiser, and we do not expect it to, either.   Literature comes to signify and promote our intensely problematic relationship to the collective.

I would like to end this chapter by giving a modern counterpart to the sublime nostalgia of Montaigne and the Princesse de Clèves.   It is the para-theological dream of the "city of the immediate," of "real presences," in the recent essay of that name by George Steiner.[92] According to Steiner, art, literature, music are being smothered by the "Byzantine dominion of secondary and parasitic discourses" (p. 38), by the proliferation of interest, by draining commentary. We are losing, Steiner says, the very essence of the humane in the cancer of the secondary. This apocalyptic indictment is, I think, one of the many avatars of a sublime, anti-discursive nostalgia that ends up, sometimes unwittingly, glorifying silence, the speaking to oneself, and refuses that very human and humane activity of motivation, justification, and understanding.

---

[92] George Steiner, *Real Presences* (Chicago: Univ. of Chicago Press, 1989). See especially the first part, "A Secondary City," pp. 3-50. Steiner echoes (surely unwittingly) Blaise de Vigenère: "Commentary is without end. In the worlds of interpretative and critical discourse, book, as we have seen, engenders book, essay breeds essay, article spawns article. The mechanics of interminability are those of the locust. Monograph feeds on monograph, vision on revision. The primary text is only the remote font of autonomous exegetic proliferation" (p. 39). Later, the Bible is invoked: "It is not, as Ecclesiastes would have it, that 'of making many books there is no end.' It is that 'of making books on books and books on those books there is no end'" (p. 48). Steiner is quoting 12:12 ("Faciendi plures libros nullus est finis"), but he neglects the context of the verse, in which it has more the sense of "it is *endlessly difficult* (or wearying) to write many books, for much study wearies the body" (see the Jerusalem Bible translation).

# FRIENDSHIP AND THE POLITICAL LIFE

# CHAPTER VI

# FRIENDSHIP AND PRAGMATIC NEGOTIATION: LEON BATTISTA ALBERTI'S *DE AMICITIA*

As we move into the political arena, the varied ethics of friendship must confront two related problems: first, the world of commercial transactions, of precarious alliances in Renaissance cities and courts; second, especially in France, the often despotic power of the monarch. The vicissitudes of friendship in the first setting have been nowhere better recorded than in a fifteenth-century Italian humanist dialogue on the moral management of a family, and this chapter will be devoted to examining this often detailed conversation.

## 1. Useful Ethics

The convivial discussion of friendship that comes to constitute the fourth book of Leon Battista Alberti's *Della famiglia* (first three books composed 1433-1434) is at the same time a celebration of ancient, especially Ciceronian, wisdom and a tacit understanding of its fairly limited relevance to contemporary Italian society.[1]  The themes of

---

[1] See the discussion of Alberti's Italian dialogues in David Marsh, *The Quattrocento Dialogue: Classical Tradition and Humanist Innovation* (Cambridge, MA: Harvard Univ. Press, 1980), pp. 78-99, and especially p. 80: "Alberti seeks a stylistic, methodological, and social middle ground between the idealism of classical learning, and the realities of contemporary experience." On the dialectic between utopian and realist moments in his architectural writings, see Paul-Henri Michel, *Un idéal humain au XVe siècle: La pensée de L. B. Alberti (1404-1472)* (Paris: Belles Lettres, 1930), pp. 270-273. On the exile of the male Alberti family members from Florence, see most recently

Alberti's symposium relate to the way in which the family can maintain and increase its material and spiritual prosperity. Leon Battista's contribution to his family's welfare is one in which the usefulness of the arts plays a major role, even though the function of letters is seriously questioned by the more pragmatic members of his family (especially Gianozzo). However, the very fact that Leon Battista's learning has enabled him to compose a useful dialogue - in the vernacular, even - is a demonstration of how the arts should be an illustration of the maxim that men are born to be useful to other men. The reader senses that Leon Battista's own choice to study in Bologna, in the 1420's, rather than help preserve the exiled family's fortune, is ultimately justified by the fact that his studies led to his pedagogic writings. This is what (Leon) Battista seems to be implying, in the late dialogue *De Iciarchia* (composed ca. 1470), when he advises the younger Niccolò and Paulo that usefulness and "onestà" go hand in hand:

> Non troverrete mai che alcuna cosa sia necessaria qual non sia utile a quel suo fine; e quel fine, qual non abbia in sé onestà, non può essere all'omo prudente mai utile o da volerlo. Chi per cupidità d'imparare quello che non sa, abandonasse il padre e gli altri suoi impotenti e destituti, sarebbe impio, inumano. L'omo nacque per essere utile all'omo. E tante arte fra gli omini a che sono? Solo per servire agli omini.[2]

Learning should not be pursued for its own sake, but should always be useful, and specifically useful for the family, although it is not clear to what extent learning for its own sake is justified if it does not leave one's father and family destitute. Thus relationships of use seem to be

---

Susannah Foster Baxendale, "Exile in Practice: The Alberti Family In and Out of Florence 1401-1428," *Renaissance Quarterly* 44 (1991): 720-756.

[2] "You will never find that a thing is necessary that is not useful to its end; and this end, if it does not have in it moral goodness, can not be useful or desirable for the prudent man. Whoever, because of his desire to learn what he does not know, should leave his father and his family powerless and destitute, would be impious and inhuman. Man is born to be useful to man. And why are there so many arts among men? Only to serve men" (*Opere volgari*, ed. Cecil Grayson, vol. 2 [Bari: Laterza, 1966], Book 2, p. 243).

the norm, and are seen to be compatible with virtue. Although the *De Iciarchia* was written much later than any of the books of *Della famiglia*, the maxim of usefulness is one that characterizes the tenor of the latter, and it also renders problematic the relationship of friendship presumably celebrated in the fourth book. For friendship, in the classical account, is often a relationship that is entered into not because it provides friends with profit or utility, but because the other is loved "for his own sake."[3] Yet friendship is a key feature of classical moral philosophy, and the ideal, and also abstract, moral relationship. In some ways it functions as the emblem of theoretical moral reflection crystallized in an exclusive but existing human relationship. As such it also stands for the *possibility* of moral theoretical reflection on behavior. Given the atmosphere of "usefulness" into which *Della famiglia*'s final book is set, a theory of friendship seems a very delicate enterprise.

Although the book was written in conjunction with a poetry contest (the *certame coronario*) on the subject of friendship which Alberti had organized in 1441,[4] the topic itself was introduced earlier in *Della famiglia*, in the second book. One of the participants, Lionardo Alberti, proposes that, after virtue, friendship is to be preferred to all other forms of love:

> Giudicate niuna cosa quanto l'amicizia essere utile e molto atta a vivere bene e beato. Persuadetevi al tutto, come fo io a me stessi, questa vera una amicizia nella vita de' mortali doppo la virtù essere tale che molto sé stessi possa non solo agli altri

---

[3] Aristotle, *Nicomachean Ethics*, 1156b 10; see also the discussion of expediency in Cicero, *De amicitia*, 8.26 and ff.

[4] See Antonio Altamura, *Il certame coronario* (Naples: Silvio Viti, 1952), and the brief discussion in Joan Gadol Kelly, *Leon Battista Alberti: Universal Man of the Early Renaissance* (Chicago: Univ. of Chicago Press, 1969), 218-219; Giovanni Ponte, *Leon Battista Alberti: Umanista e scrittore* (Genoa: Tilgher-Genova, 1981), 179, 182-183. Scholarship on the *De amicitia* tends to focus on the choice of Tuscan (understandably, since the Latin-Tuscan rivalry is an issue in the contest), and the frequent use of ancient examples.

> amori, ma a qual si sia cara e pregiata cosa preferirsi e
> soprastare.[5]

The supremacy of friendship as a form of love is challenged, however,
by Battista, who makes an argument (for the sake of argument, in fact)
for the supremacy of erotic love.  Before doing so, Battista is careful to
distinguish between his own *mores* and the position he is defending in
order to "practice" himself ("per essercitarmi," p. 87); he asks Lionardo
not to think of him as immodest personally, although he is the advocate
of erotic love.[6]   The implication is, then, that the identification of
personal behavior with abstract positions espoused in a conversation is
indeed the norm, and that theory is always already "applied."  In the
case of Lionardo and Battista it also means that the outcome of the
debate is known in advance, as presumably Lionardo's celebration of
friendship is not just a "trying-out" of an argument.

But in fact the argument Battista brings forth against the
supremacy of friendship is an important one, and one that is practically
accepted by Lionardo.  The younger interlocutor gives examples of the
greater *power* of love, showing that the most virtuous have succumbed
to it:

> Non mi pare fra gli antichi istorici fatta menzione d'alcuno, per
> virtuosissimo che fusse e in ogni lode singularissimo, in cui
> amore non in gran parte monstrasse sua prova, e superasse non
> e' giovani solo, e' quali per ogni rispetto sono in questo da
> no'gli riprendere, ma vecchi ancora, e' quali nelle cose
> amatorie possono parere e sazii e inetti. (p. 89)[7]

---

[5] "Judge that nothing as much as friendship is useful and fitting in order to
live well and happily.  Be entirely convinced, as I became myself, that this true
friendship in the life of mortals after virtue is such that by much it can be
preferred to and is better than not only the other forms of love, but also any
dear and esteemed thing" (*Opere volgari*, vol. 1, p. 86).

[6] "E pure non vorrei pel dir mio più che per costumi mi riputassi però men
continente che modesto" (p. 87).

[7] "It does not seem to me that in ancient histories anyone is mentioned, as
virtuous and exceptionally praised as he may be, in whom love did not show
itself greatly, and vanquished not only the young, who are in all respects not to

All sorts of ethical norms have been sacrificed to the fulfillment of erotic love: Catilina murdered his own son in order to marry his beloved, an oriental queen had her husband killed because of her love of an ordinary barber, etc. Love is powerful enough to "renderci debole qualunque vinculo di parentado" (p. 93). In a book on the family, this is naturally a troubling argument. It is also a *practical* argument, in the sense that Battista is not arguing that love brings us closer to God, or is an imitation of the harmony of the spheres, or renders men more virtuous. Instead, love's supremacy is factual, and indifferent to ethical claims.[8] Battista had implied the interdependency of personal behavior and "theoretical" argumentation in his disclaimer about his own love life, saying that his defense of love did not mean that he was in love. In his challenge to Lionardo this interdependency is crucial: whatever your intellectual convictions, if you are in love, your moral philosophy will always be secondary to your desire. Classical friendship is, as it were, the paragon of moral philosophy, and its defense only demonstrates that, as Lionardo had suggested in his thesis, it *should* be preferred, not that in reality it *is* preferred.[9] Battista suggests that classical examples do

---

be scolded for this, but also the old, who in things concerning love can seem satisfied and inept."

[8] Battista readily concedes that friendship deserves greater praise than desire: "giudico e sento medesimo quel che tu, che mai l'innamorato sopra l'amico meriti lodo e fama" (p. 97). This debate will be developed in numerous treatises and dialogues on the nature of love and desire, ranging from Marsilio Ficino's commentary on Plato's *Symposium*, first published in 1484 (see his discussion of *amor volgaris*), to Leone Ebreo's *Dialoghi d'amore* (1535) and Louise Labé's *Débat de folie et d'amour* (1555). There is an entire industry of treatises on love in the Renaissance: see, for a list of Italian 16th-century works, Stefano Prandi, *Il 'Cortegiano' ferrarese: I "Discorsi" di Annibale Romei e la cultura nobiliare nel cinquecento* (Firenze: Olschki, 1990), pp. 212-218.

[9] See, on the humanist sense of a primacy of the will, Charles Trinkaus, *In Our Image and Likeness* and Ullrich Langer, *Divine and Poetic Freedom*, pp. 126-148; on the humanist critique of theory, Victoria Kahn, "Humanism and the Resistance to Theory," in *Literary Theory/Renaissance Texts*, eds. Patricia Parker, David Quint (Baltimore: Johns Hopkins Univ. Press, 1986), pp. 373-396.

not have their equivalents today ("Ma chi sarà, se già tu uomo eloquentissimo uno solo quello fussi, el quale mi provasse mai oggi in questa età nostra trovarsi quelle piladee e lelie amicizie?" p. 97),[10] and Lionardo ends up admitting that Battista may be right: "E quanto tu pure ne'dì nostri trovassi amicizia niuna perfetta. . ." (p. 98).[11]

Not only are perfect classical friends, such as Pylades and Orestes or Laelius and Scipio, most likely a phenomenon of the past, but friendship, as it is described in the fourth book of *Della famiglia*, is itself no longer exempt from the sort of practical impulse that governed Battista's arguments. In spite of the fact that *De amicitia* was added to the first three books several years later, the theme it treats dovetails with the end of the third book, which discusses the economic aspect of friendship: should one give money to a friend when he asks for it (p. 253 ff.)? Although the conversation recalls the Senecan question of the true *beneficium* ("Verso gli amici si vuole usare liberalità," p. 255), the advocate of true friendship, and thus of true liberality, Lionardo, is given rather short shrift by the other interlocutors, who are more interested in how to say no gracefully to a supplicant than in what a friend's real duties are. Again, it is not clear that there are any true friends, in the midst of so many flatterers and mere acquaintances: "Salutatori, lodatori, assentatori si truovono assai, amici niuno, conoscenti quanti vuoi, fidati pochissimi" (p. 254), says Adovardo. The task of the members of the family is less the determination of what friendship is than the weeding out of false friends, in imitation of Plutarch's *How to Distinguish the Friend from the Flatterer*. The underlying suspicion is, of course, that human relations are motivated

---

[10] "But who will be able to, unless you most eloquent man alone are able to, prove to me that today in our time one can find such Pyladean and Laelian friendships?"

[11] "And although you in our days do not find any perfect friendship. . ." Castiglione will echo this complaint through Pietro Bembo: "ma perché oggidì pochissimi veri amici si trovano, né credo che più siano al mondo quei Piladi ed Oresti, Tesei e Piritoi, né Scipioni e Lelii" (*Il libro del cortegiano*, ed. Ettore Bonora, Milan, Mursia, 1972, 2.29, p. 136). Federico immediately disputes this, however, claiming that there are many pairs of friends whose love is comparable to that of ancient friends (2.30).

essentially by utility, and that one can safely assume that all friends have good reasons and interests to be friends.

## 2. Piero the Flattering Courtier

The fourth book opens with a praise of Buto, a slightly buffoonish old servant of the family, who is valued as a "true friend" because he has remained a friend even during a "change" in fortune (p. 263), thus fulfilling one of Plutarch's criteria for distinguishing a true from a false friend.[12]  However, it is exactly this true friend who (in gest) denies that there is any such thing as friendship, saying that the commonplaces cited about friendship are nothing but "fables":

> Molte diceano dell'amicizia cose belle a udirle, ma cose quale a chi poi le pruova favole.   Diceano che a ben fermare l'amicizia convenia che due in uno si congiungessero, e bisognarvi non so io che moggio di sale. (p. 264)[13]

Instead, all is a matter of money: when you are rich, you have friends, but not otherwise (ibid.).  As was suggested in the second book, there is a discrepancy between theoretical moral philosophy and practical behavior, only this time it is good behavior that is possible even when the theory is cynical.

A more coherent cynicism is practiced by the main provider of contemporary *exempla* of friendship, the courtier Piero, who agrees with the connection made by Buto between money and friends.  In spite of the fact that true friendship seems difficult mostly because of the context of the merchant and banking life into which it is set, it is perhaps the courtier who represents the real problem for Alberti's moral philosophy, given the interdependence of wealth and the sometimes willful political

---

[12] *How To Distinguish the Flatterer from the Friend*, 14.

[13] "Many say things about friendship that are beautiful to listen to, but that are fables when one tests them.  They say that in order to establish well friendship two should join as one, and you need something like a handful of salt," recalling Diogenes Laertius, *Lives* 5.20, and Aristotle, *Nicomachean Ethics* 8.3 (1156b 27).

power which enables it. The problem of the prince's favor presents the
real obstacle to the practical realization of the ethics of friendship. It is
in this sense also that classical moral discourse is anachronistic even in
its celebration by the most staunchly classicizing of Alberti's family
members, Lionardo.

Piero Alberti turns the discussion away from the nature of
friendship and its duties, and emphasizes the *acquiring* of friendship,
placing himself in the position of those inopportune "friends" the
household tried to discourage in the third book. Here, however, the
family's misfortunes have forced Piero to concentrate on acquiring the
friendship of the powerful. Thus the treatise on friendship is first of all
a practical manual for courtiers eager to please a sovereign, as is shown
by the introduction of *grazia* (favor) into the conversation: "con molta
industria e sollecitudine a me acquistai la grazia di tre, come sapesti, in
Italia ottimi, e in tutte le genti famosissimi principi" (p. 265).[14] The
three examples of Piero's "friendship" will be genuinely useful to those
wishing to secure their family's fortune through relationships with the
powerful, just as much of the rest of *Della famiglia* is genuinely useful
to preserve a household. Before recounting his gaining the favor of the
three *principi* (Duke Giangaleazzo Visconti of Milan, King Ladislaus of
Naples, anti-Pope John XXIII in Bologna), Piero must clear up the
question of whether wealth or virtue is the most useful in "farsi amare"
(ingratiating oneself). Essentially he refuses to decide, leaving those
subtle questions to the "litterati," but he does say that the absence of
wealth forced him to be more resourceful:

> E non vi nego però che la industria e diligenza mia a me giovò
> non poco ad acquistarmi la grazia e benivolenza, quale io
> desiderava, di que' principi; ché credo, se la fortuna mia fusse
> stata più copiosa e abundante, a me gran parte bisognava meno
> usare quanta usai arte e sollecitudine. (p. 267)[15]

---

[14] "With much work and sollicitude I acquired the favor of three, as you
know, in Italy, excellent and among everyone most famous princes."

[15] "And I do not deny, however, that my work and diligence helped me a
lot in acquiring the favor and goodwill, which I wished for, of these princes;
on the other hand I believe that if my fortune had been more copious and
abundant, I would have had to use much less technique and sollicitude than I

The ethical choice is entirely absent from Piero's deliberations; it is now a matter of more or less "arte e sollecitudine," of more or less developed technical expertise in the manipulation of princes' affections.    The implication is that virtue is only a technique, one that, in the absence of wealth, may serve one's purpose.[16]    That technique is demonstrated through the recitation of Piero's own experiences, none of which contain overt immorality (thus avoiding the problem of what to do to please immoral princes).[17]    In fact, Piero always appears modest and willing to subordinate personal or dynastic advantage to the common good, in his speech to the Duke of Milan (p. 273), and in his behavior at the court of the King of Naples: "Non però mai commissi che persona suspicasse me usar la grazia e favore di Ladislao in cosa non tutta iustissima e lodatissima" (p. 278).[18]    He maintains the favor of Ladislaus by practicing both Ciceronian and medieval clerical-courtly virtues: "Però io con molta vigilanza, assiduità e osservanza, con onestissimi e iocondissimi essercizii, con ogni riguardo in favellare e degna moderazione d'ogni mio gesto, curava mantenermi la grazia e benivolenza di Ladislao re" (pp. 279-280).[19]    Piero's "onestissimi e iocondissimi essercizii" are a pleasing version of Cicero's *honestum*, of

---

did."

[16] See also Piero's response to Ricciardo's description of a *non sò che* which makes one lovable, and thus more likely to gain favor: "O bisognivi virtú, o sianvi necessarie le ricchezze, o convengali in prima quel dono celeste tuo, Ricciardo . . . pure lo studio però nostro e modo troverete ad aplicarvi a benivolenza non meno che qualsisia altra cosa molto giovarvi" (p. 269).

[17] A problem discussed in Castiglione, *Il libro del cortegiano* (4.6-7): bad princes are encouraged in their vices, and false opinion of themselves, by lying courtiers.

[18] "However I never did anything that would lead someone to suspect that I used the favor of Ladislaus in a matter not entirely just or praiseworthy."

[19] "Yet I took care to maintain for myself the favor and goodwill of king Ladislaus with much vigilance, assiduousness and observance, with most honest and joyous exercises, with all circumspection in talking and a dignified moderation of every gesture."

actions that are morally right (*De officiis*, 1.3.9); the "degna moderazione" recalls both Cicero's *modestia* (*De officiis*, 1.40.142) and the *moderamen, mensura*, or *moderatio*, the moderating presence, practiced by the medieval courtier bishop.[20] Piero's behavior also anticipates Castiglione's courtier's *mediocrità* (*Il libro del cortegiano*, 1.27, 2.31, etc.).[21]

Yet Piero's more or less ethical life as a courtier was not without its pitfalls and discomforts, especially in the case of Pope John, whose avarice and corruption rendered impossible any "friendship" not based on monetary gain (pp. 280-282). Yet even with the Duke of Milan and the King of Naples Piero had to be extremely assiduous, thus losing control over his private life:

> Ma come era appresso el Duca a me prima suto incommodo molestissimo el convenirmi con infinito studio di diligenza osservare e accorrere, ch'io non tardassi o perdessi quella e quell'altra ora utile a presentarmi, così con Ladislao qui m'era molestia gravissima né ozio, né certo spazio d'ora a mia privata alcuna volontà o faccenda quasi mai restarmi. . . . (p. 279)[22]

Piero's complaint is commonplace in Renaissance anti-court literature, and is echoed by his contemporary Enea Silvio Piccolomini, who was Pope (1458-1464) during Leon Battista Alberti's career in the Papal

---

[20] See C. Stephen Jaeger, *The Origins of Courtliness: Civilizing Trends and the Formation of Courtly Ideals: 939-1210* (Philadelphia: Univ. of Pennsylvania Press, 1985), pp. 46-48.

[21] See also Marsh, *The Quattrocento Dialogue*, p. 89, on moderation as a Ciceronian moral ideal of the orator.

[22] "But as it was a great trouble for me, when I was with the Duke, to accommodate myself, with infinite diligence, to observe him and come running to him, such that I would not be late or lose this or that hour that might be useful to present myself, just so with Ladislaus it was a very great nuisance to me almost never to have any leisure, any sure time for my own private will or activity."

chancery (1443-1464).[23] In his *De curialium miseriis* (comp. 1444, ed. 1472), Piccolomini writes of the difficult life of a courtier following a prince to gain wealth ("Sunt qui se posse putant divitias cumulare princibus servientes)."[24] His courtier, too, must sacrifice his private life to the prince's whims: "Si vero in curia perseveraveris, oportet te ad quaevis imperia regis esse paratum, ire in bellum, per latrones transire, navigare in mare. . . . Nulla tibi aut in verbis aut in operibus libertas supererit" (pp. 34-35).[25] The hints of the dangers of court life are not lost on Piero's listeners: his cousin Gianozzo picks up on the final, discouraging example of the corrupt Pope, and launches into a tirade against the corruption of the clergy in general and the consequent vileness of their followers (pp. 282-283).


## 3. Compromised Friendship

When the discussion of friendship resumes, it is as if the sordidness implied in Piero's practice of courtly ingratiation had allowed a space for a classical, abstract definition of friendship. The "litterati," excluded by Piero, return in the guise of Lionardo, whose dialogue with Adovardo will monopolize discussion of friendship for the remainder of the book. Lionardo begins this discussion by explaining why Piero's examples did not *please* Adovardo: this is, indeed, a great failing for a courtier so successful at pleasing various *principi*. However, as Lionardo said earlier, the powerful are "d'ogni onesto essercizio vacui, oziosi, e in tempo non poco dati alle volutà, e acercati non da amici ma

---

[23] On Piccolomini's respect for Alberti's learning, see Michel, *Un idéal humain*, pp. 82-83.

[24] "There are those who think themselves capable of amassing wealth by serving princes." Ed. Wilfred P. Mustard (Baltimore: Johns Hopkins Univ. Press, 1928), 12, p. 34.

[25] "If truly you wish to persevere at the court, you must be ready at any command of the king, to go to war, to go through thieves, to go to sea. . . . No freedom of words or of action will remain for you." See also 2 (p. 23): "principibus servientes nihil sibi libertatis relinquunt."

da simulatori e assentatori" (p. 265).[26] The implication is that men capable of being true friends are not pleased by the stories of Piero:

> Sarebbeti forse Piero piaciuto più, s'egli non in modo d'istoria, ma come sogliono e' litterati, avesse prima diffinita che cosa sia l'amicizia, poi diviso le sue spezie, e con quello ordine proseguito sue argomentazioni e sentenze, scegliendo di tutte quale e' piú approvasse. (pp. 283-284)[27]

The Aristotelian alternative to corrupt flattery is also the possibility of a theoretical alternative in general, of a relationship defined before it is realized, and when it is realized, it is *chosen* and *approved*. The theoretical is also here the ethical, in that the definition of friendship is unadulterated by the way things *are*, but sees them as they *should be*. In the dialectical movement between the theoretical and the practical, however, Lionardo's Aristotelianism is immediately modified by Adovardo, who will be the main exponent of the discussion, and who insists on learning about friendship from an experienced man, who can teach him how to acquire useful friendships, how to augment them, how to end them, preserve them, and so forth (pp. 285-286). Adovardo's reply to Lionardo underlines once again the anachronism of the classical, philosophical moment, and the subjection of "pure" friendship to interest.

We have seen, then, in this long build-up to the actual treatise on friendship, how pragmatism influences the way in which issues are defined in the Alberti family. This is explicitly related to the often tenuous political if not financial situation of the family, which had only recently been allowed to return to Florence, and, although it was still prosperous, had lived through more than three decades of exile. These

---

[26] "Empty of all honest activity, lazy, and eventually not a little given to the seeking of pleasure, and sought out not by friends but by hypocrites and flatterers."

[27] "Perhaps Piero would have pleased you more if he had not proceeded by way of a story, but in the usual way of the educated, by first defining what thing friendship is, then by dividing it into species, and in that order carrying through his arguments and maxims, choosing which of all he approved of the most."

circumstances necessitated, at least for some members of the family, a sort of friendship very much akin to the accommodation of the powerful practiced by the courtier. From the start it is questionable that disinterested relationships exist, or, on another plane, even if they did exist, would be in the family's interest. When Alberti lets Lionardo and Adovardo display their knowledge of classical moral philosophy, in the remainder of the book, it is indeed true that "nihil dictum quin prius dictum," nothing is said that has not been said before.[28] Yet in spite of Alberti's avowed respect for his sources, his specific utilization of classical ideas on friendship is skewed, in the sense that the practice-oriented, courtly problematic described above deforms their import.

Lionardo clearly is the defender of a more idealized, classical version of friendship, and it is he who will repeat the most well-known classical definition, Cicero's "Est enim amicitia nihil aliud nisi omnium divinarum humanarumque rerum cum benevolentia et caritate consensio" (*De amicitia* 6.20): "La vera amicizia nulla [è] altro che coniunzione di tutte nostre divine cose e umane, consentendosi insieme e amandosi con aperta e somma benivolenza e carità" (p. 286).[29] Adovardo, too, knows his sources, and he repeats the Aristotelian tripartite division of friendship: "Né truovasi vincoli, credo, quali tengano gli animi a noi adiunti e dedicati se non solo questi tre, quali vedesti sono o iocundi e voluttuosi, o utili e con emolumento, o lodati, onesti e pieni di virtù" (pp. 305-306).[30] The true friend is one whose "vincolo" is one of

---

[28] Terence's phrase is quoted in Alberti's *Profugiorum ab Aerumna* in *Opere volgari*, vol. 2, p. 161. On the stylistic import of this idea for Alberti, see Marsh, *The Quattrocento Dialogue*, pp. 92-94; on its relationship to Renaissance imitation, see Thomas M. Greene, *The Light in Troy: Imitation and Discovery in Renaissance Poetry* (New Haven: Yale Univ. Press, 1982), pp. 8-11, and p. 296n11.

[29] "True friendship is none other than the union of all our divine and human affairs, joining together and loving each other with open and great goodwill and charity."

[30] "There are no ties, I believe, that hold souls bound and dedicated to us except for these three: joyous or pleasurable, useful and profitable, or praiseworthy, morally good, and full of virtue." *Nicomachean Ethics*, 1156a 6-1156b 32; *Eudemian Ethics*, 1236a 30-1236b 1. The *Eudemian Ethics* became

virtue.[31]    But Adovardo is somewhat more tempered about the
usefulness of classical sources, and he emphasizes a flexible, judicious
friendship rather than open insistence on virtue.  Indeed, he finds in
Cicero himself the justification for a less dogmatic view of things: "ma
vuolsi con tempo e modo darsi a qualunque sia cose" (p. 336).[32]
Adovardo is recalling the Ciceronian explanation of the Greek and Stoic
principles of "doing the right thing at the right time," *scientia . . .
opportunitatis idoneorum ad agendum temporum* (*De officiis*, 1.142).  So
Cicero himself can be adduced to defend a more practical perspective on
friendship.

Yet Adovardo goes beyond the Ciceronian sense of *occasio* and
*modestia* in a striking passage on the conservation of friendship with
people who because of personal faults can be difficult to get along with.
When people who are well-disposed towards us have unjustified feelings
of their own worth, or are unfriendly and prefer to be alone, we must
adapt in order to conserve their good disposition towards us:

> Seclusa ogni assentazione, qual sempre fu servile e indegna
> d'animo onesto, provederemo con dolcezza e iocundi
> ragionamenti contenerli a noi molto benivoli.  E come diceano
> sapea Alcibiade, così noi imitaremo el cameleonte, animale
> quale dicono a ogni prossimo colore sé varia ad assimigliarlo.
> Così noi co' tristi saremo severi, co' iocundi festivi, co' liberali
> magnifici; e quanto dicea Cicerone al fratello, la fronte, el viso,

---

known to Italian humanists in the 1420's: Leonardo Bruni begins his dialogue
with Marcellinus by announcing that he is reading it, in the *Isagogicon moralis
philosophiae* (composed 1424-1426).  On this Aristotelian topos see also Dante,
*Il Convivio* 3.11.8 (ed. G. Busnelli, G. Vandelli, Florence, Le Monnier, 2nd
ed. 1964, vol. 1, pp. 386-387).

[31] "Amici sì troveremo iocundi e voluttuosi numero molti, e amici quali
pendano a qualche loro commodo non pochi ti si offeriranno.  Amici vero così
in noi affetti, che d'ogni nostra buona fortuna e felicità non ivi solo sieno
studiosi e cupidi, ove a sé cerchino frutto e premio del suo verso di te servigio
e officio, ma quali solo del nostro bene molto in prima che del suo
contentamento godano, saranno certo non molti, ma ben molto sopra gli altri
costantissimi in benivolenza e ottimi" (p. 306).

[32] "But one should do things in the right time and the right way."

> le parole e tutti e' costumi accomodaremo a' loro appetiti. E
> troverremo quasi niuno, per severo e solitario che sia, a cui e'
> poemi e ogni musica e ogni istoria *presertim* ridicula non diletti.
> (pp. 335-336)[33]

The passage contains a series of overlapping classical references that
underlines the problematic nature of friendship as it is conceived in
moral philosophy.  The first is Alcibiades as chameleon, which comes
from Plutarch ("Alcibiades," 4, in his *Lives*).  In Plutarch's generally
dispassionate account this quality of Alcibiades is at best of doubtful
merit, since Alcibiades imitates good and bad alike.  Elsewhere Plutarch
condemns Proteus-like changeability as remaining on the surface
($\grave{\epsilon}\pi\iota\phi\acute{\alpha}\nu\epsilon\iota\alpha$) and thus inimical to true friendship.[34]   In Adovardo's
description this flexibility is desirable.   In another reference to
Alcibiades, Adovardo praises his ability to pacify Tissaphernes through
his "lusinghe e blandizie" (deception and flattery) (p. 331), which seems
to undermine Adovardo's exclusion of "assentazione" at the beginning
of the passage quoted.

Adovardo's counsel on preserving friendship with difficult people
also contains a reference to what "Cicero said to his brother," that "la
fronte, el viso, le parole e tutti e' costumi accomodaremo a' loro
appetiti" (p. 336).  The sequence fronte-viso-parole seems to point to
Marcus Tullius Cicero's letter to his brother Quintus, where he advises
his brother to be suspicious of friends in the province whom he has not
known before, for "the brow, the eye, and the face very often lie, but
speech most often of all" ("frons, oculi, vultus persaepe mentiuntur,

---

[33] "Without any flattery, which always was servile and unworthy of an
honest soul, let us look to it with gentleness and joyous reasoning that they
remain benevolent toward us.  And as they said Alcibiades knew how to do, so
should we imitate the chameleon, an animal which, they say, changes itself to
become like any color next to it.  So we will be severe with the sad, festive
with the joyous, freely-giving with the generous, and as Cicero said to his
brother, we will accommodate our forehead, our face, our speech and our habits
to their desires.  And we will find almost no one, as severe and solitary as he
may be, whom poems and music and a story - especially if it is funny - do not
delight."

[34] In his *Moralia* (*On Having Many Friends*, 96F-97B).

oratio vero saepissime," *Ad Quintum fratrem*, 1.1.5.15).[35] Although
in a negative way the spirit of Cicero's text seems to have been
maintained by Alberti, the *advice* of Cicero was to be wary of someone's
exterior and speech, and not that one should accommodate one's own
face and speech to others' desires.

Another classical source, from another text written by a Cicero to
his brother, comes closer to the meaning of Alberti's phrase. This time
it is Quintus Cicero writing to his brother Marcus Tullius, in a letter that
more resembles a treatise, on the art of campaigning for a consulship.
The authorship by Quintus has been disputed, but only after Alberti's
time. The *Commentariolum petitionis* (or *De petitione consulatus*) was
found in some 15th-century codices among Marcus Tullius Cicero's
*Epistolae ad familiares*, although not in the famous codex of the
*Familiares* sent to Coluccio Salutati in 1392 (the Laurentian Library ms.
49,9).[36] Quintus Cicero insists on the use of *blanditia*, flattery or
ingratiation, to deal with people and gain a good public image (*species
in re publica*). This *blanditia* (recalling Alcibiades' "lusinghe e
blandizie") may be a vice in life otherwise, but is necessary in a
campaign. Cicero goes on to show why:

---

[35] Earlier Adovardo had used a similar phrase to demonstrate how one can
ingratiate oneself by maintaining a pleasing and virtuous demeanor: "Né sarà
che tu possi se non piacere, se in ogni tuo atto, detto, fatto, abito e portamento
te presenterai modesto, costumato, ornato di virtù. E raro acaderà che di dì in
dì non succedano nuove coppie a iniziar teco nuova conoscenza e assiduità, se,
come dicea Cicerone al fratello suo, el volto e fronte, quali sono quasi porte
dell'animo nostro e addito, mai saranno a persona non aperte, e quasi publice
e liberali" (p. 296). The possibility of true openness of demeanor seems,
however, to be excluded by Cicero in his letter; another source is contaminating
the meaning in Alberti.

[36] See Remigio Sabbadini, *Le Scoperte dei codici latini e greci ne' secoli
XIV e XV*, rev. ed. Eugenio Garin (Firenze: Sansoni, 1967, 1st ed. 1914), under
Quintus Cicero. See also Mary I. Henderson's introduction to her trans. of the
*Commentariolum petitionis*, p. 741, in the Loeb Classical Library edition of
Cicero's letters, and Franz Buecheler, *Quinti Ciceronis Reliquiae* (Leipzig: B.
G. Teubner, 1869), pp. 10-13, on the different manuscripts. Paul Oskar
Kristeller lists another 15th-century manuscript in the Seminario Gregoriano in
Belluno, in his *Iter italicum*, vol. 2 (London: Warburg Institute, 1967), p. 496.

> Etenim cum deteriorem aliquem adsentando facit, tum improba est, cum amiciorem, non tam vituperanda, petitori vero necessaria est, cuius et frons et vultus et sermo ad eorum quoscumque convenerit sensum et voluntatem commutandus et accommodandus est.[37]

The sequence *frons-vultus-sermo* is imbedded in a phrase whose meaning is much closer to Alberti's sentence than the phrase in *Ad Quintum fratrem*: we have to accommodate our appearance and speech to the dispositions of those whose friendship we need or value. In addition, the movement from *adsentari* to *accommodare* in the Latin anticipates Alberti's *assentazione* and *accommodare* in Adovardo's advice. Thus it seems more likely that the *Commentariolum petitionis* is Alberti's source.

  The *Commentariolum* is in fact much closer in spirit to the sort of courtier politics Piero Alberti describes, than to the idealized, disinterested view of friendship we have in Cicero's *De amicitia* or Seneca's *De beneficiis*. It acknowledges the necessity of interested friendship, and of flattery to obtain and to maintain friends, in the campaign to be elected consul. The exclusive, rarefied friendship described in moral philosophy is hardly relevant here, just as, in the case of fifteenth-century Italy, the Alberti family's interest is hardly defended by gratuitous virtue. Another classical reference in Adovardo's advice to be accommodating confirms the move into the sort of courtier politics we find later associated with Castiglione. Illustrating his counsel to imitate the chameleon, Adovardo states: "Così noi co' tristi saremo severi, co' iocundi festivi, co' liberali magnifici" (p. 335).[38] The enumeration recalls Cicero's speech in defense of Caelius: when Caelius is accused of having associated with Catilina, Cicero defends him by saying that Catilina was friends with many people, and Caelius should not be singled out. Catilina knew how to ingratiate himself with

---

[37] "For it is vile when flattery is used to corrupt a man, but less execrable when used to conciliate friendship, and indispensable for a candidate, whose facial expression and conversation must be modified and adapted to the humour and inclination of all whom he meets." [Q. Cicero], *Commentariolum petitionis*, 11.42, ed. Loeb Classical Library, trans. M. I. Henderson.

[38] "So we will be sad with the severe, festive with the joyous, freely-giving with the generous."

everyone, since he was able to change himself and "be serious with the austere, gay with the lax, grave with the old, amiable with the young, daring with criminals, dissolute with the depraved" ("cum tristibus severe, cum remissis iucunde, cum senibus graviter, cum iuventute comiter, cum facinerosis audaciter, cum libidinosis luxuriose vivere," *Pro Caelio*, 6.13). In Cicero's speech this flexibility both explains Caelius's friendship with Catilina and distinguishes the gullible but virtuous Caelius from the wicked Catilina. In Adovardo's advice, however, it is only the practical effectiveness of such behavior that counts: once again, what is at best of dubious ethical value in Cicero is given as counsel in Alberti.

Alberti's deformation of Cicero is all the more telling when one compares Adovardo's use of the *Pro Caelio* speech with that of Enea Silvio Piccolomini's, in his anti-court treatise *De curialium miseriis*. Piccolomini observes that some people may justify their courtier career by claiming that they want to give good counsel to princes, in order to help the disadvantaged, promote the public good, etc. However, the court is such a corrupt place that it is impossible to remain virtuous: you must accommodate yourself to others, and perforce take on their vices. It is at this point that Piccolomini quotes the passage from *Pro Caelio* just cited (ed. Mustard, 28, p. 52). Thus the flexibility of Catilina is given an even greater negative value in the epistle of Alberti's contemporary.

The courtier-like flexibility suggested by Adovardo also includes the ability to cheer up those who are sad: "E troverremo quasi niuno, per severo e solitario che sia, a cui e' poemi e ogni musica e ogni istoria *presertim* [especially] ridicula non diletti" (p. 336). The *istoria ridicula* not only recalls the section on laughter initiated by Julius Caesar in Cicero's *De oratore* (2.57.235-2.61.290), but it also announces the long section on *facezie, burle, motti*, etc. that any capable courtier should be able to master, in the second book of Castiglione's *Libro del cortegiano*. The friend becomes, then, a self-interested entertainer, and in spite of Adovardo's denials, very close to a flatterer.

Alberti himself did not endorse unequivocally such a view of human relations; in his later, more Stoic *De Iciarchia*, the sort of flexibility required for political success is incompatible with the ideal of *tranquillità* and *riposo*, and he echoes Piccolomini's condemnation of the life of the *ambiziosi*. If you desire the reputation of being "first,"

> Sempre fu faccenda e condizion tale che per ottenerla [reputazione] bisogna ostinata sollecitudine, rissosa importunità, servile summissione e confederazion d'ingegni fallaci, maligni, petulanti. Poi per mantenerla continuo ti conviene agitar te stessi concitando in te sospetti, fingendo, simulando, dissimulando, sofferendo, temendo più e più cose indegne e gravi a chi voglia vivere con tranquillità e grato riposo.[39]

The ideal life is one in which no simulation is necessary, and it is in fact the good man, refraining from false appearances, who will end up being listened to, although the masses may for a while prefer the appearance of competence to the real thing (see pp. 248-249). Alberti is rejecting here the advice given by Quintus Cicero to his brother, to cultivate his public image, and to persuade himself to simulate having that which by nature he does not have ("Deinde id quod natura non habes induc in animum ita simulandum esse ut natura facere videare," *Commentariolum petitionis*, 11.41).

In the earlier dialogue on friendship, however, Alberti seems to have more doubts about the practical use of classical moral philosophy, and, although he invokes classical sources such as Cicero frequently and, on the surface, reverently, their actual use in his text often shows the extent to which the ideal has been submitted to the exigencies of interest. The exemplary, useful accounts are essentially those of Piero the courtier, and the only parallel to them in classical sources are the life of Alcibiades and the relatively cynical, disabused advice by Quintus Cicero to his brother on how to make lots of friends and win an election. Already in early humanism the discourse on friendship is an occasion to display the delights of classical learning, but that discourse is also suspected to be anachronistic, and true friendship takes on the thoroughly secular characteristics of nostalgia.

---

[39] "Conditions and affairs are always such that in order to obtain a reputation you need obstinate sollicitousness, aggressive importuneness, servile submission and a lot of deceptive, evil, shameless tricks. Then, in order to maintain it, you must entertain in yourself suspicions, deceiving, feigning, hiding, suffering, fearing more and more things unworthy and difficult for whomever wants to live in tranquility and agreeable calm" (*Opere volgari*, vol. 2, p. 189). Battista is speaking.

The secular nature of friendship is nowhere clearer than in the discussion of its extension: should one be friends with many or with a few? The classical answer is clear: since thorough knowledge of, and long familiarity with the person are necessary, true friendships will be rare.[40] This is the gist of what Adovardo says, in a distinction he makes between *amicizia* and *benivolenza* (pp. 303 ff.). His explanation, however, is occasioned by a very pertinent question of Lionardo: does charity not exhort you to love your neighbor as yourself?

> E chi ricusasse non da tutti essere amato? Chi non molto diletasse trovarsi amici numero quasi infinito? Sempre a me piacque quella nostra appresso de' nostri sacerdoti sacra e divina sentenza, quale comanda tanto ami el prossimo quanto te stessi: processo di carità con quale puoi avere a te commendatissimi tutti gli uomini. (p. 303)[41]

The connection between classical friendship and Christian charity is, as one may expect, the subject of medieval theological reflection,[42] and will be the subject of evangelical humanist reflection as well.[43] Adovardo's rather secular response takes up the Aristotelian distinction between good will and friendship (*Nicomachean Ethics*, 1166b 30 -

---

[40] See Aristotle, *Nicomachean Ethics*, 1156b 25-32, *Eudemian Ethics*, 1237b 35, and *supra*, Introduction.

[41] "And who would refuse to be loved by everyone? Who would not delight in acquiring an almost infinite number of friends? I always liked the maxim which is for our priests holy and divine, and which commands that you love our neighbor as yourself: an application of charity by which you can hold all men to be recommended to you."

[42] See both Ethelred of Rievaulx, *De spirituali amicitia* in *PL*, vol. 195, 664D, 670A, and Pierre de Blois, *De amicitia christiana et de dilectione Dei et proximi* in *Un traité de l'amour du XIIe siècle*, ed. and trans. M.-M. Davy (Paris: E. de Boccard, 1932), 1.1, pp. 108-110, 1.17, p. 192, and 2.1, p. 234. Friendship is considered to be inferior to true charity that is the love of God through the creature.

[43] See Erasmus, *Adagia* 1.1.2.

1167a 20).[44]    Adovardo in effect dismisses the question, implicitly equating charity with good will, *benivolenza*, which allows you to be "friends" with many, without requiring you to be in continuous contact with them.   Even good will combined with familiarity is not always sufficient to produce "vera e perfetta amicizia," as the true friend will be such only in the practice of virtue (pp. 305-307), and the virtuous are rare.  Adovardo's dismissal of charity only repeats, however, the quirky way in which the question is introduced by Lionardo: who would not be delighted to have lots of friends, to be loved by all?  Yet the precept of charity is in principle one that commands love of all, irrespective of their love for you.   In theory, thus, charity is not a means of gaining popularity, for the love of your *proximus* does not guarantee that he should love you.  By inverting the sequence, placing all others' love for you first, Lionardo emphasizes the self-interest underlying the question, and sets up Adovardo's response.

In its independence from charity friendship is part of a secular order.  But in that order, as a relationship with someone "for his own sake," classical friendship seems weak in the face of relationships governed by expediency.  This weakness emblematizes the delicate and unstable place of moral philosophy in a world governed by favor and interests.  In the end, in order to function in the social order, friendship cannot be rare and exclusive, it cannot rely on long familiarity, it must rely on interpretation and calculation.   In other words, it must be *benivolenza*, that watered-down and perhaps easily corrupted version of charity, or the *blanditia* practiced by the campaigning Cicero.

Alberti's *De amicitia* ends on a note that announces the pedagogical function of the courtier, in Castiglione's *Libro del cortegiano*.[45]  Adovardo suggests that there is a way in which princes can make themselves beloved, although almost no prince is interested in finding out how:

---

[44] See also Cicero, *De amicitia*, 5.19-20.

[45] See the discussion in the first half of the fourth book; Cesare Gonzaga responds to Ottaviano's pedagogical program: "se voi formaste con quelli [documenti] il vostro principe, più presto meritareste nome di bon maestro di scola che di bon cortegiano" (4.36).

> Oh! felicissimo quel principe quale così vorrà acquistarsi
> benivolenza, e meno essere temuto che amato, quanto con una
> sola facile e piena di voluttà cosa possono tutti, ma non curano
> in questa parte insieme acquistarsi benivolenza e lode
> immortali. (p. 341)[46]

The education of princes will, presumably, proceed through the advice of proto-courtiers such as Piero or Battista himself, and perhaps this "cosa" would be the most useful of all the information Adovardo can give to his listeners. It is here, however, that the discussion is interrupted and the book ends. In spite of frustrating the audience's expectations, Alberti has concluded on what will become an important aspect of the discourse on friendship in the Renaissance, the choice of being loved or feared that is given to princes. In his preference for the former Alberti presages 16th-century anti-Machiavellianism and its rejection of Machiavelli's answer to his question, "an sit melius amari quam timeri, vel e contra" (*Il principe*, 17).

The writing of the fourth book of *Della famiglia* was undoubtedly motivated in large part by the poetry contest on the theme of friendship. Yet Alberti did not simply write a treatise, but attached it thematically and structurally to the rest of a useful book on the management of families, and gave his own family members often very sympathetic voices. In doing so Alberti seems to have made a gesture of friendship toward his own family that is a demonstration of his later maxim, "l'omo nacque per essere utile all'omo." It is not clear that his family *deserved* such a gesture, given that they had repudiated him during his Bologna studies, and that Leon Battista had been forced to seek patrons and employers to survive. In 1441, when he composed the friendship addition to *Della famiglia*, he had been employed in the pontifical chancery for nine years, and seems to have been in a more independent position vis-à-vis his family.[47] The very gesture of composing the

---

[46] "Oh, that prince will be happiest who will in this way wish to acquire for himself goodwill [of others], and to be less feared than loved, as all can, with a single, easy thing that is full of pleasure: but here they do not care to acquire goodwill and with it immortal praise."

[47] On Alberti's career in these years see Michel, *Un idéal humain au XVe siècle*, pp. 55-75.

dialogue seems, then, without immediate interest, and the sort of a gratuitous, classical *beneficium* that the text itself finds improbable in this difficult world.

# CHAPTER VII

# FRIENDSHIP IN AN ABSOLUTE MONARCHY: PIERRE CORNEILLE'S *CINNA* AND *RODOGUNE*

We have seen how grand gestures - offers of friendship, refusals to explain, offers of radical honesty - entail a reordering of ethical imperatives and generally of ways of understanding ethical behavior. This is nowhere more obvious than in the theater, where the conditions of representation favor the concentrated, dazzling physical incarnation of a moral choice. In Corneille's theater the demonstration of utter generosity by an emperor is one such example, as are a series of gestures by the fraternal friends Antiochus and Séleucus, the postponed designation of a first-born successor by the tyrant Cléopâtre, but especially her self-poisoning at the conclusion of her struggle to maintain her power. These moments suppose a whole fabric of ethical thought on the possibilities of friendship in the realm of absolute power, and on the practical consequences of the bond between equals.

## 1. The Emperor's Generosity

At the conclusion of Pierre Corneille's tragedy *Cinna ou la Clémence d'Auguste* (first staged in December 1640), the emperor Augustus pardons the conspirator Cinna, grandson of Pompey, and his co-conspirator and lover, Emilie. His act toward Cinna is doubly generous, as Cinna had once before benefitted from his good will (2.1.637-645), but had persisted in his plot to kill the emperor. When he confronts the conspirators in the final scene, he chooses to accept them as *friends*:

> Soyons amis, Cinna, c'est moi qui t'en convie:
> Comme à mon ennemi je t'ai donné la vie,

Et malgré la fureur d'un lâche destin,
Je te la donne encor comme à mon assassin.
Commençons un combat qui montre par l'issue
Qui l'aura mieux de nous donnée ou reçue.
Tu trahis mes bienfaits, je les veux redoubler,
Je t'en avais comblé, je t'en veux accabler.
Avec cette beauté que je t'avais donnée,
Reçois le consulat pour la prochaine année.
Aime Cinna, ma fille, en cet illustre rang,
Préfères-en la pourpre à celle de mon sang,
Apprends sur mon exemple à vaincre ta colère:
Te rendant un époux, je te rends plus qu'un père.
(5.3.1701-1714)[1]

Augustus proposes to replace the conflict between enemies with the "combat" between friends, in a virtuous rivalry that recalls Lucian's *Toxaris*, a friendly competition in exemplary friendships between a Scyth and a Greek. His words recall as well an allegorical painting described in a section of Honoré d'Urfé's *L'Astrée*, under an oak tree in the "Temple d'amitié," in which two children are wrestling with each other, and in which victory belongs to the one who loves the other most.[2]

----

[1] "Let us be friends, Cinna, it is I who invite you to do so: as to my enemy I have given you your life, and in spite of the fury of a cowardly destiny, I give you your life again as to my assassin. Let us begin a struggle that will show by its outcome which one will have better given or received it [your life]. You betray my favors, I want to double them, I had showered favors on you, I want to crush you with them. With this beauty that I had given you, receive the consulate for next year. Love Cinna, my daughter, in this illustrious rank, prefer the purple [of the consular robe] to the purple of my blood, learn from my example how to vanquish your anger: giving you a spouse I give more than a father back to you." All quotations from Corneille's plays are taken from his *Oeuvres complètes*, ed. André Stegmann (Paris: Seuil, 1963). Augustus uses the term "amis" (as opposed to the "courtisans" who do nothing but flatter) to refer to Maximus and Cinna (see 2.1.362 and 2.1.393-394).

[2] See *L'Astrée*, Part 2, Book 5 (ed. Hugues Vaganay, Lyons, P. Masson, 1926, pp. 179-180): "Si est-ce qu'à leur visage on connoissoit bien qu'il n'y avoit point d'inimitié entre eux, ayant meslé parmy leur combat je ne sçay quoy de doux et de riant aux yeux et en la bouche de tous les deux." Their torches

When Augustus "crushes" Cinna with good deeds, "bienfaits," he also evokes the Senecan *beneficium* that solidifies friendship, although his generosity, self-indulgently emphasized, seems to go beyond Seneca's warning against excess (*De beneficiis*, 1.4.2, and *passim*). In his demonstration of friendship toward his vengeful adopted daughter Emilie, Augustus proposes his behavior as an example to her. This gesture, too, partakes of the rhetoric of friendship, especially in its political aspect, as emulation of exemplary virtue in the prince can lead to the strengthening of the ties of friendship among his subjects. The friendly gesture toward Augustus's daughter is a literal instance of what is called "civil friendship" in what will come to be anti-Machiavellian political theory, the "commune benevolenza" (common good will) that binds inhabitants of the same state ("quella, per laquale i cittadini di ciascheduna città si congiungono insieme per un certo ordine de la patria," according to the fifteenth-century political theorist Francesco Patrizi).[3] It is this type of "amicitia civile" that belongs particularly to the prince, as he resembles the father of a family,[4] which Augustus

---

were put aside, still burning, and their flames have combined into one, illustrating the classical principle, "nos volontez de mesme ne sont qu'une." The painting is interpreted in the following way: "ce tableau ne nous veut representer que les efforts de deux amants pour emporter la victoire l'un sur l'autre, non pas d'estre le mieux aymé, mais le plus remply d'amour, nous faisant entendre que la perfection de l'amour n'est pas d'estre aimé, mais d'estre amant."

[3] "The one through which the inhabitants of each city join together through a certain order of the fatherland" (Francesco Patrizi [da Siena], *Il sacro regno de'l gran Patritio, de'l vero reggimento, e de la vera felicità de'l principe, e beatitudine humana* [Vinegia: Aldi filii, 1553], trans. of *De regno et regis institutione* [composed in the 1470's, first published in Paris in 1518], Book 8, Chap. 10, f. 307v). Patrizi's work was translated into French in 1577.

[4] "Questa tal amicitia s'appartiene piu a'l Principe, che à nessuno altro, perche egli ha una certa somiglianza col padre d'una famiglia," Patrizi, *Il sacro regno*, f. 308r. See, on the French side, Guillaume Budé, *De l'institution du prince* (Troyes: Nicole Paris, 1547), Chap. 48: "A ce propos disoit Aristote au viii. livre des Ethiques [*Nicomachean Ethics*, 1160a 36 and 1160b 24-26], que le Royaulme bien ordonné est loué sur touts les aultres gouvernemens dont on use envers les peuples. Car il a quelque similitude & proportion convenable de

emphasizes by his addressing of Emilie as "ma fille," and by giving her away in marriage, thus replacing her own father, C. Toranius, for whose death he had been responsible.[5] Augustus is putting into practice what Montaigne recommends, in his essay "De l'affection des pères aux enfans" (2.8), in a maxim that, as we will see, echoes Machiavelli: "Quand je pourroy me faire craindre, j'aimeroy encore mieux me faire aymer."[6]

The emperor's offer of friendship to his subject Cinna is an example of a particularly delicate sort of friendship, that between superior and inferior. For Aristotle, although it is possible for a ruler to be friends with a subject, there should be a certain proportion of love: the ruled should love the ruler more than the ruler the ruled (*Nicomachean Ethics* 1158b 12-1159a 5, *Eudemian Ethics* 1238b 18-29). In fact, loving someone undeserving can be a reproach to the ruler (*Eudemian Ethics* 1239a 6-7). Augustus's clemency toward the ungrateful Cinna comes close to this situation; Corneille's formulation of the emperor's clemency in terms of a dazzling victory over himself and the universe ("Je suis maître de moi comme de l'univers," 1. 1696) seems partly designed to overcome that sort of an objection. Indeed, the emperor's gesture has the force of divine grace, causing his subjects to convert their anger into love and admiration: "Et je me rends, Seigneur, à ces hautes bontés. / Je recouvre la vue auprès de leurs clartés" (ll.

---

l'accomparer au gouvernement dont use le pere envers ses enfans: & est de pareille façon honoré & redoubté le Roy envers ses Subiects, comme est le pere de ses enfans, desquelz il veult avoir reverence & obeïssance procedente d'une honneste affection d'amour estant enraciné dedans le coeur des Hommes, plus que de creincte servile, qui ne se doibt nommer obeïssance" (p. 202).

[5] Although Emilie and Cinna are depicted as lovers in the play, the giving away or exchange of women sometimes underlies male friendship, as the supreme *beneficium* that one friend can do for another. See the analysis of the second book ("De re uxoria") of Alberti's *Della famiglia*, and of Boccaccio's *Decameron* (10.8) in Constance Jordan, *Renaissance Feminisms* (New York: Columbia Univ. Press, 1990), pp. 49-50.

[6] "Even if I could make myself feared, I would rather make myself loved." *Essais*, ed. Pierre Villey, Verdun-L. Saulnier (Paris: Presses univ. de France, 1965), p. 393.

1715-1716), says Emilie, echoing the language of religious conversion.[7] Even more obviously, Livie's divinely inspired speech ("Oyez ce que les Dieux vous font savoir par moi," l. 1755)[8] predicts an exemplary reign, and a glorious conversion of Roman citizens to subjects of a monarchy.

## 2. Friendship as a Political Choice of the Sovereign

The splendidly efficacious gesture of friendship toward the most undeserving subjects is, however, especially important as a demonstration of Corneille's anti-Machiavellian political philosophy.[9] The play illustrates the effectiveness of clemency by taking the most extreme case: a would-be assassin is not only pardoned, but made consul and son-in-law literally in the same breath. Augustus's startling "soyons amis" is a precise refutation of a chapter of *Il Principe* (ed. 1532) that poses the question of whether a ruler should make himself feared or loved: "De crudelitate et pietate; et an sit melius amari quam timeri, vel e contra" (On cruelty and piety, and whether it is better to be loved than feared, or the contrary) (Chap. 17). Machiavelli's answer is that both are desirable, but that it is much safer for the prince to be feared than loved, if one must choose. This is because men generally are "ingrati, volubili, simulatori e dissimulatori, fuggitori de' pericoli, cupidi di

---

[7] "I surrender, Lord, to these superior acts of good will. I recover my sight beside their luminousness."

[8] "Listen to what the Gods tell you through me."

[9] See, for a useful account of anti-Machiavellian theory that was available to Corneille, André Stegmann, *L'héroïsme cornélien: Genèse et signification* (Paris: Armand Colin, 1968), vol. 2, part 1, pp. 158-202. See also the interesting study by Werner Krauss, *Corneille als politischer Dichter* (Marburg: Adolf Ebel, 1936), "Marburger Beiträge zur romanischen Philologie, 18" (pp. 33-36 on *Cinna*, pp. 39-42 on *Rodogune*), who sees Augustus's clemency as a concession to the feminine, an attempt at "humanization" of the absolutist state.

guadagno,"[10] and they will do everything for you when you do good to them, but when you are in dire straits, they will revolt. For their relationship to the ruler is based on utility:

> Perché le amicizie che si acquistano col prezzo e non con grandezza e nobilità di animo, si meritano, ma le non si hanno, e a' tempi non si possono spendere. E li uomini hanno meno respetto a offendere uno che si facci amare, che uno che si facci temere; perché l'amore è tenuto da uno vinculo di obligo, il quale, per essere li uomini tristi, da ogni occasione di propria utilità è rotto; ma il timore è tenuto da una paura di pena che non ti abbandona mai. (pp. 85-86)[11]

On the surface Machiavelli does not seem to be doing anything scandalous here: he carefully distinguishes between friendships gained through "prezzo" and utility to the friend, from friendships gained through "grandezza e nobilità di animo." It is a commonplace that friendships determined by utility do not last beyond that utility (see Aristotle, *Nicomachean Ethics*, 1156a 14-24). Augustus's gesture is exactly one that proposes friendship out of spiritual nobility and greatness, so he seems to be acting in a way compatible with Machiavelli's advice. However, the general condemnation of men's motives that preceded this distinction makes any friendship caused by spiritual greatness highly unlikely, all the more so because men not only are generally interested in their welfare to the exclusion of all else, but they are ungrateful, fickle (i.e., hardly capable of "nobilità di animo"), and "simulatori e dissimulatori": Machiavelli is implying that if the

---

[10] "Ungrateful, volatile, hypocritical, dissimulators, fearful of danger, desirous of gain." Niccolò Machiavelli, *Il Principe. Scritti politici*, ed. Luigi Fiorentino (Milano: Mursia, 1969), p. 85.

[11] "Because friendships that are acquired through money and not with greatness and nobility of soul are merited, but one does not possess them, and one cannot spend them when one wants to. And men have less compunction about offending someone who makes himself loved, than one who makes himself feared; for love is held by a tie of obligation which, since men are evil, is broken by any conflict with self-interest; but fear is held by a fear of punishment that never abandons you."

appearance of nobility is in their interest, they will simulate such an appearance to gain the favor of the ruler. In other words, given the general condition of mankind, one must proceed on the assumption that there are only friendships based on utility.[12] Machiavelli's pessimistic view finds its echo in later treatises on "reason of state," such as Giovanni Botero's *Della ragion di stato libri dieci* (1589), who is generally critical of Machiavelli, but who grants that one of the principles of prudence is to distrust friendships.[13]

In the most famous sixteenth-century French anti-Machiavellian treatise, Innocent Gentillet's *Discours contre Machiavel* (1576), we find Machiavelli's deliberations condensed and simplified into a maxim: "Le Prince ne se doit fier en l'amitié des hommes."[14] Gentillet does not

---

[12] Something already suggested by Patrizi, who cites the proverb, "amico è la borsa, e chi fa utile" (*Il sacro regno*, 8.11, f. 309r), and by Leon Battista Alberti, albeit "[per] motteggiare," in the beginning of his *De amicitia*: "cosa niuna tanto nuoce a farsi amare quanto trovarsi povero; porgetevi ricchi, e ivi più arete amici che voi non vorrete" (*Della famiglia*, Book 4, in *Opere volgari*, vol. 1, ed. Cecil Grayson, Bari, Laterza, 1960, p. 264).

[13] "Tenga per cosa risoluta, che nelle deliberazioni de' principi l'interesse è quello che vince ogni partito. E perciò non deve fidarsi d'amicizia, non di affinità, non di lega, non d'altro vincolo, nel quale, chi tratta con lui non abbia fondamento d'interesse" (in *Scritti politici*, Milano, Ubicini, 1839, "Biblioteca enciclopedica italiana," vol. 6, p. 462). There are French translations in 1599 and 1606 of Botero's work. See Robert Bireley, *The Counter-Reformation Prince: Anti-Machiavellianism or Catholic Statecraft in Early Modern Europe* (Chapel Hill: Univ. of North Carolina Press, 1990).

[14] "The Prince should not rely on the friendships of men." Ed. A. D'Andrea, P. D. Stewart (Florence: Casalini Libri, 1974), X. Maxime, p. 317. This "maxim" is a commonplace in the ecclesiastical reception of Machiavelli: Antonio Possevino, S.J., in his *Bibliotheca selecta* (Rome: Typ. Apostolica Vaticana, 1593) condemns, among others, the sentence "Amicitiae haud fidendum" in his judgment on Machiavelli (Book 1, Chap. 26, pp. 121-129). The love-fear alternative proposed by Machiavelli is discussed before Gentillet by Guillaume Budé, *De l'institution du prince*, Chap. 26, p. 105: "Et ceste obeïssance [of the people] ne peult venir que par deux moyens: l'un, par l'amour & affection, que les bons & graves personnes de se Subiects, portent à la vertu de leur Prince. Et par l'affection que le peuple a envers luy, pour la

hesitate to deform Machiavelli by eliminating, in his translation of the Italian passage on friendship, all mention of a friendship based on spiritual nobility and greatness.[15] This simplification allows Gentillet to associate Machiavelli's "maxim" with traditional criticism of tyranny: "Ceste Maxime . . . est un vray precepte tyrannique" (p. 317). He quotes Aeschylus, and provides an example from the life of Dionysos the tyrant. In part this criticism is related to Aristotle's discussion of friendship in different political systems: there is little or no friendship in tyranny, for there is nothing common to the tyrant and his subjects, who are equivalent to slaves (*Nicomachean Ethics* 1161a 30-1161b 5).[16] The lack of commonality means that there can be no justice, and thus no friendship, which assumes equality or at least proportionality of friends. Aristotle's distinction between the tyrant and the king is based on a definition of the king as one who looks to the interests of his subjects, whereas the tyrant looks only to his own interests (1160b 5-9). If, as

---

bonne estime qu'il en faict. Et l'aultre, par la creincte qu'il introduict par sa puissance, quand il veult user plus de cruaulté & de force, que d'honneste persuasion, & de clemence. Mais l'une [i.e., cruelty and force] n'est pas de si longue durée & defense, comme l'aultre."

[15] Claiming to quote Machiavelli, Gentillet writes: "Le Prince qui se fondera là dessus [l'amitié des hommes], tombera du premier coup en ruine. Et mesmes ils l'offenseront plustost quand il voudra user d'amitié envers eux, que si par rigueur il se fait craindre. Parce que les hommes font moins cas d'offenser celuy qui se fait aimer, que celuy de qui ils ont crainte, d'autant que *l'amitié est fondée seulement sur quelque obligation* qui se peut aisément rompre. . ." (p. 317, my italics). Gentillet, in one of his examples refuting Machiavelli, quotes a speech by Micipsa to Jugurtha from Sallust, in which the old king exhorts his children to love each other ("Or qui doit estre plus loyal amy que le frere au frere?" etc., p. 318). In Sallust, Jugurtha realizes immediately that the speech was insincere ("tametsi regem ficta locutum intellegebat," *Iugurtha*, 11.1), which is conveniently left out by Gentillet.

[16] See also Cicero, *De amicitia*, 15.52: "Haec enim est tyrannorum vita, nimirum in qua nulla fides, nulla caritas, nulla stabilis benevolentiae potest esse fiducia, omnia semper suspecta atque sollicita, nullus locus amicitiae." This sentence is also quoted by Marc Fumaroli, on p. 619 in "Tragique païen et tragique chrétien dans 'Rodogune'," *Revue des sciences humaines* 38 (1973): 599-631, who does not link it to anti-Machiavellian political thought.

Gentillet makes Machiavelli say, the prince must instill fear in his subjects in order to prolong their "friendship" and thus his own interests, he is by definition a tyrant. Etienne de la Boétie's *De la servitude volontaire ou contr'un*, whose first version probably was composed in 1548, but was known in manuscript form and published in Protestant polemical literature in the 1570's, also contains passages on the impossibility of friendship with tyrants:

> C'est cela que certainement le tiran n'est jamais aimé ni n'aime. L'amitié, c'est un nom sacré, c'est une chose sainte: elle ne se met jamais qu'entre gens de bien et ne se prend que par une mutuelle estime. ( . . . ) Il n'i peut avoir d'amitié là où est la cruauté, là où est la desloiauté, là où est l'injustice.[17]

For La Boétie and Gentillet, it is the absence of friends that characterizes the tyrant. In Corneille's play Augustus proves, by his offer of friendship, that he is precisely not the tyrant depicted in anti-Machiavellian literature.

The choice to encourage friendship is also essential in the maintenance of the ties that bind subjects to the prince. Friendship is intimately connected to fidelity, which is part of the feudal contract linking the lord to his vassals. In Traiano Boccalini's *Ragguagli di Parnaso* (1612), one of the allegorical scenarios described by the satirist-commentator is the departure of the Virtue of Loyalty from the world, and the consequent decision of Friendship no longer to inhabit the hearts of men:

---

[17] "It is certain that the tyrant is never loved and never loves. Friendship is a holy name and a holy thing: it only occurs between good persons and is only taken by mutual esteem. ( . . . ) There can be no friendship where there is cruelty, where there is disloyalty, where there is injustice." Ed. Malcom Smith (Geneva: Droz, 1987), pp. 73-74. On the public usefulness of friendship and its absence in tyranny, see also Pierre Charron, *De la sagesse*, rev. ed. 1604 (repr. Paris: Fayard, 1986), 3.7: "Et ne faut penser que l'amitié soit utile et plaisante qu'en privé, et pour les particuliers: car encores l'est elle plus au public, c'est la vraye mere nourrice de la societé humaine, conservatrice des états et polices. Et n'est suspecte ny ne desplaist qu'aux tyrans, et aux monstres. . ." (pp. 637-638).

[After the departure of "Fedeltà"] facevano maggiori le
afflitioni di lui [del mondo] i disordini bruttissimi, che in ogni
Principato continuamente si udivano nascere tra i Popoli, e la
stessa Sacratissima Amicitia, unica delitia del genere Humano,
vedendosi abbandonata dalla pregiata Virtù della Fedeltà, per
non ricevere dalla Fraude qualche segnalato smaccho, negò di
più voler habitar nel cuor degli huomini. . .[18]

The result is disastrous, for when friendship departs, men are freed from
the social bonds that ensure the survival of the common order (the
"consortio humano").[19]   They become not only "selvaggi nelle
seditione" toward their princes, but also cruel toward each other.[20]  The
princes protest to Apollo that "per la scelerata infedeltà de' Vassalli loro
erano necessitati abbandonar il governo del genere Humano" (p. 110).[21]
The ties of friendship are related to the feudal order of mutual succor

---

[18] "After the departure of Loyalty the afflictions of the world were made
worse by horrible disorders, which in all sovereignties were heard to arise
between peoples, and most sacred Friendship herself, seeing herself abandoned
by the esteemed virtue of loyalty, in order not to receive from Deceit some
signal humiliation, refused to inhabit the hearts of men any longer" (*De'
Ragguagli di Parnaso* [Venice: Pietro Farri, 1612], 1.30, pp. 109-110). The
departure of a virtue from the world is a theme of Golden Age writing; see for
example Aratus, *Phaenomena*, 96-136 (the departure of Justice).

[19] Boccalini's "consortio" is an extension of Seneca's maxim: "Consortium
rerum omnium inter nos facit amicitia, nec secundi quicquam singulis est, nec
adversi" (*Epistolae ad Lucilium*, 48, quoted from *Lucii Annaei Senecae
sanctissimi philosophi lucubrationes omnes, . . . Erasmi Roterodami cura . . .*,
Basel, Johannes Frobenius, 1515, p. 234).

[20] "Liberi dal vincolo di quel sincero amore, col quale co' privati amici loro
sono ligati, . . . divennero fieri nella perfidia," etc. (p. 110). The *vinculum* of
social order is a commonplace of the Roman legal tradition as well; the tie of
benevolence harks back to Aristotle (*Nicomachean Ethics*, 1166b 30 - 1167a 20,
also 1155a 21-22). See also Seneca, *Epistolae ad Lucilium*, 9: "Quomodo
[through friendship] hominem homini natura conciliat."

[21] "Because of the evil infidelity of their vassals they were constrained to
abandon the governing of the human race."

and loyalty in a way that makes Augustus's offer to his vassal-subject slightly anachronistic in absolutist France.

This nostalgic component of the discourse on friendship is also clear in Gentillet's polemic against Machiavelli. When Gentillet lists examples of the political effectiveness and advantages of "se faire aimer," he proposes that one benefit of friendly relations with subjects is the absence of a need for many guards:

> L'amitié et les amis qu'un Prince se doit acquerir par bon et juste gouvernement, luy peuvent servir pour s'asseurer tellement de chascun en son estat, qu'il ne luy seroit besoin d'aucune garde ny satellites [bodyguards] s'il s'en vouloit passer. Comme faisoit ce bon Empereur Trajan qui bien souvent alloit voir et visiter ses amis, acompaigné seulement de quatre ou cinq gentilshommes, sans aucune garde de soldats. Et le semblable faisoyent nos anciens Rois de France, qui mesmes ne savoyent que c'estoit de ceste scopeterie [firearms] et autre militie de garde qui est aujourd'huy usitée, ains marchoyent ordinairement sans autre compaignie que de gentilshommes, qui portoyent seulement l'espée. (pp. 318-319)[22]

Friendship constitutes a link between the Roman emperor Trajan who cultivates direct contact with his friends, without the protection of guards, the old French kings who needed only a few noblemen with swords, and the contemporary French king who could choose to do the same. Along with the nostalgia for old French kings, protected by a feudal network of noble friends armed with the symbol of their caste, comes a rejection of modern weapons, the "scopeterie" or rifles, from

---

[22] "The friendship and the friends a prince must acquire by a good and just government can be useful to him in trusting so much everyone in his state, that he would have no need of bodyguards if he wished to do without them. This is what the good emperor Trajan did, he who often went to see and visit his friends, accompanied only by four or five nobles, without any soldiers guarding him. And our old kings of France did the same thing; they did not even know what these bodyguards armed with firearms are that are used today, but they went ordinarily without any accompaniment except some nobles who carried only their swords."

the Italian *scoppio* (modern "schioppo").[23]    Anti-Machiavellism is
perhaps inevitably a nostalgic discourse, and Corneille's depiction of
Augustus participates in a feudal-religious critique of Machiavellian
absolutism.[24] Friendship is a key element in that critique.


## 3. Friends as Absolutism's Subjects

Although *Cinna* contains the most spectacular gesture of
friendship, from an Emperor to his foiled assassin, and the theme
emerges in other plays,[25] the most sustained representation of a
friendship is found in *Rodogune, Princesse des Parthes* (staged in the
winter of 1644-1645). It is here that Corneille produces in an almost

---

[23] See Ariosto, *Orlando furioso*, 11.24.7-8: "qual nomina scoppio, / qual
semplice cannon, qual cannon doppio." These various types of firearms
constitute "la crudele arte" of the king Cimosco.

[24] Compare Augustus's gesture of love with the discussion of friendship with
kings in Madeleine de Scudéry's *La Morale du monde, ou conversations*
(Amsterdam: Pierre Mortier, 1686), p. 195: "J'ay eu raison de dire [says
Poliante] qu'on ne doit pas attendre des Rois amitié pour amitié, & qu'il y
auroit trop d'audace à cette pretention.   En effet, il suffit qu'ils souffrent
agreablement d'estre aimez, & qu'ils aiment mieux estre aimez que d'estre
craints." The king is entirely absolved of any friendship tie; the best one can
hope for is that he permits his subjects to love him.

[25] Such as the late *Suréna, Général des Parthes*, staged in 1674.   The
eponymous hero is in love with, and loved by, Eurydice, who has been chosen
to marry the king's son. Suréna's sister, Palmis, is his friend and confidant;
she attempts to save his life by combatting Eurydice's love for her brother,
which has made him sacrifice a marriage arranged by the king to his daughter
Mandane. By refusing to marry Mandane Suréna provokes his own death. The
friendship between the siblings is not strong enough to overcome the love of
Suréna and Eurydice for each other, and Palmis vows revenge for her brother's
death.   She is thus a more active friend than the brothers in *Rodogune*.

uncanny way the logical *reductio ad absurdum* of friendship theory, and its political and literary consequences.[26]

Corneille found his material in the historiography of Appian of Alexandria, in an episode concerning Antiochus VIII and Seleucus V. The choice of Antiochus and Seleucus as fraternal friends is ironic, as their names are associated with the civil war fought by their ancestors, Antiochus Hierax and Seleucus II, and used as examples of fraternal violence.[27] *Rodogune* is the story of the two brothers, Antiochus and Séleucus, whose mother, the queen of Syria, Cléopâtre, will in the course of the play designate one or the other as the first-born, and thus as her successor to the throne. As part of a peace-making deal between Syria and the Parthians, one of the brothers also gets to marry Rodogune, a captured princess of the Parthians, and former fiancée of the brothers' deceased father Démétrius Nicanor. At the beginning of the play the brothers decide that the successor to the throne will also be the one to marry Rodogune. Although Cléopâtre has announced, as part of the agreement, that she will relinquish the throne to the first-born son, she is at heart unwilling to do so. By manipulating her sons she hopes to retain real power over the kingdom; the fact that only she knows which one is the first-born gives her the means to do so. Cléopâtre announces to them that she will designate that son as a successor who is willing to kill Rodogune, the enemy princess and the betrothed of her former husband. Neither son is willing to do so, as they both love Rodogune. The situation is complicated further by the fact that Rodogune herself is bent on avenging the death of her fiancé Nicanor,

---

[26] For a good overview of criticism of this unjustly neglected play, see Derek A. Watts, "A Further Look at 'Rodogune'," in *Ouverture et Dialogue: Mélanges offerts à Wolfgang Leiner*, eds. Ulrich Döring, Antiopy Lyroudias, Rainer Zaiser (Tübingen: Gunter Narr, 1988), pp. 447-463. Marc Fumaroli has drawn attention to several of the classical sources of the representation of friendship in *Rodogune*, in "Tragique païen et tragique chrétien dans 'Rodogune'," especially pp. 617-619. Fumaroli reads the play as a Christian humanist "tragedy," and Antiochus as its proto-Christian hero.

[27] See Plutarch, *De l'amitié fraternelle* in *Les oeuvres morales & meslees de Plutarque*, trans. Jacques Amyot (Paris: M. de Vascosan, 1572) (repr. Mouton, Johnson, S.R. Publishers, 1971), fs. 86r C [486A] and 88r A-B [489A-B].

who was ambushed by Cléopâtre's soldiers. When asked by the sons
whom she prefers, she announces that he who kills Cléopâtre will win
her in marriage. Unwilling to sacrifice their mother, the brothers decide
on separate courses of action, as Séleucus proposes that they abandon the
women to their quarrel, whereas Antiochus retains some hope that one
or the other can be mollified. Antiochus turns out to be the one
Rodogune really prefers, and she gives up her project of revenge when
he confesses his love for her. Cléopâtre, after some difficulty,
apparently also is willing to make peace, and she announces to Antiochus
that he is indeed the first-born and will marry Rodogune. The queen is
not ready to give up yet, and she attempts to play off Séleucus against
his brother by claiming that in fact Séleucus was the first-born, and that
she is punishing his disloyalty to her. None of this works, however;
Séleucus remains faithful to his brother, and Cléopâtre in a fit of rage
decides to murder them all. She does have Séleucus killed, but when
she tries to murder the couple at the wedding ceremony through a
poisoned drink, the news of Séleucus's murder interrupts the ceremony.
Antiochus has trouble deciding which one of the women is responsible,
and finds suicide an attractive alternative. At the last moment, before
he is about to drink from the cup, Rodogune realizes that it may be
poisoned and wants to have a servant try it, first. Recognizing that her
plot will be uncovered, Cléopâtre drinks from it herself and before going
off stage to die, she curses the couple and its future offspring.

This long recounting of the play's action is necessary in part
because the plot is at the same time complicated and neatly symmetrical:
on the surface the two women differ in very little, and neither do the
brothers, which helps in establishing the central political allegory of the
play, the destructiveness of absolutism. Given so few "natural"
differences among the brothers, a point to which I shall return, only a
willful instance of authority can distinguish between them. This instance
will make one the king, the other the subject, as Laonice announces
during the exposition:

> Ce grand jour est venu, mon frère, où notre reine,
> ( . . . )
> [Doit] [d]e deux princes gémeaux nous déclarer l'aîné;
> Et l'avantage seul d'un moment de naissance,
> Dont elle a jusqu'ici caché la connaissance,
> Mettant au plus heureux le sceptre dans la main,

Va faire l'un sujet, et l'autre souverain.  (1.1.7-14)[28]

Two equals will become *absolutely* different from each other, becoming antitheses through the declaration of the queen.  Whereas as equals they each had some inherent value ("deux *princes*"), as sovereign only one of them does, and the other becomes a "sujet," that is, functionally indistinct from the mass of subjects in a kingdom.  This is the situation in which fraternal friendship is most endangered, for, as we read in Jacques Amyot's 1572 translation of Plutarch's *Moralia*, "il fault que un frere ne soit pas comme le bassin d'une balance qui fait le contraire de son compagnon, quand l'un se haulse, l'autre se baisse."[29]

Instead of being based on nature, that is, on the physical precedence in birth of one or the other twin, Cléopâtre's decision is in fact based on her will, since it is she alone who knows who preceded whom.  Real precedence does not matter, of course; all that is important is that she be *alone* in her knowledge, in which case knowledge does not matter either.  This is precisely the paradox of absolute sovereignty, as absolutism always produces an instance of decision *prior* to any constraining knowledge.  Cléopâtre is an incarnation of the willfulness

---

[28] "This great day has come, my brother, on which our queen shall declare for us the eldest of two twin brothers; and the sole advantage of a moment of birth, the knowledge of which she has not divulged until now, placing the scepter in the hand of the most fortunate, will make one a subject, the other the sovereign."

[29] "One brother should not be like a dish in a pair of scales that is opposite to the other brother, such that when one rises, the other is lowered." *De l'amitié fraternelle*, f. 86r B [485 E].  Once inequality installs itself, it can lead to ever greater violence: "Toute inegalité est bien dangereuse de mettre dissension & querelle entre les freres, & est toutefois impossible qu'ils soient en toutes choses egaulx ny pareils, d'autant que ou la nature des la naissance, ou depuis la fortune leur departent inegalement leurs graces & faveurs, d'où procedent les envies, & jalousies entre-eulx, maladies & pestes mortelles, non seulement aux familles & maisons, mais aussi aux villes & citez" (f. 85r D [484C-D]).  One of the examples Plutarch gives is of "Antiochus" and "Seleucus" (f. 86r C [486A], and again f. 88A-B [489A-B]), referring, however, to Antiochus Hierax ("the hawk") and Seleucus II.  Fumaroli confuses these figures with Corneille's characters, Antiochus VIII and Seleucus V, in "Tragique païen et tragique chrétien," pp. 602-603.

that absolutism signifies to Corneille: the choice between the two sons is one of the elements added by Corneille to the narrative that he found in Appian of Alexandria.[30]    Towards the end of the play the arbitrariness of Cléopâtre's decision is made clear in an exchange with Séleucus.  The queen announces: "Je puis, comme je veux, tourner le droit d'aînesse" (4.6.1423).[31]  Séleucus is justifiably suspicious of her motives, and asks: "Je le veux croire ainsi, mais quel autre intérêt / Nous fait tous deux aînés quand et comme il vous plaît?" (4.6.1457-1458).[32]  The queen refuses to reveal her "interest": "Comme reine, à mon choix je fais justice ou grâce, / Et je m'étonne fort d'où vous vient cette audace, / D'où vient qu'un fils, vers moi noirci de trahison, / Ose de mes faveurs me demander raison" (4.6.1463-1466).[33]  The language used by the two characters closely matches the language vehemently criticized by anti-absolutist political writers in the late sixteenth and early seventeenth centuries.  They objected to the formula *Tel est nostre plaisir*, used by kings to ward off requests for explanation of their decrees.  Henri Estienne, in his collection of commonplace epigrams, gives a neat summary of this criticism:

> Bien qu'un prince soit grand, ces mots sont odieux
> Aux aureilles d'aucuns, *Tel est nostre plaisir*.
> Ou ces mots, leurs cousins, *Car ainsi je le veux*.
> Ou, *Ainsi le voulons*.  Maints ont à desplaisir
> D'ouir ainsi parler, au lieu de raison rendre,

---

[30] See Corneille's preface (pp. 415-416): "L'ordre de leur naissance incertain" is among the "embellissements de l'invention."

[31] "I can, as I wish, turn around the right of the eldest."

[32] "I am willing to believe you, but what other interest makes of one or the other of us the eldest when and how it pleases you?"

[33] "As queen, I render justice or favor as I choose, and I am surprised by your audacity; how does it come about that a son, blackened with treason toward me, dares to ask the reason for my favors?"

Et faire le motif que l'on a eu, entendre.[34]

Cléopâtre's own insistence on her will ("comme je veux"), and her son's words "comme il vous plaît," make obvious the parallel with absolutism Corneille is establishing in the play.

When, after having failed to incite Séleucus's jealousy of his more fortunate brother, Cléopâtre reflects on her situation, and deliberates her horrible revenge, she uses language that recalls Augustus's offer of friendship to Cinna: "Leur amour m'offensait, *leur amitié m'accable*, / Et contre mes fureurs je trouve en mes deux fils / Deux enfants révoltés et deux rivaux unis" (4.7.1476-1478).[35] Augustus, too, "crushes" Cinna with his friendship and his favors (5.3.1708). Apparently, then, friendship has the power of vanquishing tyranny, and the play's mitigated happy ending seems to imply that the two brothers' unwillingness to betray each other either for love of Rodogune or desire of the throne has brought about the end of Cléopâtre and absolutism.

## 4. Similarity and Equality

Yet the picture becomes more complicated when one considers Antiochus and Séleucus in themselves, as friends. Their relationship is clearly designated from the very beginning as friendship: Antiochus speaks of their "sainte amitié" (1.2.81) before their meeting. There is no mention of their friendship in Corneille's source; this addition must have been of particular significance to the playwright. The most striking thing about their presentation at the beginning of the play is their

---

[34] "Even though a prince may be great, these words are odious to the ears of some: 'Such is our pleasure.' Or these words, their cousins: 'For I wish it to be this way.' Many feel displeasure when they hear these words being spoken instead of a reason given and one's motivation explained." *Les premices, ou le I livre des proverbes epigrammatizez, ou, des epigrammes proverbializez* (1593) (repr. Geneva: Slatkine, 1968), epigram 97, p. 71. On the debates surrounding this formula, see also Ullrich Langer, *Divine and Poetic Freedom in the Renaissance*, pp. 155-160.

[35] "Their love offends me, their friendship crushes me, and against my rage I find in my two sons two rebellious children and two united rivals."

*similarity* to each other.[36]   Without having consulted the other, they both choose to relinquish the throne in order to marry the princess Rodogune.  Before explaining his choice to his brother, Séleucus reflects on the dangers to their relationship that the succession to the throne represents.  This is because the resulting inequality will destroy its basis:

> L'égalité en [i.e., de notre amitié] est le ferme appui,
> C'en est le fondement, la liaison, le gage,
> Et voyant d'un côté tomber tout l'avantage,
> Avec juste raison je crains qu'entre nous deux
> L'égalité rompue en rompe les doux noeuds,
> Et que ce jour, fatal à l'heur de notre vie,
> Jette sur l'un de nous trop de honte ou d'envie. (1.3.110-116)[37]

Antiochus immediately confirms this sense of equality: "nous n'avons eu jamais qu'un sentiment," they have always felt the same way (1.3.117). Whereas both Séleucus and Antiochus are thinking here about the political equality they have enjoyed as equal princes, their sameness extends, unbeknownst to them, to their emotions.   The choice of

---

[36] This has been interpreted as a sign of their weakness, and has provoked rather scathing remarks by critics: "The rule of the game requires that each [of the leading women] should reach the other only by using the two passive men who niggardly hesitate between them.  To make the ceremony as symmetric as possible, the princes act as one single character. . . . As such, they incessantly exchange pledges of fraternal love -- presumably as a device for making plausible their identical attitudes" (Thomas G. Pavel, "*Rodogune*: Women as Choice Masters," in ed. Claude Abraham, *Actes de Davis*, Paris, Papers on French Seventeenth Century Literature, 1988, pp. 161-165; quoted from p. 164).  Pavel, I think, has it the wrong way around.

[37] "Equality is the firm support of our friendship, its foundation, its bond, its token, and seeing the advantage falling entirely to one of us, justifiably I fear that destroyed equality will destroy its sweet ties between us, and that this day, fatal to our happiness, will cast on one of us too much shame or too much envy."  Compare Plutarch imagining Eteocles admonishing his children, "De conserver entre eulx egalité, / Laquelle joinct cité avec cité, / Amis avec leurs amis secourables, / Confederez en ligues perdurables: / Et n'y a rien qui en fermeté seure, / Qu'egalité, en ce monde demeure," in *De l'amitié fraternelle*, f. 83r C-D [481A].

Rodogune and the sacrifice of the throne by both brothers constitute a real demonstration of their psychological as well as social equality, and specifically of the equality of their will: given similar situations, they will choose the same things, and they will love the same person.[38] This sameness is even emphasized in their language: they echo each other in their dismayed discoveries of the other's love.  "Quoi? l'estimez-vous tant?"  "Quoi? l'estimez-vous moins?"  "Que ne ferais-je point contre un autre qu'un frère?"  "Que ne ferais-je point contre un autre que vous?" (ll. 134, 144, 146).[39]

The equality of the brothers is, as Séleucus says, the foundation of their friendship; although this is also specifically true of their situation, he is repeating a commonplace of the discourse on friendship, where equality and resemblance are often linked.  This commonplace is present both in the moral philosophical tradition and in chivalric romance.  The two brothers are a figure of the celebrated Ciceronian definition of friendship, "omnium divinarum humanarumque rerum cum benevolentia et caritate consensio" (De amicitia, 6.20).  Plutarch, in his little treatise on fraternal friendship, emphasizes the infrequency in his times of such friendship by saying that nowadays people are amazed to see brothers who seem to have their bodies "collez ensemble," glued together, and they find it hard to believe and "monstrueux" that "des freres usent en commun des biens, des amis, & des esclaves que leurs

---

[38] "[V]rays amis ont mesme vouloir, et ce que l'un veult l'autre le doit vouloir en toutes choses honnestes et licites" is a commonplace comment on the equally commonplace phrase, the friend is "ung autre moy" (taken from Les Parolles Joyeuses et Dictz Memorables des Nobles et saiges hommes anciens Redigez par le Gracieulx et Honneste Poete Messire François Petrarque (1531) in Le Parangon de Nouvelles, ed. Gabriel-A. Pérouse, Geneva, Droz, 1979, p. 215).  The saying is not from Petrarch, but from Diogenes Laertius; Zeno says that a friend is an ἄλλος ἐγώ (Lives 7.23).  Although this sameness of choice is a logical consequence of perfect friendship, it is also, according to Plutarch, something to be avoided, in order to minimize envy: friends should not select the same profession, and should avoid being "amoureux d'une mesme maistresse" (De l'amitié fraternelle, f. 86v E [486C]).

[39] "What? do you respect her so much?  What? do you respect her less? What would I not do against someone other than a brother?  What would I not do against someone other than you?"

peres leur ont laissez, comme ils feroient que une seule ame regist les
pieds, les mains, & les yeulx de deux corps."[40]   There are many
discussions on the necessity of friends to resemble each other in their
goodness in classical moral philosophy.[41]    Early modern moral
philosophy repeats these classical commonplaces; Erasmus lists "Amicitia
aequalitas. Amicus alter ipse" as one of his first adages.[42]  Erasmus
includes a long digression on the attraction of the similar in his *De
ratione studii* (1510); the like find joy in the like as the equal love the
equal: "et simile gaudet simili; et aequalis aequalem delectat."[43]   The
absence of friendship in tyranny is explained by the radical inequality of

---

[40] "Brothers use in common the possessions, the friends, and the slaves that
their fathers have left them, as if only one soul governed their feet, their hands,
and the eyes of both bodies." *De l'amitié fraternelle*, f. 81v G [478C-D].

[41] See Plato's *Lysis* (214d and ff.), and Aristotle's *Nicomachean Ethics*
(1156b 7-9, 1158a 1), and *Eudemian Ethics* (1235a 6, 1240b 1-2, etc.).  Cicero
echoes these sentiments in his *De amicitia* (14.50), as does Plutarch in his
insistence on the likeness of friends, and thus on the exclusivity of friendship
(*On Having Many Friends*, 96D).  Some commonplaces are Plato's "equality
gives birth to friendship" (*Laws* 6.757a), and Aristotle's "friendship is said to
be equality" (*Nicomachean Ethics* 1158a 1).

[42] "Friendship is equality. The friend is another self" (*Adagia* 1.1.2). In the
novella tradition, too, one finds examples of friendship as "another oneself"; see
Marguerite de Navarre, *Heptaméron*, 47: "y avoit deux gentilz hommes qui, dès
le temps de leur enfance, avoient vescu en si grande et parfaicte amityé, que ce
n'estoit que un cueur, que une maison, ung lict, une table et une bource.  Ilz
vesquirent long temps, continuans cest parfaicte amityé, sans que jamays il y eut
entre eulx deux une volunté ou parolle où l'on peut veoir difference de
personnes, tant ilz vivoient non seulement comme deux freres, mais comme ung
homme tout seul" (ed. Michel François, Paris, Garnier, 1967, pp. 311-312).
Trouble arrives, though, when one of them marries, and the husband becomes
jealous of his friend for no reason.

[43] In his *Opera omnia*, 1.2, ed. Jean-Claude Margolin (Amsterdam: North
Holland Publishing Co., 1971), p. 139.  The most striking example of the love
for the similar is Narcissus: "Quid enim nostri similius quam ipsa imago?" (p.
141).  Narcissus is indeed the literalization of the "other self."

tyrant and slave-like subjects.[44]   In his representation of Séleucus and Antiochus Corneille has fused equality with identity, and has furthermore chosen, according to Plutarch, the most "natural" friendship.[45]

Antiochus and Séleucus are an example of moral equality; in addition, in the similarity of their emotional investments they are a psychological version of the similarity of some chivalric romance friends.  Taking its cue perhaps from one of the many versions of the medieval *Ami et Amile*, the popular *roman-fleuve* of chivalry *Amadis de Gaule* (gradually translated into French during the sixteenth century) stages a friendship between the eponymous hero and his brother Galaor in which the two resemble each other not only in their virtues and prowess but even in their physical appearance.  During one episode the queen calls on Amadis to sit next to Galaor so that the ladies of the court may judge their differences, but this proves to be very difficult:

> Mais ilz [Amadis and Galaor] se ressembloient tant bien qu'elles n'y sceurent que contrarier.   Ains furent toutes d'opinion que Dieu les avoit renduz perfaitz entre tous aultres chevaliers, feust en beaulté, noblesse, bonté, et bonne grace, et de visaige, et corsaige si conformes, qu'il eust esté difficile y mettre difference, excepté que Galaor estoit ung petit plus blanc, Amadis de plus gros ossemens, les cheveulx crespes et blonds, et le visaige plus rouge que Galaor. . . .[46]

---

[44] Aristotle, *Nicomachean Ethics*, 1161a 30-1161b 8.

[45] "Ce sont ombres veritablement la plus part de noz amitiez, images & semblances de celle premiere que la nature imprime aux enfans envers leurs pere & meres, & aux freres envers leurs freres" (*De l'amitié fraternelle*, f. 82r D [479D]).

[46] "But they resembled each other so well that the ladies could only disagree.  Rather, they were all of the opinion that God had rendered them so perfect among all the other knights, whether in beauty, nobility, goodness, or grace, and so alike in face and body, that it would have been difficult to distinguish between them, except that Galaor was a bit whiter, Amadis had larger bones, and curly blond hair, and a redder face than Galaor." *Le premier livre d'Amadis de Gaule*, vol. 2, ed. Hugues Vaganay, rev. ed. Yves Giraud (Paris: Nizet, 1986), chap. 31, pp. 343-344.  There is an earlier mention of their physical resemblance in chap. 24 (p. 291).  The medieval legend of Ami

Moral and social qualities flow into physical attributes and esthetic qualities; the real physical differences enumerated at the end of the passage seem to be minimized by the equalizing effect of knightly perfection.    Whereas the degree to which Amadis and Galaor bear physical resemblances to each other can be explained by the fact that they were brothers, the physical identity of two friends can also be found outside of fraternal friendship.    This is the case in a story based on chivalric romance by Vérité Habanc, in his *Nouvelles histoires tant tragiques que comiques* (1585).    The protagonist of the story, Tyron, is saved from bandits by a Duke who believes him to be his nephew Branfil (from whom he has just been separated during a hunt).    Branfil and Tyron become perfect friends: in fact it is *because* they resemble each other so perfectly that they become friends.    The Duke, upon saving Tyron, brings him before his nephew and says:

> Mon nepveu, si avez envie de sçavoir quelle est votre figure plus naifvement qu'avec un mirouer, regardez ce jouvenceau, car l'eau cheante du Ciel n'est point si semblable que vous à luy.  Et par ce je vous conseille l'aymer, tant à cause de ceste conformité que parce qu'il me semble estre bien nay. . . .[47]

Physical resemblance here clearly precedes in importance resemblance in birth, but the two together produce the perfect conditions for the perfect friendship.    The friends are encouraged in their relationship through discussion of moral philosophy and examples such as Pylades

---

and Amile is based on the miraculous physical resemblance and beauty of the two protagonists.    In the thirteenth-century French version we read: "Il s'entresamblent de venir et d'aler / Et de la bouche et dou vis et dou nés, / Dou chevauchier et des armes porter, / Que nus plus biax ne puet on deviser. / Dex les fist par miracle" (*Ami et Amile: Chanson de geste*, ed. Peter F. Dembowski, Paris, Champion, 1987, p. 2, 39-43).

[47] "My nephew, if you wish to know what you look like more faithfully than with a mirror, look at this young man, for the water falling from the sky is not as alike as you are to him.  And because of this I advise you to love him, as much because of this similarity as because he seems to me to be well born." *Nouvelles histoires tant tragiques que comiques*, eds. Jean-Claude Arnould, Richard A. Carr (Geneva: Droz, 1989), Histoire 3, p. 115.

and Orestes (p. 116). The physical resemblance of the two is so great that they can substitute for each other in bed and in battle. Tyron is truly an "autre moymesme" (another myself) to Branfil, and vice-versa.[48] This is a version without anxiety of the *Doppelgänger* motif. The doubling of the self enables heroic feats, such as judiciary combat in place of the friend (when he is in a compromised position). Chivalric romance, then, functions as a literalization of the equality that moral philosophy requires of friends.

Corneille's sets up this traditional equality both psychologically and dramatically. Not only do Cléopâtre's sons fulfill the requirement for perfect friendship of equality, but they demonstrate, in a classical way, their friendship through the favors or good deeds they perform for each other throughout the play, even when their reactions to the events are different. Their friendship is cemented by mutual *beneficia*, from the very beginning: both are willing to cede the throne, to accept the other as master ("je consens de l'accepter comme maître," 1.2.96; "[je] vous cède / Tout ce que la couronne a de charmant en soi," 1.3.120-121), in return for Rodogune. These offers are interested in the sense that each feels that Rodogune is of greater worth to themselves, but the trade-off would also maintain the equality of their relationship and thus their friendship. As soon as they realize that the other is in love with the same woman, however, they do the only logical thing: Rodogune should marry whoever is chosen to be king ("Elle doit épouser, non pas vous, non pas moi, / Mais de moi, mais de vous, quiconque sera Roi," 1.3.157-158). The chiasmus-like repetition vous-moi-moi-vous highlights the *consensio* that this solution in fact represents. Either one of the friends is willing to give up *everything* for the other, fulfilling the strictest requirement for the *beneficium* of friendship, as one in which there is no hope for anything in return: *nunc est virtus dare beneficia non utique reditura* (Seneca, *De beneficiis*, 1.1.12).[49] Far from being

---

[48] In the first story of Habanc's collection, the protagonist selects what he thinks is a perfect friend, calls him "un autre moymesme" (p. 61), but is soon betrayed by him when his friend falls in love with the same woman. This is what Corneille's brothers *avoid* doing.

[49] Corneille is pushing to the limit Plutarch's counsel to accustom brothers to "ceder l'un à l'autre reciproquement, & à se laisser vaincre, & à s'esjouir plus tost de leur complaire, que non pas de les vaincre" (*De l'amitié fraternelle*,

a sign of weakness, this is the closest a relationship comes to the classical ideal of friendship of the virtuous. Antiochus's solution is enthusiastically accepted by Séleucus, who foresees the triumph of friendship and love on the wedding day, and who celebrates the power of *amicitia*:

> Malgré l'éclat du trône et l'amour d'une femme,
> Faisons si bien régner l'amitié sur notre âme,
> Qu'étouffant dans leur perte un regret suborneur,
> Dans le bonheur d'un frère on trouve son bonheur.
> Ainsi ce qui jadis perdit Thèbes et Troie
> Dans nos coeurs mieux unis ne versera que joie,
> Ainsi notre amitié, triomphante à son tour,
> Vaincra la jalousie en cédant à l'amour,
> Et de notre destin bravant l'ordre barbare,
> Trouvera des douceurs aux maux qu'il nous prépare.
> (1.3.191-200)[50]

Through the "union" of hearts friendship will avoid the bitter epic struggles between brothers and lovers of the same woman, and this triumph is paradoxical: by conceding friendship vanquishes. Indeed, it will "suffocate" ("étouffant") jealousy, just as it "crushes" ("accable") Cléopâtre and Cinna. This is precisely what happens just before Séleucus's death, when he refuses to be jealous of his brother in spite of his mother's goading: "n'espérez voir en moi / Qu'amitié pour mon frère, et zèle pour mon roi" (4.6.1473-1474).[51] There, too, Séleucus

---

f. 87v E [488A]).

[50] "In spite of the splendor of the throne and the love of a woman, let us have friendship so well govern our soul that, smothering a pernicious regret over their loss, we will find happiness in the happiness of our brother. Thus what formerly destroyed Thebes and Troy will pour only joy into our better-united hearts; thus our friendship, triumphant, will vanquish jealousy by ceding to love, and, defying the barbarous order of our destiny, will find pleasures in misfortunes destiny prepares for us."

[51] "Do not hope to see in me anything other than friendship for my brother and zeal for my king."

is willing to "cede" to Antiochus, and by this act of renunciation he triumphs over the enraged queen.

Antiochus and Séleucus appear then, in their similarity and their practice of *beneficia*, as the incarnation of perfect friendship in a classical sense, set in a world of absolutist tyranny. Corneille's play, however, makes obvious certain problems entailed by this perfect friendship, and, in spite of Antiochus's survival and the Parthian ambassador Oronte's expression of hope for a better reign, at the conclusion of the play one does feel that the classical ideal is somehow compromised.

Partly, this is because friendship *itself* contains contradictions. If *amicitia* is the union of two wills into one, and thus the identity of choices, then it is important that the crucial events in the friends' lives not be determined by their own choice. For if each chooses the same object or course of action, there inevitably will be fundamental conflicts. Both friends are in love with the same woman, both friends want to give up the throne in favor of the other, etc. It is immaterial to decide whether their love for Rodogune is a matter of blind destiny or a product of their will, for destiny would only reproduce what was logically entailed by their equality. The relative "weakness" of the friends is perhaps the only way in which fundamental conflict between them can be avoided. It is important that there be a Cléopâtre or a Rodogune who will impose decisions from the outside, for the more classically perfect friends Antiochus and Séleucus are, the less will they be able to keep their interests apart.

The necessity of an outside instance of decision is a curious feature of the self-sacrificing passivity of other friendship couples, exemplified perhaps most memorably in Cicero's account of the stirring effect of Pylades announcing to the king that he was Orestes and should be put to death.[52] The very structure of friendship, the reproduction of the self, leads to an heroic interchangeability, allowing for the greatest of *beneficia*, the giving of one's life for the other. This is only possible when someone will *take* the one life for the other, in all senses of the word. A classic example is that of Damon and Phintias whose friendship

---

[52] See *De amicitia*, 7.24: "The people in the audience rose to their feet and cheered this incident in fiction; what, think we, would they have done had it occurred in real life?"

was so strong that when Dionysius the tyrant wanted to execute one of them, the other willingly served as hostage while the other attended to family matters. Instead of abandoning his friend to the tyrant, the first returns on the appointed day.[53] In a story that is the inverse of Corneille's plot, Boccaccio's protagonists Gisippo and Tito in novella 8 of the tenth day of the *Decameron*, prove themselves to be friends first in respect to love, then in respect to death.[54] In both cases they become substitutable for each other, if not literally mistaken for each other. In Cicero's allusion to Orestes and Pylades in the *De amicitia*, the king, who wants to have Orestes killed, does not know which is Orestes, and each one asserts steadfastly that he is the one. In Boccaccio's story, moreover, Gisippo offers his bride to his friend, as Tito has fallen desperately in love with her, and will die, wasting away, unless Gisippo, who is less in love, makes the required sacrifice. Tito literally replaces Gisippo in the wedding bed, and the bride Sofronia does not recognize him until it is too late. At the end of the story Gisippo, poverty-stricken and disconsolate over Tito's imagined slighting of him in Rome, takes responsibility for a murder which he did not commit. Tito, having arrived by chance at the praetor's office, identifies himself as the murderer, and the astonished praetor must choose between two murderers who are trying to outdo each other in wanting to be punished. Their rivalry is truly a stalemate until the real murderer is inspired by their heroism to confess; the ruler Octavian (not yet called Augustus) hears of this epidemic of self-sacrifice and determines the first two friends to be innocent and pardons the real murderer. Tito and Gisippo go on to share Tito's possessions; Gisippo becomes a Roman and marries Tito's young sister. Their heroic similarity is contagious and effective, in the sense that the real murderer experiences a profound

---

[53] See, among various versions, Cicero, *De officiis* 3.10.45.

[54] This tale, which derived from a story of two merchants in Egypt and Syria, was well-known in Renaissance Europe. It was translated into Latin by Filippo Beroaldo, whose version is the basis of a French translation in rhyme by François Habert (1551). Alexandre Hardy (1622) and Urbain Chevreau (1638) both made dramatic versions of it, and there are imitations in England and Germany, as well. See A. C. Lee, *The Decameron: Its Sources and Analogues* (London: David Nutt, 1909), pp. 330-343.

conversion ("da grandissima compassion mosso"), and Octavian is moved to a gesture of noble *liberalitas*.[55]

In Alexandre Hardy's dramatic version of Boccaccio's story, *Gesippe ou les deux amis* (1622), heroic similarity is also underlined. When the two friends propose themselves as murderers, their judges, the senators Antoine and Luculle find the case to be unique, and uniquely confusing.[56] Both friends act in one way:

> Au lieu que chacun craint, que chacun fuit la mort,
> Deux à se l'avancer bandent tout leur effort,
> Deux qu'unit l'amitié brûlent de même envie,
> De perdre, s'accusans, l'un pour l'autre la vie.[57]

---

[55] Giovanni Boccaccio, *Decameron*, 10.8, ed. Charles Singleton (Bari: Laterza, 1966), pp. 289-290. The final generosity of the ruler is prefigured in the Damon-Phintias story, at the end of which the tyrant Dionysius asks the friends to accept him as a third member of the friendship (see Cicero, *De officiis*, 3.10.45). The story of Gisippo and Tito is not always taken to show the triumph of friendship: in Estienne Pasquier's *Le Monophile*, a Neoplatonic colloquium between the self-explanatory characters Monophile, Glaphire, and Philopole, the interpretation given to the Boccaccian story is that it demonstrates the greater power of love or desire, as Tito's desire is so great that it overcomes his feelings of friendship, causing him to waste away (in Pasquier's *Oeuvres*, Amsterdam, Compagnie des Libraires associez, 1723, vol. 2, 732-733). For a scene of self-sacrifice similar to Boccaccio's, see Habanc's third tale of the *Nouvelles histoires*: captured by cruel pirates, Tyron and Branfil compete with each other in offering their lives for the other. The pirates are very impressed, free them, and ask to be accepted as their friends.

[56] In Urbain Chevreau's version of the story, Anthoine also admits to be taken aback: "Mon esprit est confus, quelle humeur les transporte, / Je ne me vis jamais surpris de cette sorte" (*Les Deux Amis: Tragi-comedie*, Paris, Augustin Courbé, 1638, 5.4, p. 101).

[57] "Instead of fearing and fleeing death, as everyone does, two persons concentrate all their effort in hastening death; two whom friendship unites burn with the same desire, to lose, accusing themselves, their life for the other," *Le théâtre d'Alexandre Hardy*, ed. E. Stengel, vol. 4 (repr. of the 1626 ed., Marburg: Elwert'sche Verlagsbuchhandlung, 1883), 5.1.1499-1502.

Their eagerness to sacrifice themselves elicits religious adoration in the real murderer, who is moved to pity at the sight of an example of perfect friendship: "Conservons aux humains un couple où l'amitié / Ses merveilles produit, parfaite se contemple, / Et s'érige l'honneur d'un venerable temple" (5.1.1528-30).[58] The senator Luculle praises Jupiter for his miraculous intervention ("son miracle intervient," 5.1.1551) and the friends' sacrifice causes the other senator Antoine to intone a similar praise of the "souverain moteur," and to consider the virtuous actions of Gesippe and Tite worthy of immortal praise (5.1.1641-48). They indeed cause a general euphoria. In all these cases the action comes from the outside; friends tend to demonstrate their interchangeable availability, and that moves others to act.[59]

In contrast to the *exemplum*-like novella and the quasi-utopian tragicomedy, Corneille has worked out brilliantly the subtleties and contradictions of true friendship. More troubling than the passivity of Antiochus and Séleucus is the suggestion that their friendship was made possible by the very tyranny they must combat. As Séleucus emphasizes at the outset of the play (1.3.110-116), equality is the basis for their relationship; this equality was the product of Cléopâtre's willful decision not to reveal the precedence in birth of the brothers. The absolutist queen's suspension of biological difference produced an artificial equality of the princes that in turn produced their friendship. The suggestion is, then, that friendship here is the equality of *subjects*, not the proto-feudal relationship that, on the surface, seems more likely in the case of Corneille. For, as we have seen, anti-Machiavellian political theory demonstrates the incompatibility of friendship and tyranny, and the atmosphere of interestedness and distrust tyranny engenders. Gestures of generosity as grandly staged as that of Augustus become strangely naïve, and perhaps even counterproductive, in the light of tyranny's *usefulness* in creating the equality of subjection.

---

[58] "Let us conserve for humans a couple in which friendship produces its marvels, can be contemplated in its perfect state, and where the honor of a venerable temple is erected."

[59] Chevreau's Anthoine proclaims general participation in the friend's glory: "Sus, il faut qu'un chacun participe à leur gloire. . ." (*Les Deux Amis*, 5.4, p. 106).

## 5. Friendship and Absolutism's Self-Destruction

When one takes a further step in this reasoning, though, the enabling of friendship in absolutism that *Rodogune* demonstrates cannot be read as a legitimation of absolutism. The artificial equality of Antiochus and Séleucus is indeed a product of Cléopâtre's will, but it also leads to her downfall. In other words, the internal dynamics of absolutism produce its own destruction, by engendering the sort of subjection that will prove impenetrable to the attempts by absolute power to reestablish self-serving distinctions. If Cléopâtre has bound the brothers to each other in passivity, she also must contend with the fact that neither is willing to betray the other. This loyalty of friends leads on the one hand to Séleucus's death, but on the other does ensure the succession to the throne of the virtuous Antiochus. If, then, friendship contains within itself the logical problem of identical choice, absolutism contains the greater problem (to its own survival) of identical subjects. Corneille's "tragedy" is profoundly optimistic in thinking of tyranny as necessarily self-destructing.

In the end, the somewhat frustrating passivity of Antiochus also allows of a positive reading, and one consonant with the notion of the *beneficium* that is a large part of friendship theory. In the final and climactic scene of the play he must decide between believing his mother and believing his future bride. Although the tyrannical and Machiavellian ways of Cléopâtre, revealed in her monologues, have not made her the audience's favorite, Antiochus's loyalty to his mother is linked by nature with his friendship for his brother.[60] Séleucus' dying words were of no help to him; his brother only designates "une main qui nous fut bien chère" (5.3.1643), a hand that was very dear to them, as the murderer. As both Cléopâtre and Rodogune will hold out their hands to him, one to offer the nuptial cup filled with the poisonous drink ("Recevez de ma main la coupe nuptiale," 5.3.1591), the other to offer herself in marriage, not even the synecdoche is a clue in distinguishing between the women. It is only through the gesture of sacrificing *himself* that Antiochus can establish the distinction between guilt and innocence. He draws his own sword once ("je préviens ses coups," 5.4.1690) and

---

[60] See Plutarch, *De l'amitié fraternelle*: "aimer son frere est demonstration certaine d'aimer aussi son pere & sa mere" (f. 83r B [480A]).

then is willing to go ahead blindly with the ceremony: "Pour m'exposer à tout achevons l'hyménée. / Cher frère, c'est pour moi le chemin du trépas" (5.4.1772-1773).[61] This unwillingness to decide between the women is in some ways a reflection of the brothers' unwillingness to betray each other, but it is also, in fact, a very efficacious way of resolving the situation. When Rodogune asks to have the wedding drink tested, as it came from the queen, Cléopâtre drinks from it herself, and agonizes. The gesture of literal self-destruction duplicates the logical self-destruction that her willful reign entails. Just as the internal contradiction in the perfect friendship was mirrored in absolutism's larger contradiction, so Antiochus's gesture of self-destruction leads to the queen's real suicide.

The ultimate *beneficium*, the giving of his own life, produces an external resolution to a conflict that Antiochus could not have resolved himself. This final gift repeats the favors the brothers have done to each other from the beginning of the play, favors which, as I have shown, are so imitative of each other that only outside resolution (Cléopâtre's choice, Rodogune's choice) will bring about any real action. While the brothers' refusal to act is frustrating to spectators and critics, it is also supremely efficacious, as it brings about the fall of absolutism *without replicating it*. Neither one follows Rodogune's request and kills his mother. Antiochus's difficult triumph is precisely not usurpation of power by a willful agent, but a sort of renunciation that emulates his brother's renunciation of the throne and Rodogune, at the end of the previous act, and that is similarly effective in "crushing" the tyrant through friendship.

When Corneille represents the generous and dazzling gesture of friendship, in both *Cinna* and *Rodogune*, he uses a discourse on *amicitia* that he inherited from Cicero, Aristotle, and Plutarch. But his obvious classical borrowing belies a Christian influence. The exemplary friendships depicted in classical moral philosophy, Orestes and Pylades, Castor and Pollux, Achilles and Patroclus, Theseus and Perithous, are *active* friendships, in the sense that the friends together wage war, rescue each other, take revenge, combat tyrants. Séleucus, the seemingly less gullible of the two brothers, does advocate active resistance to the cruel

---

[61] "In order to expose myself to all dangers let us go through with the wedding. Dear brother, that is for me the path to death."

demands of Rodogune and Cléopâtre: "Lorsque l'obéïssance a tant d'impiété, / La révolte devient une nécessité" (3.5.1061-1062).[62] But his call for revolt is in reality a call for total renunciation: "Dérobons-nous, mon frère, à ces âmes cruelles, / Et laissons-les sans nous achever leurs querelles" (3.5.1091-1092).[63] He simply withdraws from the playing field, finding in this act of withdrawal itself his happiness ("J'ai trouvé mon bonheur" 3.5.1112). The willingness of both Séleucus and Antiochus to become victims, to abandon active intervention, is a martyr-like impulse, an echo of his Christian tragedy *Polyeucte* (probably staged 1640-1641). Corneille recasts, though, the renunciation of the world as a politically effective tool *in the world*: fraternal friendship is not charity, or love of God through the friend; it can really bring about the self-destruction of tyranny here and now.

Whether or not anti-Machiavellian friendship can bring about the permanent exclusion of tyrannical usurpation is, however, another question. The ending of the play is ambivalent; there is no conversion of the tyrant, only her self-destruction. Although Antiochus has avoided, in his hesitant succession to the throne, a reduplication of the tyranny he replaces, the danger of a literal rebirth of tyranny still exists. When Cléopâtre makes her exit to die offstage, she curses the reign of her son by wishing that her grandson resemble herself, in an ironic reversal of the resemblance of friends: "Et pour vous souhaiter tous les malheurs ensemble, / Puisse naître de vous un fils qui me ressemble" (5.4.1823-1824).[64] Although she does not formulate it in these terms, this is in some ways a logical thing for the queen to say, for tyranny also makes an implicit historical claim: the willful exercise of power is merely a reflection of the way things *are*. When Machiavelli says, "degli uomini si può dire questo generalmente: che sieno ingrati, volubili, simulatori e dissimulatori" etc., he is offering a good reason for princes to act accordingly. Cléopâtre's curse on Antiochus's and Rodogune's child is more realistic than one imagines, especially if one

---

[62] "When obeisance contains so much impiety, revolt becomes a necessity."

[63] "Let us escape, my brother, from these cruel souls, and let them finish their quarrels without us."

[64] "And in order to wish for you all misfortunes together, may a son be born from you who resembles me."

considers the following history of the Syrian kings. Rodogune is only mentioned in connection with Antiochus's father Demetrius, and drops out of sight after his death, but Antiochus does have a son. According to Appian, the child of Antiochus (and, in other accounts, Cleopatra Tryphaina), Seleucus VI, waged war with his uncle and is described by the chronicler as violent and extremely tyrannical ($\beta i \alpha \iota o \varsigma$ $\kappa \alpha i$ $\tau \upsilon \rho \alpha \nu \nu \iota \kappa \acute{\omega} \tau \alpha \tau o \varsigma$). He was burned to death in the gymnasium of Mopsuestia in Cilicia.[65] For that matter, the entire history of the house of Seleucus is characterized by furious internecine warfare.

The response to Cléopâtre's curse is divided: the ambassador of the Parthians, Oronte, dismisses the queen's railings and sees in her death the punishment imposed by a just destiny and favorable auspices for Antiochus's reign. His interpretation is, of course, interested, as the wedding between Antiochus and Rodogune is part of his diplomatic strategy. Antiochus on the other hand is not so sure, for he sees "malheurs sans exemple" in his mother's life and death. He decides not to proceed with the wedding until sacrifices are made and the will of the gods is consulted. Antiochus hesitates as he has hesitated all during the play. But on a larger level Corneille has refused here the sort of conversion rhetoric that characterized Augustus's gesture of friendship with Cinna, and that characterized his predecessors Boccaccio and Alexandre Hardy in their paeans to friendship. Antiochus wants, in effect, Cléopâtre to convert, to change hate into love: "Ah! vivez pour changer cette haine en amour!" (5.4.1825). Cléopâtre stubbornly refuses, and so does, on a certain level, Corneille. He has thus, I think, inserted the renunciation that friendship represents into the contingent world of politics, made it a part of politics, rather than offer it as a transcendent and entirely nostalgic solution.

---

[65] Appian, *Roman History*, 11: *The Syrian Wars*, 69. Seleucus VI is described as *violentus & supramodum tyrannicus* in Sigismundus Gelenius's Latin translation (ΑΠΠΙΑΝΟΥ ΑΛΕΞΑΝΔΡΕΩΣ ΡΩΜΑΙΚΩΝ . . . *Appiani Alexandrini Romanorum Historiarum*, Paris, Charles Estienne, 1551, p. 88). The suggestion of *tyranny* is maintained. In Appian Antiochus is shown to be as cruel as his mother Cleopatra.

# CONCLUSION

     The central question with which most of the preceding pages have tried to deal is, "How does one talk about loving another person as a friend?" Another two questions seem to be implied in the larger one, namely, "Whom do you love?" and "Why do you love your friend?" The *object* of your love is always also the *reason* for your love, in the sense that to provide a description of your friend is also necessarily to provide a motivation for your love. The converse is no less true: to provide a reason for your love of someone is also to sketch out the object of your love, the other person. What this means is that talking about a friendship in these terms necessarily involves attempting to define the identity of another person, as someone unlike any other potential object of your choice. The designation of a person through your love appears to imply inevitably that the person loved is not loved because he or she is a member of a group, all of whose members could be loved by you, but because the person is who he or she is, as an individual. This necessity for a radical individuality in the definition of the object of your love conflicts, however, with answers to the other ancillary question one asks when talking about friendships, namely, why you are friends with a particular person. To the extent that you may give coherent answers to that question you are enumerating attributes of the person, attributes which, while providing the person with a semantic density, also connect the person with the members of groups defined by the possession of those attributes. This sharing of attributes can be perceived as lessening the person's individuality.

     I think that the problems just formulated are produced in part by the way we conceive of persons and by the way we conceive of friendship with another person. These conceptions are not "false," but they do arise in part out of historical and cultural circumstances. It seems clear to me, for example, that one of the reasons why we conceive of motivation of love for another to be a corruption, a muddying of that love, is that our conception reflects the way in which theological paradigms silently took over ethical paradigms after Antiquity. It also seems clear to me that the separating-out of the person vis-à-vis his or her attributes is connected to a sense of the radically distinct subject which emerges, very unevenly, in the early modern period, and which is very different from the "person" in classical ethical thought. These two developments are briefly summarized in my first two chapters, concerning the "ethics" of representation on the one hand, and the "object" of friendship on the other.

Yet it is in the imaginary worlds of literature that a more complex, varied, and in the end, useful, picture of friendship appears. For literature presents us with accounts of situations that draw on various areas of experience, including the esthetic and cultural, emotional, religious, political, sexual, moral. I have the feeling that I am saying the obvious when I find that very complexity to present the best trying-out of human relations, a testing of the codes through which persons understand their lives and, perhaps more importantly, their situation in a culture. The fact that literary worlds are for the most part fictional, that is, strictly speaking, not the recording of real events, does not invalidate their usefulness.

For the purposes of this book it is of limited usefulness, on the other hand, to investigate the degree of correspondence there may be between the fictional world and the real experiences of the author. The kind of intellectual work a piece of literature does is a question independent of the degree to which it reflects personal experience. There is a sense in which personal experience is irrelevant, although that irrelevance marks in no way a complete separation between the modalities of the work's genesis and the meaning of the final product. To the contrary: the meaning of the fictional situations represented in the literary work can be conveyed only through an understanding of what it was possible for these situations to mean when they were represented.

In Rabelais's world the friendship between Pantagruel and Panurge offers an example of the way in which literature tests the discourses available in a certain culture to understand a "perfect" relationship. The insufficiency of feudal, classical ethical, evangelical-humanist, and scholastic depictions of love between creatures appears in the fiction of the unequal devotion of unequal friends to each other. Rabelais's protagonists mark the emergence of a kind of "thingness" of representations of the Other; he has chosen not ineffability as a sign of the perfect relationship, but the very irreducibility of the bewildering variety of the creature. Pantagruel just loves Panurge, period, and Panurge is both useful and useless to Pantagruel; he both merits and does not merit his immense love. Since no unitary motivation, no coherent signifying of their relationship is possible, in a curious way *all* is possible, all representations will have value. Rabelais opens the relationship to the contingent, the plural.

Montaigne's "fiction" of La Boétie is perhaps the other extreme. The weight of motivation is such that the ineffable seems the only solution, the only escape; to refuse to describe or to signify is the most adequate gesture to convey the power of a unique friendship. Although the language of love for the other evokes the Real by its very sparseness, and effectively communicates the *feeling* of the absent friend, I think that we arrive at a sublime dead end. The silently present Other enables the garrulous and immensely entertaining self-involvement Montaigne displays in his *Essais*. When the focus is the Other, Montaigne's quasi-theological treatment of the friend is indistinguishable from a retreat into a nostalgic solipsism.

Whereas Rabelais and Montaigne in their different ways celebrate friendship, and provide their own testimonies to its success, both Marguerite de Navarre and Madame de Lafayette offer examples of failed friendships. In the case of Amadour and Monsieur de Clèves the man is unable to equal the *beneficium*, the gift, the woman is able to offer him. In part, these men are shown to be determined, in their relationships with the women they love, by an economy and teleology of love that render impossible the emotional sacrifice that, for example, male friends are capable of toward each other. The logical conundrums evoked above are equally present, in the sense that the men tend to demonstrate only love of themselves, by means of the woman, whereas the women are able to love those who love themselves above all. When Madame de Clèves loves her husband as a friend, what, precisely, does she love? When Floride continues to love a friend whose desire for her leads him to prefer his satisfaction to her life, what, precisely, does she love?

Friendship is also, however, a *practice*, in the sense that the set of theoretical considerations determining friendship can be inserted into a narrative involving a greater set of persons than the two friends. The translation of an ideal, often lyrical and self-directed, relationship into the world of political relationships is not obvious. Literary friendship couples are mostly anachronistic, epic protagonists whose relationship is demonstrated more by the repetition of sacrifice for each other than a consistent opening-up towards a collective entity. The *usefulness* of friendship is tested in the two environments crucial to the political evolution of Renaissance France (and of much of Europe), the compromising, negotiating world of merchants and princely and papal courts, and the absolutist court. Alberti's symposium *Della famiglia* provides us with a theoretical discussion of friendship that is constantly aware of the pitfalls of a moral, disinterested stance in a highly interested world. ˙Pierre Corneille's representation of friends in his play *Rodogune* brilliantly evokes the paradoxes of the weakness and effectiveness of friendship in an environment of entirely brutal despotism. Corneille's play is a peculiar return to classical values that, to its credit, refuses an anachronistic utopian solution and allows for the contingent world of political life.

In both Alberti's symposium and Corneille's dramas the moral and logical issues friendship theory often entails are submerged in the negotiations that experience demands. The lyrical, arresting "pastness" of friendship is subordinated to a future-oriented narrative of desire, interest, motivation. The theoretical problems are not, however, entirely forgotten: the similarity of friends, in *Rodogune*, and the interplay of virtue and usefulness, in the *Libri della famiglia*, arise from a tradition of moral theoretical reflection, and have profound practical consequences in the political and domestic realms. In a sense, this is the purpose of moral philosophy. As opposed to metaphysics or epistemology, it is poised on the brink of experience: if it cannot be "applied," it is not moral philosophy.

Yet can one say the same thing about the issues I discussed in the literary worlds of Rabelais, Marguerite de Navarre, Madame de Lafayette and Montaigne? These representations of friendship do not really involve *exemplary* narratives or discussions, as does the work of Corneille and Alberti.[1] The Princesse de Clèves is explicitly

---

[1] For an interesting discussion of humanist concepts of exemplarity and the relationship of exemplarity to narrative and imitation, see Timothy Hampton, *Writing from History: The Rhetoric of Exemplarity in Renaissance Literature*

"inimitable," Montaigne makes sure we cannot come close to the excellence of his friendship, Rabelais's friends are a giant with unlimited means and a protean trickster, and Marguerite de Navarre's tale is highly pessimistic about the value and possibilities of relationships in a fallen world. Yet in their way these works provide us with a perhaps more profound account than Alberti and Corneille of how early modern culture "made sense" of a particular moral relationship, and how that account is determined by historical constraints and possibilities. Analyzing the modalities of friendship as they precipitate from our readings of both literary and non-literary sources we find, first of all, the notion that teleology governs all relationships to the Other. We are friends in order that something may be attained, and we know beforehand what it is we want to attain. In addition, the mere description of the friend implies a certain motivation or instrumentality of the person. The "perfect" relationship is, however, in the tradition I have sketched out, the one in which the Other is the ultimate end, where nothing outside the Other can function as another, more important end. The literary texts demonstrate in complicated ways the consequences of the conflict between motivation or teleology and a kind of sublime but remote perfection, and make the modern reader question either one or the other notion. Having come to understand the difficulties caused by the conflict between a dominant teleological model and a radical notion of love "for someone's own sake," one could either abandon the teleological model or reject the radicalized notion of ideal love. I suggest that in Rabelais's and Montaigne's literary worlds there are attempts to dispense with teleology, in the celebration of a quirky perfection. We have seen, however, how in one case friendship becomes a manifestation of abundant incoherence and is marked in another by silence and the retreat from the exemplary. Perhaps more consistently, in both Marguerite de Navarre's and Madame de Lafayette's works human relationships are simply entirely resistant to perfection. If perfection means a sublime

---

(Ithaca: Cornell Univ. Press, 1990), especially pp. 1-30; for a detailed definition of the example, see John D. Lyons, *Exemplum: The Rhetoric of Example in Early Modern France and Italy* (Princeton: Princeton Univ. Press, 1989), pp. 3-34. Exemplary narrative and reading are, after an all-too-brief period of innocence, always a problem, according to Hampton and Lyons.

emptying-out of the person, that resistance is perhaps not a totally unfortunate option.

For in the early modern ethical scenario that friendship provides, the alternative to the abandoning of teleology is, I think, the abandoning of the deification of the Other, a refusal of the theological paradigm. For, as we have seen, radicalized friendship theory becomes the paroxysmal union of two selves into one, unfettered by the constraints of obligations except to each other. When the Other is an end unto itself, absolved of the network of the ethical, and thus communicable, activity of our social existences, then in effect the Other is only an ineffable mirror to the Self. It seems important to insist on the imperative to communicate the modalities and conditions of the experience of the "perfect" relationship, an insistence that is natural to the literary world.[2] Narrative seems necessary to the communication of the ethical choices that make up one's life, and narrative is inseparable, at some level, from teleology. As we have learned from the Ancients, teleology does not have to mean what we tend to assume it means, an entirely instrumental or utilitarian determination of one's relationships with others. Instead, the motivation for one's relationships may *also* be the common orientation toward something like virtue or the good life, may be a complex of choices from which the individual self is not separable.

---

[2] For a fruitful demonstration of the importance of rational communication in the "making sense" of one's life, and in the narrative that constitutes both our identity and our orientation to the good, see Charles Taylor, *Sources of the Self: The Making of Modern Identity* (Cambridge: Harvard Univ. Press, 1989), especially pp. 25-52.

# BIBLIOGRAPHY

## 1. Primary Literature

Ailly, Pierre d'. *Quaestiones super libros sententiarum cum quibusdam in fine adjunctis*. Strasburg, 1490. Repr. Frankfurt: Minerva, 1968.

Alberti, Leon Battista. *Opere volgari*. Vols. 1 & 2. Ed. Cecil Grayson. Bari: Laterza, 1960, 1966.

Alciatus, Andreas. *Emblematum libellus*. Paris: Chr. Wechel, 1542. Repr. Darmstadt, Wissenschaftliche Buchgesellschaft, 1980.

Almain, Jacques. *Aurea clarissimi et acutissimi Doctoris theologi Magistri Iacobi Almain Senonensis opuscula / omnibus theologis perquam utilia*. Paris: Claude Chevallon, 1518.

-- *Moralia acutissimi et clarissimi Doctoris theologi magistri Jacobi almain: cum eiusdem Jacobi: et David Cranston Scoti additionibus*. Paris: Claude Chevallon, 1520.

Altensteig, Johannes. *Opusculum de amicicia* . . . Hagenau: Henricus Gran, 1519.

-- *Lexicon Theologicum* (1517, rev. Johannes Tytz, 1617). Repr. Hildesheim: G. Olms, 1974.

*Amadis de Gaule*. Book 1. 2 Vols. Ed. Hugues Vaganay, rev. ed. Yves Giraud. Paris: Nizet, 1986.

*Le neufiesme livre d'Amadis de Gaule*. Trans. Claude Colet. Paris: Jean Longis, 1557.

*Le vingtiesme livre d'Amadis de Gaule*. Trans. Jean Boyron. Lyons: Antoine Tardif, 1582.

Amantius, Bartholomaeus. *Flores celebriorum sententiarum graecarum ac latinarum, definitionum, item virtutum et vitiorum*. . . . Dilinga: Sebaldus Mayer, 1556.

*Ami et Amile: Chanson de geste*. Ed. Peter F. Dembowski. Paris: Champion, 1987.

Andreas Capellanus. *De amore libri tres*. Ed. E. Trojel. Munich: W. Fink, 1972.

Appian. ΑΠΠΙΑΝΟΥ ΑΛΕΞΑΝΔΡΕΩΣ ΡΩΜΑΙΚΩΝ . . . *Appiani Alexandrini Romanorum Historiarum*. Trans. Sigismundus Gelenius. Paris: Charles Estienne, 1551.

Aquinas, St Thomas. *Opera omnia*. 1st ed. 1852-1873. Repr. New York: Musurgia, 1949.

Ariosto, Lodovico. *Orlando furioso*. Ed. Lanfranco Caretti. Torino: Einaudi, 1971.

*Aristotelis Ethicorum Nicomachiorum Paraphrasis, incerto auctore, antiquo & eximio peripatetico. . . .* Ed. and trans. Daniel Heinsius. Lyons: 1607.

Aristotle. *Complete Works*. 2 Vols. Ed. Jonathan Barnes. Princeton: Princeton Univ. Press, 1984.

-- *Nicomachean Ethics*. Ed. and transl. Howard Rackham. Loeb Classical Library. Cambridge, MA: Harvard Univ. Press, 1926.

-- Αριστοτέλους ἅπαντα *Aristotelis summi semper philosophi . . . opera . . . omnia*. Basel: Johannes Bebel, 1550.

-- *Decem librorum Moralium Aristotelis, tres conversiones: Prima Argyropyli Byzantii, secunda Leonardi Aretini, tertia vero Antiqua. . .* Paris: Simon Colin, 1535.

-- *Aristotelis de moribus ad Nicomachum libri decem. Nunc primum e graeco et latinè & fideliter, quod utrunque querebantur omnes praestitisse adhuc neminem, à Dionysio Lambino expressi*. Venice: Vincentius Valgrisius, 1558.

-- *L'Ethica d'Aristotile ridotta in compendio da Ser Brunetto Latini: Et altre Traduttioni, & scritti di quei tempi*. Lyons: Jean de Tournes, 1568.

-- *Petri Victorii commentarii in X. Libros Aristotelis De Moribus ad Nicomachum*. Florence: Ex officina iunctarum, 1584.

-- *L'Ethica d'Aristotile tradotta in lingua vulgare fiorentina. Et commentata per Bernardo Segni*. Vinegia: Bartholomeo detto l'Imperadore, 1551.

-- *Auctoritates Aristotelis. . . .* Cologne, 1487.

-- ibid., Paris, 1522.

Augustine, St. *On Christian Doctrine*. Trans. D. W. Robertson, Jr. Indianapolis: Bobbs-Merrill, 1958.

-- *De diversis quaestionibus*. In *Oeuvres complètes*. Vol. 10. Paris: Desclée de Brouwer.

Auvray, Jean. *Modele de la perfection religieuse en la vie de la venerable Jeanne Absolu dite de S. Sauveur, religieuse de Hautes-Bruyères, de l'Ordre de Fontevrault*. Paris: Adrian Taupinart, 1640.

Béda, Noël. *Apologia Natalis Bedae, theologi, adversus clandestinos lutheranos*. Paris: J. Badius, 1529.

Bembo, Pietro. *Gli asolani*. Milan: Società de' classici italiani, 1808.

Beroaldus, Philippus. *Varia opuscula*. [Paris: F. Regnault, n.d.].

*The Jerusalem Bible*. New York: Doubleday, 1966.

*Biblia sacra iuxta Vulgatam Clementinam nova editio*. Eds. Albertus Colunga, O.P., Laurentius Turrado. Madrid: Biblioteca de autores cristianos, 1976.

Boaistuau, Pierre. *Bref discours de l'excellence et dignité de l'homme* (1558). Ed. Michel Simonin. Geneva: Droz, 1982.

Boccaccio, Giovanni. *Il Decameron*. 2 vols. Ed. Charles Singleton. [Bari]: Laterza, 1966.

-- *Decameron; Filocolo; Ameto; Fiammetta*. Eds. Enrico Bianchi, Carlo Salinari, Natalino Sapegni. Milan: Riccardo Ricciardi, 1952.

Boccalini, Traiano. *De' Ragguagli di Parnaso*. Venice: Pietro Farri, 1612.

Boileau, Nicolas. *Oeuvres complètes*. Eds. Antoine Adam, Françoise Escal. Paris: Gallimard, 1966. "Bibliothèque de la Pléiade."

Botero, Giovanni. *Scritti politici*. Milan: Ubicini, 1839. "Biblioteca enciclopedica italiana, 6."

Briçonnet, Guillaume, and Marguerite d'Angoulême. *Correspondance (1521-1524)*. Vol. 2. Eds. Christine Martineau, Michel Veissière. Geneva: Droz, 1979.

Bruni, Leonardo. *The Humanism of Leonardo Bruni: Selected Texts*. Trans., eds. Gordon Griffiths, James Hankins, David Thompson. Binghamton, N.Y.: Medieval & Renaissance Texts & Studies, 1987.

Budé, Guillaume. *De l'institution du prince*. Troyes: Nicole Paris, 1547.

Buridan, John. *Questiones . . . super decem libros ethicorum aristotelis ad nicomachum*. Paris: Ponset le Preux, 1513.

Carbone da Costacciaro, Lodovico. *Trattato dell'amore et concordia fraterna*. Trans. R. D. Leonardo Cernoti. Trevisi: Aurelio Righettini, 1592.

Castiglione, Baldassarre. *Il libro del cortegiano*. Eds. Ettore Bonora, Paolo Zoccola. Milano: Mursia, 1972.

Charron, Pierre. *Trois livres de la sagesse* (1601, 1604). Repr. Paris: Fayard, 1986.

Chevreau, Urbain. *Les deux amis. Tragi-comedie*. Paris: Augustin Courbé, 1638.

Christine de Pisan. *Livre de la cité des dames*. Ed. Maureen Cheney Curnow. Ph. D. Thesis. Vanderbilt Univ., 1975.

Cicero, Marcus Tullius. *Laelius de amicitia*. Ed. and trans. W. A. Falconer. Loeb Classical Library. Cambridge, MA: Harvard Univ. Press, 1979.

-- *Les oeuvres de M. T. Cicero pere d'eloquence latine. Les offices. Livres III. Le livre d'amitié. Le livre de vieillesse. Les paradoxes. Le songe de Scipio*. 2 vols. Rev. ed. Paris: Denys Janot, 1539.

-- *M. Tul. Ciceronis Laelius, sive de Amicitia dialogus ad T. Pomponium Atticum, cum doctissimi viri Xysti Betuleii commentariis, adiectis Desid. Erasmi, P. Victorii, & Petri Balduini adnotationibus*. Paris: Odoënus Parvus, 1556.

-- *De officiis libri III. Cato Maior, vel de Senectute: Laelius, vel de amicitia . . . cum annotationibus Pauli Manutii*. Venice: Aldus, 1564.

-- *Opera philosophica*. Venice: Luca Antonius Iunta, 1536.
  See also Collin, Vigenère, Du Perron.

Cicero, Quintus Tullius. *Commentariolum petitionis.* Ed., trans. M. I. Henderson. Loeb Classical Library. Cambridge, MA: Harvard Univ. Press.

Cintio, Giovambattista Giraldi. *Dialogues philosophiques et tres-utiles, Italiens-François, touchant la vie Civile.* Trans. Gabriel Chappuis. Paris: Abel l'Angelier, 1584.

Collin, Jean, trans. *Le livre de amytie de Ciceron.* Paris: Anthoine Bonnemere, 1537.

Corneille, Pierre. *Oeuvres complètes.* Ed. André Stegmann. Paris: Seuil, 1963.

Crenne, Helisenne de [Marguerite de Briet]. *Les Angoisses douloureuses qui procedent d'amours* in her *Oeuvres*, rev. ed. Claude Colet, 1540. Repr. Geneva: Slatkine, 1977.

Dante Alighieri. *Il convivio.* Vol. 1 of *Opere di Dante.* Eds. G. Busnelli, G. Vandelli. Florence: Le Monnier, 2nd. ed. 1964.

Denisot, Nicolas (?), ps. Théodose Valentinian Françoys. *L'Amant resuscité de la mort d'amour.* Lyon: Maurice Roy, Loys Pesnot, 1558, repr. Johnson, Mouton, 1971. 1st ed. 1555.

Des Caurres, Jean. *Oeuvres morales et diversifiées en histoires, pleines de beaux exemples, enrichies d'enseignements vertueux, & embellies de plusieurs sentences & discours.* Rev. ed. Paris: Guillaume Chaudiere, 1584.

Des Périers, Bonaventure. Translation of Plato's *Lysis.* In *Oeuvres françoises.* Vol. 1. Ed. Louis Lacour. Paris: P. Jannet, 1866.

Diogenes Laertius. *De vita et moribus philosophorum libri X. recens opera Ioannis Boulieri ad fidem Graeci codicis diligenter recogniti.* Lyons: Antoine Vincent, 1556.

-- ΔΙΟΓΕΝΟΥΣ ΛΑΕΡΤΙΟΥ ΠΕΡΙ ΒΙΩΝ . . . *Diogenis Laertii de vitis, dogmatis, & apophthegmatis.* . . . Paris: Henri Estienne, 1570.

-- ΔΙΟΓΕΝΟΥΣ ΛΑΕΡΤΙΟΥ ΠΕΡΙ ΒΙΩΝ . . . *Diogenis Laertii de vitis, dogmatis, & apophthegmatis clarorum philosopharum libri X.* Paris: Henri Estienne, 1593.

Du Moulin, Charles. *Sommaire du livre analytique des Contrats, usures, Rentes constituées, Interests, & Monnoyes.* Paris: Jean Houzé, 1586.

Duns Scotus. *Opera omnia.* Vol. 2. Ed. P. Carolus Balic. Vatican: Typis polyglottis vaticanis, 1950.

Du Perron, Jacques Davy, trans. *Laelius ou de l'Amitié.* Paris: Antoine Estiene, 1618.

Du Vair, Guillaume. *La Philosophie morale des Stoïques.* Ed. G. Michaut. Paris: Vrin, 1946.

Eck, Johannes. *In primum librum sententiarum annotiunculae* (1542). Ed. Walter L. Moore, Jr. Leiden: E. J. Brill, 1976.

Equicola, Mario. *Libro di natura d'amore.* Vinegia: Gioanniantonio & Fratelli de Sabio, 1526.

Erasmus, Desiderius. *Adagia.* In *Collected Works of Erasmus.* Vol. 31. Trans. Margaret Mann Philipps. Toronto: Univ. of Toronto Press, 1982.

-- *Colloquies*, trans. Craig R. Thompson. Chicago: Univ. of Chicago Press, 1965.

-- *Opera omnia.* Loudun: P. Vander Aa, 1705.

-- *De ratione studii.* In *Opera omnia*, 1.2. Ed. Jean-Claude Margolin. Amsterdam: North Holland Publishing Co., 1971.

Estienne, Charles. *Paradoxes, ce sont propos contre la commune opinion: debatus, en forme de Declamations forenses: pour exerciter les jeunes advocats, en causes difficiles.* Paris: Charles Estienne, 1553.

Estienne, Henri. *La precellence du langage françois.* Ed. Léon Feugère. Paris: Jules Delalain, 1850.

-- *Les premices, ou le I livre Des Proverbes epigrammatizez, ou, Des Epigrammes proverbializez. C'est à dire, Signez & scellez par les proverbes François: aucuns aussi par les Grecs & Latins, ou autres, pris de quelcun des langages vulgaires. Rengez en lieux communs.* (1593) Repr. Geneva: Slatkine, 1968.

-- *Thesaurus linguae graecae.* Rev. ed. Paris: Firmin Didot, 1831.

Ethelred of Rievaulx. "De spirituali amicitia," in *Patrologiae cursus completus,* vol. 195, col. 659-702.

Ficino, Marsilio. *Commentaire sur le Banquet de Platon.* Trans. Raymond Marcel. Paris: Belles lettres, 1978.

Figliucci, Felice. *Della filosofia morale libri dieci: sopra i dieci libre dell'etica d'Aristotile.* Vinegia: Giovanmaria Bonelli, 1552.

*Flores doctorum insignium, tam graecorum, quam latinorum, qui in Theologia ac Philosophia claruerunt, sedulò per Thoman Hybernicum collecti & postrema hac editione à mendis quàm plurimis vindicati.* Antwerp: J. Bellerus, 1576.

*Flores poetarum de virtutibus et viciis.* Cologne (?), 1490.

Fonte, Moderata [Modesta Pozzo di Zorzi]. *Il merito delle donne.* Venice: Domenico Imberti, 1600.

François de Sales, Saint. *Introduction à la vie dévote.* Ed. Charles Florisoone. Paris: Les Belles Lettres, 1961.

Fregoso, Battista. *Baptistae Fulgosi opus incomparabile, in IX libros digestum, de dictis & factis memorabilibus. . ..* Trans. Camillus Gilinus. Basel: Bartholomaeus Westhemerus, 1541.

Gentillet, Innocent. *Discours contre Machiavel.* Ed. A. d'Andrea, P. D. Stewart. Florence: Casalini Libri, 1974.

Giambelli, Cipriano. *Il Diamerone ove si ragiona della natura, e qualità de' sogni, e della perfettione, et eccelenza dell'amicitia humana.* Venice: Giorgio Angelieri, 1589.

Gournay, Marie de. "Préface à l'édition des *Essais* de Montaigne." Ed. François Rigolot. In *Montaigne Studies* 1 (1989).

Gregory of Rimini. *Lectura super primum et secundum sententiarum.* Eds. A. Damasus Trapp OSA, Venicio Marcolino. Berlin: Walter de Gruyter, 1981.

Habanc, Vérité. *Nouvelles histoires tant tragiques que comiques.* Eds. Jean-Claude Arnould, Richard A. Carr. Geneva: Droz, 1989.

Habert, François. *L'Histoire de Titus, et Gisippus, et autres petiz oeuvres de Beroalde latin.* Paris: Michel Fezandat & Robert Gran Ion, 1551.

Hardy, Alexandre. *Le théâtre d'Alexandre Hardy.* Ed. E. Stengel. Marburg: Elwert'sche Verlagsbuchhandlung, 1883.

Héroet, Antoine. *Oeuvres poétiques.* Ed. Ferdinand Gohin. Paris: Droz, 1943.

Hotman, Antoine. *Deux paradoxes de l'amitié et de l'avarice* (1598) in *Opuscules francoises des Hotmans.* Paris: Veuve Matthieu Guillemot, 1616.

-- ΠΩΓΩΝΙΑΣ, *sive de barba, dialogus.* Antwerp: Christophorus Plantinus, 1586.

-- *Observationum, quae ad veterem nuptiarum ritum pertinent.* Jean le Preux, 1585.

Jean de Meung. *Le Roman de la rose.* Version attributed to Clément Marot. 2 vols. Ed. Silvio F. Baridon. Milan: Istituto Editoriale Cisalpino, 1957.

Jodelle, Etienne. *Oeuvres complètes.* 2 vols. Ed. Enea Balmas. Paris: Gallimard, 1965.

Labé, Louise. *Oeuvres complètes.* Ed. François Rigolot. Paris: Flammarion, 1986.

La Boétie, Estienne de. *De la servitude volontaire ou contr'un.* Ed. Malcolm Smith. Geneva: Droz, 1987.

Lactantius. *Lactance Firmian des Divines institutions, contre les gentilz & idolatres.* Trans. René Fame. Paris: Galliot du Pré, 1543.

Lafayette, Madame de. *La Princesse de Clèves.* In *Romanciers du XVIIe siècle.* Ed. Antoine Adam. Paris: Gallimard, 1958. "Bibliothèque de la Pléiade."

Landi (or Lando), Ortensio. *Paradossi. Cioè, sententie fuori del comun parere novellamente venute in luce.* Lyons: Gioanni Pullon da Trino, 1543.

La Primaudaye, Pierre de. *Academie francoise, en laquelle il est traicté de l'institution des Moeurs, & de ce qui concerne le bien & heureusement vivre en tous Estats & conditions: Par les Preceptes de la doctrine, & les exemples de la vie des anciens sages, & hommes illustres.* Paris: Guillaume Chaudiere, 1581.

Lefèvre d'Etaples, Jacques, trans. *Epistolae Beatissimi Pauli, adiecta intelligentia ex Graeco, cum commentariis Jacobi Fabri Stapulensis.* Paris: Henri Estienne, 1512.

-- *Moralis Iacobi Fabris Stapulensis in Ethicen introductio, Iudoci Clichtovei Neoportuensis familiaris commentario elucidata.* Paris: Simon Colin, [1535?].

Leone Ebreo. *Dialogues d'amour.* Trans. Pontus de Tyard (?), Lyons, 1551. Ed. T. Anthony Perry. Chapel Hill: Univ. of North Carolina Press, 1974.

Le Roy, Louis. *De la vicissitude ou variété des choses en l'univers, et concurrence des armes et des lettres par les premires et plus illustres nations du monde, depuis le temps où a commencé la civilité, et memoire humaine jusques à present. Plus s'il est vray ne se dire rien qui n'ayt esté dict paravant: et qu'il convient par propres inventions augmenter la doctrine des anciens, sans s'arrester seulement aux versions, expositions, corrections, et abregez de leurs escrits.* Paris: Pierre l'Huillier, 1575, repr. Paris: Fayard, 1988.

Loisel, Antoine. *Divers opuscules tirez des Memoires de M. Antoine Loisel advocat en parlement. Ausquels sont joints quelques ouvrages de M.M. Baptiste Du Mesnil, Advocat General du Roy; de M. Pierre Pithou, Sieur de Savoye, Advocat en la Cour; & de plusieurs autres celebres Personnages de leur temps.* Ed. Claude Joly. Paris: Veuve J. Guillemot, J. Guignard, 1652.

Lombardelli, Orazio. *Le Condizioni del vero amico et altri discorsi in materia d'Ammistà.* Florence: Georgio Marescotti, 1590.

Lonicer, Johannes. *Librorum Aristotelis . . . compendium.* Marburg: Christian Egenolph, 1540.

Lucian. *Toxaris.* See Vigenère.

Luther, Martin, and Desiderius Erasmus. *Luther and Erasmus: Free Will and Salvation.* Trans., eds. E. Gordon Rupp, A. N. Marlow, P. S. Watson, B. Drewery. Philadelphia: The Westminster Press, 1969.

Machiavelli, Niccolò. *Il Principe. Scritti politici.* Ed. Luigi Fiorentino. Milan: Mursia, 1969.

Major, John. *Ethica Aristotelis Peripateticorum principis, Cum Ioannis Maioris Parisiensis Commentariis.* Paris: Jean Petit, impr. Iodocus Badius, 1530.

Marguerite de Navarre. *L'Heptaméron.* Ed. Michel François. Paris: Garnier, 1967.

-- *Chansons spirituelles.* Ed. Georges Dottin. Geneva: Droz, 1971.

-- *Théâtre profane.* Ed. V.-L. Saulnier. Geneva: Droz, 1963.

Marot, Clément. See Jean de Meung.

Montaigne, Michel de. *Essais.* Ed. Pierre Villey, V.-L. Saulnier. Paris: Presses universitaires de France, 1965.

Nietzsche, Friedrich. *Die fröhliche Wissenschaft.* In *Werke.* Vol. 3. Ed. Karl Schlechta. Munich: Carl Hanser, 1966.

Ockham, William of. *Opera theologica,* vol. 2. Eds. Gedeon Gál, Stephen Brown. St. Bonaventure, N.Y.: Franciscan Institute, 1967.

Oresme, Nicole, trans. *Le livre de ethiques d'Aristote* (1488). Ed. Albert Douglas Menut. New York: G. E. Stechert, 1940.

*Les Paroles Joyeuses et Dictz Memorables des Nobles et saiges hommes anciens Redigez par le Gracieulx et Honneste Poete Messire Françoys Petrarque* (1531). In *Le Parangon de Nouvelles*. Ed. Gabriel-A. Pérouse. Geneva: Droz, 1979.

Pascal, Blaise. *Pensées sur la religion et quelques autres sujets*. Ed. Louis Lafuma. Paris: Editions du Luxembourg, 1952.

Pasquier, Estienne. *Oeuvres complètes*. Amsterdam: Compagnie des Libraires associez, 1723.

Patrizi [da Siena], Francesco. *Il sacro regno de'l gran Patritio, de'l vero reggimento, e de la vera felicità de'l principe, e beatitudine humana*. Vinegia: Aldii filii, 1553.

Peter Abailard. *Sic et Non*. Eds. Blanche Boyer, Richard McKeon. Chicago: Univ. of Chicago Press, 1976-1977.

Peter Lombard. *Sententiae in IV libris distinctae*. Grottoferrata: Collegium S Bonaventurae, 1971.

Petrarca, Francesco. *Epistolarum familiarum libri XIV*. . . . Lyons: Samuel Crispin, 1601.

-- *Epistolae de rebus familiaribus et variae*. Ed. Joseph Fracassetti. Vol. 2 Florence: Le Monnier, 1862.

-- *De remediis utriusque fortunae*. . . Cremona: Bernardinus Misinta & Caesar of Parma, 1492.

Piccolomini, Enea Silvio (Pius II). *De curialium miseriis*. Ed. Wilfred P. Mustard. Baltimore: Johns Hopkins University Press, 1928.

Pierre de Blois. *De amicitia christiana*; *De dilectione Dei et proximi* in *Un traité de l'amour du XIIe siècle*. Ed. and trans. M.-M. Davy. Paris: E. & Boccard, 1932.

Plato. *Lysis*. See Des Périers, Vigenère.

Plutarch. *Les oeuvres morales & meslees de Plutarque*. Trans. Jacques Amyot. Paris: M. de Vascosan, 1572. Repr. The Hague: Mouton et al., 1971.

Poggio Bracciolini. *Opera omnia*. Torino: Bottega d'Erasmo, 1964.

*Polyanthea: Opus suavissimus floribus exornatum compositum per Dominicum Nanum Mirabellium*. Venice: 1507.

*Polyanthea. Hoc est, opus suavissimus floribus celebriorum sententiarum tam graecarum quam latinarum exornatum quos ex innumeris fere cum sacris, tum prophanis Authoribus, iisque Vetustioribus & Recentioribus, summa fide collegere, ad communem studiosae iuventutis utilitatem, eruditissimi viri Dominicus Nanus Mirabellius, Bartholomaeus Amantius, & Franciscus Tortius*. Rev. ed. S. Gervasius: Ex Typis Vignonianis, 1604.

Possevino, Antonio, S.J. *Bibliotheca selecta*. Rome: Typ. Apostolica Vaticana, 1593.

Rabelais, François. *Pantagruel*. Ed. V.-L. Saulnier. Geneva: Droz, 1965.
*Gargantua*. Eds. M. A. Screech, Ruth Calder. Geneva: Droz, 1970.
-- *Le Tiers livre*. Ed. M. A. Screech. Geneva: Droz, 1974.
Riccobono, Antonio. *Aristotelis doctrina de amicitia . . . in ethicis latine conversa, & partitionibus, ac periochis ornata*. Padova: Laurentius Pasquato, [1595].
Rinuccini, Annibale. *Quattro lezzioni . . . Lette publicamente da lui nell'Academia Fiorentina*. Florence: Lorenzo Torrent., 1561.
Ronsard, Pierre de. *Oeuvres complètes*. Vol. 11. Ed. Paul Laumonier. Paris: Didier, 1946.
Sainct Julien, Pierre de. *Meslanges historiques, et recueils de diverses matieres pour la pluspart Paradoxalles, & neantmoins vrayes*. Lyons: Benoist Rigaud, 1588.
Sainte-Marthe, Scevole (Ier) de. *Eloges des hommes illustres, qui depuis un siecle ont fleury en France dans la profession des lettres*. Trans. Guillaume Colletet. Paris: A. de Sommaville, Aug. Courbé, Fr. Langlois, 1644.
Salviati, Lionardo. *De dialogi d'amicizia*. Florence: i Giunti, 1564.
Sarcerius, Erasmus. *Dictionarium scholasticae doctrinae, in quo & horrendos abusus, & multa alia ad sacram scripturam rectè intelligendam non inutilia, cernere licebit*. Basel, 1546.
Scudéry, Madeleine de. *Clelie, Histoire Romaine*. Part 5, Book 1. Paris: Augustin Courbé; Amsterdam, Jean Blaev, 1660.
-- *La Morale du monde, ou conversations*. Amsterdam: Pierre Mortier, 1686.
Seneca the Younger. *De beneficiis*. Ed., trans. John W. Basore. Loeb Classical Library. Cambridge, MA: Harvard Univ. Press, 1939.
-- *Lucii Annaei Senecae sanctissimi philosophi lucubrationes omnes . . . .* Basel: Johannes Frobenius, 1515.
-- *Les Oeuvres morales et meslees de Seneque*. Trans. Simon Goulart. Paris: Jean Houzé, 1595.
Teresa of Avila. *The Life of Saint Teresa of Avila by Herself*. Trans. J. M. Cohen. London: Penguin, 1957.
*Thesaurus Magistri Sententiarum cum plenis sententiis in ordinem alphabeticum redactus*. [Speier: Peter Drach], 1495.
Thevet, André. *Les vrais pourtraits et vies des hommes illustres* (1584). 2 vols. Repr. Delmar, N.Y.: Scholars' Facsimiles & Reprints, 1973.
[Thomas à Kempis]. *De imitatione Christi*. Paris: Imprimerie royale, 1640.
Thou, Jacques Auguste de. *Historiarum sui temporis opera*. Frankfurt: P. Kopffius, 1621.
Urfé, Honoré d'. *L'Astrée*. Ed. Hugues Vaganay. Lyons: P. Masson, 1926.
Vigenère, Blaise de, trans. *Trois dialogues de l'amitié: Le Lysis de Platon, & le Laelius de Ciceron; contenans plusieurs beaux preceptes, & discours philosophiques sur ce subject: Et le Toxaris de Lucian; ou sont amenez*

*quelques rares exemples de ce que les amis ont fait autresfois l'un pour
l'autre.* Paris: Nicolas Chesneau, 1579.

Zwinger, Theodor. *Theatrum vitae humanae, omnium fere eorum, quae in
hominem cadere possunt, Bonorum atque Malorum exempla historica, ethicae
philosophiae praeceptis accommodata, & in XIX libros digesta,
comprehendens: Ut non immeritò Historiae promptuarium, vitaeque humanae
speculum nuncupari possit.* Basel: Frères Frobenius, 1565.

-- *Theatrum humanae vitae.* Basel: E. Episcopius, 1586.

## 2. Secondary Literature

Altamura, Antonio. *Il certame coronario.* Naples: Silvio Viti, 1952.

Ascoli, Albert Russell. *Ariosto's Bitter Harmony: Crisis and Evasion in the
Italian Renaissance.* Princeton: Princeton University Press, 1987.

Baxendale, Susannah Foster. "Exile in Practice: The Alberti Family In and Out
of Florence 1401-1428," *Renaissance Quarterly* 44 (1991): 720-756.

Bellenger, Yvonne. *Le jour dans la poésie française au temps de la
Renaissance.* Tübingen: Gunter Narr, 1979.

Bireley, Robert. *The Counter-Reformation Prince: Anti-Machiavellianism or
Catholic Statecraft in Early Modern Europe.* Chapel Hill, NC: University of
North Carolina Press, 1990.

Boyle, Marjorie O'Rourke. *Rhetoric and Reform: Erasmus' Civil Dispute with
Luther.* Cambridge, MA: Harvard University Press, 1983.

Bradley, Marshell Carl, and Philip Blosser, eds. *Of Friendship: Philosophic
Selections on a Perennial Concern.* Wolfeboro, N. H.: Longwood, 1989.

Buecheler, Franz. *Quinti Ciceronis Reliquiae.* Leipzig: B. G. Teubner, 1869.

Caron, Elisabeth. *Les 'Essais' de Montaigne ou les échos satiriques de
l'humanisme.* Montreal: Editions CERES, 1993.

Cazauran, Nicole. *"L'Heptaméron" de Marguerite de Navarre.* Paris: Société
d'Enseignement Supérieur, 1976.

-- "'Honneste,' 'honnesteté' et 'honnestement' dans le langage de Marguerite de
Navarre," in *La Catégorie de l'Honneste dans la culture du XVIe siècle.*
Actes du colloque international de Sommières, 2. Saint Etienne: Institut
d'études de la Renaissance et de l'âge classique, 1985. Pp. 149-164.

Céard, Jean. "La culture du corps: Montaigne et la diététique de son temps,"
in *Le parcours des Essais: Montaigne 1588-1988.* Eds. Marcel Tetel, G.
Mallary Masters. Paris: Aux amateurs du livre, 1989. Pp. 83-96.

Certeau, Michel de. "L'énonciation mystique," *Recherches de science
religieuse* 64, no. 2 (1976): 183-215.

Charpentier, Françoise, Céard, Jean, and Mathieu-Castellani, Gisèle. "Préliminaires," in *La curiosité à la Renaissance.* Ed. Jean Céard. Paris: SEDES, 1986. Pp. 7-23.

Cholakian, Patricia Francis. *Rape and Writing in the* Heptaméron *of Marguerite de Navarre.* Carbondale, IL: Southern Illinois University Press, 1991.

Coleman, Dorothy Gabe. "Notes sur l'édition grecque de Diogène Laërce que possédait Montaigne," *Bulletin de la société des amis de Montaigne* 27-28 (1978): 93-95.

Colie, Rosalie L. *Paradoxia Epidemica: The Renaissance Tradition of Paradox.* Princeton: Princeton University Press, 1966.

Cornilliat, François. "Morales du sonnet: le vers et la vertu dans les sonnets de Jodelle à M. de Fauquemberge," *RHR (Réforme, Humanisme, Renaissance)* 24 (1987): 47-63.

Couloubaritsis, Lambros. "L'amitié selon Montaigne et les philosophes grecs," in *Montaigne et la Grèce.* Ed. Kyriaki Christodoulou. Paris: Aux amateurs des livres, 1990.

D'Amico, John. "Humanism and Pre-Reformation Theology," in *Renaissance Humanism: Foundations, Forms, and Legacy.* Vol. 3. Ed. Albert Rabil, Jr. Philadelphia: University of Pennsylvania Press, 1988. Pp. 349-379.

Defaux, Gérard. *Pantagruel et les sophistes: Contribution à l'histoire de l'humanisme chrétien au XVIe siècle.* The Hague: M. Nijhoff, 1973.

-- *Le curieux, le glorieux, et la sagesse du monde: L'exemple de Panurge (Ulysse, Démosthène, Empédocle).* Lexington, KY: French Forum, 1985.

-- Introduction to Clément Marot, *Oeuvres poétiques.* Vol. 1. Paris: Bordas, 1990.

-- "Les deux amours de Clément Marot," *Rivista di letterature moderne e comparate* 46 (1993): 1-30.

-- "Montaigne et la rhétorique de l'indicible: l'exemple 'De la tristesse' (I, 2)," *Bibliothèque d'Humanisme et Renaissance* 55 (1993): 5-24.

Desan, Philippe. Ed. *Humanism in Crisis: The Decline of the French Renaissance.* Ann Arbor: University of Michigan Press, 1991.

-- *Les commerces de Montaigne: le discours économique des 'Essais'.* Paris: Nizet, 1992.

Duval, Edwin M. *The Design of Rabelais's Pantagruel.* New Haven: Yale University Press, 1991.

Fanlo, Jean-Raymond. *Tracés, ruptures: la composition instable des 'Tragiques.'* Paris: Champion, 1990.

Farge, James K. *Orthodoxy and Reform in Early Reformation France: The Faculty of Theology in Paris: 1500-1543.* Leiden: E. J. Brill, 1985.

Fraisse, Jean-Claude. *Philia: La notion d'amitié dans la philosophie antique.* Paris: Vrin, 1974.

Freccero, John. "The Fig Tree and the Laurel: Petrarch's Poetics," in *Literary Theory/Renaissance Texts*. Eds. David Quint, Patricia Parker. Baltimore: Johns Hopkins Univ. Press, 1986. Pp. 20-32.

Friedrich, Hugo. *Montaigne*. Trans. Dawn Eng. Berkeley: University of California Press, 1991.

Fumaroli, Marc. "Tragique païen et tragique chrétien dans 'Rodogune'," *Revue des sciences humaines* 38 (1973): 599-631.

Godin, André. "Erasme: 'Pia/impia curiositas'," in *La curiosité à la Renaissance*. Ed. Jean Céard. Paris: SEDES, 1986. Pp. 25-36.

Gray, Floyd. "Montaigne's Friends." *French Studies* 15 (1961): 203-212.

Greene, Thomas M. *The Light in Troy: Imitation and Discovery in Renaissance Poetry*. New Haven: Yale University Press, 1982.

Hampton, Timothy. *Writing From History: The Rhetoric of Exemplarity in Renaissance Literature*. Ithaca: Cornell University Press, 1990.

-- "'Turkish Dogs': Rabelais, Erasmus, and the Rhetoric of Alterity," *Representations* 41 (1993): 58-82.

Harris, Margaret A. *A Study of Théodose Valentinian's 'Amant resuscité de la mort d'amour': A Religious Novel of Sentiment and Its Possible Connexions with Nicolas Denisot du Mans*. Geneva: Droz, 1966.

Henry, Patrick. *Montaigne in Dialogue: Censorship and Defensive Writing, Architecture and Friendship, the Self and the Other*. Saratoga, CA: ANMA Libri, 1987.

Irigaray, Luce. *Ce sexe qui n'en est pas un*. Paris: Minuit, 1977.

Jaeger, C. Stephen. *The Origins of Courtliness: Civilizing Trends and the Formation of Courtly Ideals: 939-1210*. Philadelphia: University of Pennsylvania Press, 1985.

-- "L'amour des rois: structure sociale d'une forme de sensibilité aristocratique," *Annales: Economies, Sociétés, Civilisations* 3 (1991): 547-571.

Jordan, Constance. *Renaissance Feminism: Literary Texts and Political Models*. Ithaca: Cornell University Press, 1990.

Jugé, Clément, abbé. *Nicolas Denisot du Mans (1515-1559): Essai sur sa vie et ses oeuvres*. Le Mans: A. Bienaimé-Leguicheux, 1907.

Kahn, Victoria. "*Stultitia* and *Diatribe*: Erasmus' Praise of Prudence," *German Quarterly* 55 (1982): 349-369.

-- "Humanism and the Resistance to Theory," in *Literary Theory /Renaissance Texts*. Eds. Patricia Parker and David Quint. Baltimore: Johns Hopkins University Press, 1986. Pp. 373-396.

Kelley, Donald R. *François Hotman: A Revolutionary's Ordeal*. Princeton: Princeton University Press, 1973.

Kelly, Douglas.  "Amour comme amitié: De Jean de Meung à Christine de Pisan," in *Anteros*. Eds. Jan Miernowski, Ullrich Langer. Orléans: Editions Paradigme, 1994.

Kelly, Joan Gadol. *Leon Battista Alberti: Universal Man of the Early Renaissance*. Chicago: University of Chicago Press, 1969.

Kirkham, Victoria.  "The Classic Bond of Friendship in Boccaccio's Tito and Gisippo (*Decameron* 10.8)," in *The Classics in the Middle Ages*. Eds. Aldo S. Bernardo, Saul Levin. Binghamton, NY: Center for Medieval and Early Renaissance Studies, 1990.  "Medieval & Renaissance Texts and Studies, 69."  Pp. 223-235.

Kooper, Erik.  "Loving the Unequal Equal: Medieval Theologians and Marital Affection," in *The Olde Daunce: Love, Friendship, Sex, and Marriage in the Medieval World*. Eds. Robert R. Edwards, Stephen Spector. Albany, NY: State Univ. of New York Press, 1991.  Pp. 44-56.

Krauss, Werner. *Corneille als politischer Dichter*. Marburg: Adolf Ebel, 1936.

Kristeller, Paul Oskar. *Iter italicum*. Vol. 2. London: Warburg Institute, 1967.

Kritzman, Lawrence D. *The Rhetoric of Sexuality and the Literature of the French Renaissance*. Cambridge: Cambridge Univ. Press, 1991.

Kupisz, Kazimierz.  "La femme 'honneste' dans l'*Heptaméron*," in *La Catégorie de l'Honneste dans la culture du XVIe siècle*. Actes du colloque international de Sommières, 2.  Saint Etienne: Institut d'études de la Renaissance et de l'âge classique, 1985.  Pp. 165-177.

Lafond, Jean, and André Stegmann, eds. *L'Automne de la Renaissance 1580-1630*. Paris: Vrin, 1981.

Lajarte, Philippe de.  "L'*Heptaméron* et le ficinisme: Rapports d'un texte et d'une idéologie," *Revue des sciences humaines* (1972): 339-371.

Langer, Ullrich. *Divine and Poetic Freedom in the Renaissance: Nominalist Theology and Literature in France and Italy*. Princeton: Princeton University Press, 1990.

-- "*L'honneste amitié* et le refus du désir dans la tradition morale latine." In *Anteros*. Eds. Jan Miernowski, Ullrich Langer. Orléans: Editions Paradigme, 1994.

Lee. A. C. *The Decameron: Its Sources and Analogues*. London: David Nutt, 1909.

Leff, Gordon. *William of Ockham: The Metamorphosis of Scholastic Discourse*. Manchester: Manchester Univ. Press, 1975.

Lewis, Philip.  "L'anti-sublime, ou la rhétorique du progrès," in *Rhétoriques fin de siècle*. Eds. François Cornilliat, Mary Shaw. Paris: Christian Bourgois, 1992.  Pp. 117-145.

Lotz, Johannes B. *Drei Stufen der Liebe: Eros, Philia, Agape*. Frankfurt a. M.: J. Knecht, 1971.

Lyons, John D. *Exemplum: The Rhetoric of Example in Early Modern France and Italy*. Princeton: Princeton University Press, 1989.

MacNamara, Marie Aquinas O.P. *L'amitié chez Saint Augustin*. (transl. from English) Paris: P. Lethielleux, 1961.

MacPhail, Eric. "Friendship as a Political Ideal in Montaigne's *Essais*," *Montaigne Studies* 1 (1989): 177-187.

Marin, Louis. "Une rhétorique 'fin de siècle': Pascal: *De l'art de persuader* (1657-1658?)," in *Rhétoriques fin de siècle*. Eds. François Cornilliat, Mary Shaw. Paris: Christian Bourgois, 1992. Pp. 83-96.

Marsh, David. *The Quattrocento Dialogue: Classical Tradition and Humanist Innovation*. Cambridge, MA: Harvard University Press, 1980.

McGrade, Arthur S. "Ockham on Enjoyment: Towards an Understanding of Fourteenth-Century Philosophy and Psychology," *Review of Metaphysics* 34 (1981), pp. 706-28.

-- "Enjoyment at Oxford after Ockham: Philosophy, Psychology, and the Love of God," in *From Ockham to Wyclif*, ed. A. Hudson, M. Wilks. Oxford: Basil Blackwell, 1987. Pp. 63-88.

McGuire, Brian Patrick. *Friendship and Community: The Monastic Experience 350-1250*. Kalamazzo, MI: Cistercian Publications, 1988.

Michel, Paul-Henri. *Un idéal humain au XVIe siècle: La pensée de L. B. Alberti (1404-1472)*. Paris: Les Belles Lettres, 1930.

Miernowski, Jan. "The Law of Non-Contradiction and French Renaissance Literature: Skepticism and Negative Theology," *South Central Review* 10, no. 2 (1993): 49-66. Special issue on *Reason, Reasoning, and Literature in the Renaissance*.

Moretti, Walter. *Cortesia e furore nel rinascimento italiano*. Bologna: Pàtron, 1970.

Nakam, Géralde. *Les 'Essais' de Montaigne, miroir et procès de leur temps: Témoignage historique et création littéraire*. Paris: Nizet, 1984.

Noonan, John T. *The Scholastic Analysis of Usury*. Cambridge: Harvard University Press, 1957.

Nussbaum, Martha C. *Love's Knowledge: Essays on Philosophy and Literature*. New York, Oxford: Oxford University Press, 1990.

-- *The Fragility of Goodness: Luck and Ethics in Greek Tragedy and Philosophy*. Cambridge: Cambridge University Press, 1986.

Pakaluk, Michael, ed. *Other Selves: Philosophers on Friendship*. Indianapolis: Hackett Publishing Co., 1991.

Pavel, Thomas G. "*Rodogune*: Women as Choice Masters," in *Actes de Davis*. Ed. Claude Abraham. Paris: Papers on French Seventeenth Century Literature, 1988. Pp. 161-165.

Perreiah, Alan. "Humanistic Critiques of Scholastic Dialectic," *The Sixteenth Century Journal* 13 (1982): 3-22.

Pétré, Hélène. *Caritas: Etude sur le vocabulaire latin de la charité chrétienne.* Louvain: Spicilegium sacrum Lovaniense, 1948. Etudes et documents, 22.

Ponte, Giovanni. *Leon Battista Alberti: Umanista e scrittore.* Genoa: Tilgher-Genova, 1981.

Prandi, Stefano. *Il 'Cortegiano' ferrarese: I "Discorsi" di Annibale Romei e la cultura nobiliare nel cinquecento.* Florence: Olschki, 1990.

Price, A. W. *Love and Friendship in Plato and Aristotle.* Oxford: Clarendon, 1989.

Proctor, Robert E. *Education's Great Amnesia: Reconsidering the Humanities from Petrarch to Freud: With a Curriculum for Today's Students.* Bloomington: Indiana University Press, 1988.

Regosin, Richard L. *The Matter of My Book: Montaigne's 'Essais' as the Book of the Self.* Berkeley: University of California Press, 1977.

Rigolot, François. "L'amitié intertextuelle: Gournay, La Boétie, et Montaigne," in *L'esprit et la lettre: Mélanges offerts à Jules Brody.* Ed. Louis van Delft. Tübingen: Gunter Narr, 1991. Pp. 57-68.

-- "Quand le géant se fait homme: Rabelais et la théorie de la *condescendance*," *Etudes rabelaisiennes* 29 (1993): 7-23.

Sabbadini, Remigio. *Le Scoperte dei codici latini e greci ne' secoli XIV e XV.* Rev. ed. Eugenio Garin. Florence: Sansoni, 1967.

Saccone, Eduardo. *Il "soggetto" del 'furioso' e altri saggi tra quattro e cinquecento.* Napoli: Liguori, 1974.

Schleiner, Winfried. "Le feu caché: Homosocial Bonds Between Women in a Renaissance Romance," *Renaissance Quarterly* 45 (1992): 293-311.

Schnell, Rüdiger. *Causa amoris: Liebeskonzeption und Liebesdarstellung in der mittelalterlichen Literatur.* Bern: Francke, 1985.

Schönberger, Axel. *Die Darstellung von Lust und Liebe im 'Heptaméron' der Königin Margarete von Navarra.* Frankfurt a. M.: Domus Editoria Europaea, 1993.

Sharp, Ronald A. *Friendship and Literature: Spirit and Form.* Durham: Duke Univ. Press, 1986.

Simonin, Michel. "Autour du *Traicté paradoxique en dialogue* de Bénigne Poissenot: dialogue, foi et paradoxe dans les années 1580," in *Le paradoxe à la Renaissance.* Ed. M. T. Jones-Davies. Paris: Jean Touzot, 1982. Pp. 23-39.

-- "*Rhetorica ad lectorem*: lecture de l'avertissement des *Essais*," *Montaigne Studies* 1 (1989): 61-72.

Sitterson, Joseph C. "Allusive and Elusive Endings: Reading Ariosto's Vergilian Ending," *Renaissance Quarterly* 45 (1992): 1-19.

Stegmann, André. *L'héroïsme cornélien: Genèse et signification.* 2 vols. Paris: Armand Colin, 1968.

Stegmüller, Friedrich. *Repertorium in commentariorum in sententias Petri Lombardi.* 2 vols. Würzburg: F. Schöningh, 1947.

Steiner, George. *Real Presences.* Chicago: Univ. of Chicago Press, 1989.

Struever, Nancy S. *Theory As Practice: Ethical Inquiry in the Renaissance.* Chicago: Univ. of Chicago Press, 1992.

Taylor, Charles. *Sources of the Self: The Making of the Modern Identity.* Cambridge, MA: Harvard University Press, 1989.

Thompson, Craig R. "Better Teachers than Scotus or Aquinas," in *Medieval and Renaissance Studies.* Proceedings of the Southeastern Institute of Medieval and Renaissance Studies, vol. 2. Ed. John L. Lievsay. Durham, NC: Duke University Press, 1968.

Tomarken, Annette H. *The Smile of Truth: The French Satirical Eulogy and Its Antecedents.* Princeton: Princeton University Press, 1990.

Traverso, Edilia. *Montaigne e Aristotele.* Florence: Le Monnier, 1974.

Trinkaus, Charles. *Adversity's Noblemen: The Italian Humanists on Happiness.* New York: Columbia University Press, 1940.

-- *In Our Image and Likeness: Humanity and Divinity in Italian Humanist Thought.* 2 vols. London: Constable, 1970.

Trusen, Winfried. "Handel und Reichtum: Humanistische Auffassungen auf dem Hintergrund vorangehender Lehren in Recht und Ethik," in *Humanismus und Ökonomie.* Ed. Heinrich Lutz. Weinheim: Acta humaniora, 1983. Pp. 87-103.

Wadell, Paul J. *Friendship and the Moral Life.* Notre Dame, Ind.: Notre Dame University Press, 1989.

Watts, Derek A. "A Further Look at 'Rodogune'," in *Ouverture et dialogue: Mélanges offerts à Wolfgang Leiner.* Eds. Ulrich Döring, Antiopy Lyroudias, Rainer Zaiser. Tübingen: Gunter Narr, 1988. Pp. 447-463.

Weller, Barry L. "The Rhetoric of Friendship in Montaigne's *Essais,*" *New Literary History* 9 (1977-78), pp. 503-23.

-- "The Other Self: Aspects of the Classical Rhetoric of Friendship in the Renaissance." Ph. D. Thesis. Yale University, 1974.

Worth, Valerie. *Practising Translation in Renaissance France: The Example of Etienne Dolet.* Oxford: Clarendon, 1988.

# INDEX

# INDEX

# CONTENTS